EDUCATION IN
THE EMERGING INDIAN SOCIETY

EDUCATION IN THE EMERGING INDIAN SOCIETY

Babu Muthuja
M.A., M.A., M.Ed.
Educational Advisor,
Arcot Sri Mahalakshmi Matric Hr. Sec. School,
Villapakkam, Vellore Dist.-632521 T.N.

R. Usharani
M.A., M.Ed.
Principal, Arcot Sri Mahalakshmi Matric Hr. Sec. School,
Villapakkam, Vellore Dist.-632521 T.N.

Prof. Vijay Kumar Rai
Principal, SM College of Education,
Patna

CENTRUM PRESS
NEW DELHI-110002 (INDIA)

CENTRUM PRESS
H.O.: 4360/4, Ansari Road, Daryaganj,
New Delhi-110 002 (India)
Ph.: 23278000, 23261597

B.O.: No. 1015, Ist Main Road, BSK IIIrd Stage
IIIrd Phase, IIIrd Block,
Bangalore - 560 085 (India)
Tel.: 080-41723429
Visit us at: www.centrumpress.com

Education in the Emerging Indian Society

First Edition, 2009

PRINTED IN INDIA

Printed at Balaji Offset, Delhi

Contents

Preface

India's recent economic growth rates have generated much optimism about its general social and economic development. But has there been accompanying progress in indicators of educational outcomes? How good are Indian educational achievements in relation to China's, the country with which it is increasingly compared? What are the most significant developments in Indian school education and what has been the impact of various education policy initiatives?

The story of India's educational achievements is one of mixed success. On the down side, India has 22 per cent of the world's population but 46 per cent of the world's illiterates, and is home to a high proportion of the world's out of school children and youth. On the positive side, it has made encouraging recent progress in raising schooling participation. While the base of India's education pyramid may be weak, it has emerged as an important player in the worldwide information technology revolution on the back of substantial (absolute) numbers of well educated computing and other graduates. At independence, India inherited a legacy of large-scale illiteracy and lack of proper provision

for education. At the first post-Independence Census of 1951, only 9 per cent of women and 27 percent of men were literate. It was resolved by the framers of the constitution that the new Indian state would endeavour to provide free and compulsory education to all children up to age 14 by 1960. This goal turned out to be elusive and the deadline for its achievement has been put back repeatedly in the past 60 years. While even today this goal remains unfulfilled, there has been very encouraging progress in schooling participation and other educational outcome indicators in recent times.

This book comprehensively covers the different aspects of education in the emerging Indian society. This book provides an exhaustive treatment of the subject in a very lucid and cogent manner.

— *Prof. Vijay Kumar Rai*

Unit-I

Philosophy and Education in India

Education : Nature, Meaning and its Objectives in Indian Context

Education in its broadest sense is any act or experience that has a formative effect on the mind, character, or physical ability of an individual (e.g., the consciousness of an infant is educated by its environment through its interaction with its environment); and in its technical sense education is the process by which society deliberately transmits its accumulated knowledge, values, and skills from one generation to another through institutions. Teachers in such institutions direct the education of students and might draw on many subjects, including reading, writing, mathematics, science and history. This technical process is sometimes called schooling when referring to the compulsory education of youth. Teachers in specialized professions such as astrophysics, law, or zoology may teach only a certain subject, usually as professors at institutions of higher learning. There is also instruction in fields for those who want specific vocational skills, such as those required to be a pilot. In addition there is an array of education possible at the informal level, e.g., at museums and libraries, with the Internet, and in life experience.

The right to education has been described as a basic human right: since 1952, Article 2 of the first Protocol to the European Convention on Human Rights obliges all signatory parties to guarantee the right to education. At world level, the United Nations' International Covenant on Economic, Social and Cultural Rights of 1966 guarantees this right under its Article 13.

The Meaning of Philosophy and its Relation to Education

Philosophy of education is a field of applied philosophy, drawing from the traditional fields of philosophy (ontology, ethics, epistemology, etc.) and its approaches (speculative, prescriptive, and/or analytic) to address questions regarding education policy, human development, and curriculum theory, to name a few. Put another way, philosophy of education is the philosophical study of the purpose, process, nature and ideals of education. For example, it might study what constitutes upbringing and education, the values and norms revealed through upbringing and educational practices, the limits and legitimization of education as an academic discipline, and the relation between educational theory and practice.

Philosophy of education can be considered a branch of both philosophy and education. The multiple ways of conceiving education coupled with the multiple fields and approaches of philosophy make philosophy of education not only a very diverse field but also one that is not easily defined. Although there is overlap, philosophy of education should not be conflated with educational theory, which is not defined specifically by the application of philosophy to questions in education.

Although philosophers around the world have asked questions regarding education for millenia, as an academic discipline with its own place in the university it is relatively new. Nonetheless, it is an internationally well-established field, with departments and programs around the world.

Implications of the Impulses for Philosophy of Education

Given the existence of these three impulses, how can they help in providing an overview of the field of philosophy of education that does not fall into arguments about disciplinary boundary maintenance? First, these very broad orientations are in many respects easier to generalize within the field than would be any specific set of disciplinary criteria; many different kinds of philosophy of education can manifest these sorts of inclinations. Indeed, it makes for strange bedfellows when people consider that despite their vigorous paradigmatic differences they are actually motivated by very similar underlying philosophical commitments. Perhaps this recognition might create a stronger incentive for them to engage one another respectfully across those differences.

Second, it is beneficial for philosophers to consider that the validity they attribute to certain kinds of arguments may not be driven simply by the objective force of those arguments, but also by a particular appeal those kinds of arguments have *for them.* This sort of reflectiveness might be fruitful for various reasons, but a significant benefit could be in raising a person's appreciation for why others may not be moved by the arguments that seem so patently obvious to that person; and why the force of argument alone may not be sufficient to generate philosophical agreement or reconcile disagreement. Given the pervasively eclectic and interdisciplinary nature of the field of philosophy of education, such a spirit of tolerance and inclusiveness, while not needing to be unbounded entirely, would be a valuable corrective to the historical tendency to establish *the* methodsor *the* philosophical school that will separate proper philosophy of education from the imposters.

Advocates of more prescriptive approaches typically buttress their case for dominance by reference to canonical Great Works (Plato, ancient Greek philosopher Aristotle, Locke, Rousseau, Dewey). This sort of system-building across epistemological, ethical, and social/political issues is what the great philosophers *do,* and it is revealing that for them philosophy of education was rarely seen as a distinct area of inquiry but merely the working out in practice of implications for teaching and learning that were derived from their larger positions about truth, value, justice, and so on.

Advocates of more analytical approaches, as noted, tend to put more reliance upon the tools of philosophical investigation, and less on particular authors or sources. In the twentieth century, versions of these approaches tended to dominate philosophy of education, especially in the English-speaking world, as they have many departments of philosophy itself. Indeed, when one surveys accounts of the field of philosophy of education from the 1990s forward, they nearly all chart the history as one of the rise to dominance of an analytical approach and then a succession of critiques and attacks upon it.

Advocates of more critical approaches suffer from a particular difficulty–carrying out their philosophical work in a way that is consistent with their broader commitments. Naturally, any philosophical approach aspires to consistency of some sort; but to the extent that critically oriented philosophers are concerned with challenging power structures, hegemonic belief systems, and universalisms that obscure, not to say squelch, the particular beliefs, values, and experiences of those whom they seem to empower, such philosophers must also endeavour to avoid these potentially oppressive tendencies in their own writing and teaching. This tension is perhaps felt most acutely by contemporary post-modern philosophers of education, but it can be seen in much of the work of neo-Marxists, critical theorists, feminists, and Foucauldians as well: how to argue for and promote an emancipatory approach to education that does not itself fall into the habits of exclusionary language, authoritative (if not authoritarian) postures, and universalizing generalizations that are excoriated when detected in the work of others.

Where is the Proper Meaning of Education in India?

Our country needs to introduce a uniform pattern of education in all places. If the parents have a transferable job or changing jobs in private sector, then such children suffer the most as they do not have proper domicile papers in any state and they have to apply in private colleges for professional studies. Moreover these entrance exams are a big hindrance for students with our huge population, the competition is too much, and very few seats, it creates a lot of stress and tension.

We have reservations, thanks to our politicians and our higher castes, especially in villages where these higher castes exploit the less privileged, and the politicians exploit these people for their votes. But the general category is the most affected in these entrance exams, especially in the medical entrances, where the numbers of seats are less and lakhs of students write these exams. Let us put the poor students under so much stress and tension. Let us control our population growth especially in the rural sector. Let us get the India of Mahatma Gandhi who desired to see a liberated India wherein anyone who wanted to study any course could get the seat with the required marks.

Many students get seats in colleges paying so much money, but to get the money back, which they used for education loans or entry donation, those candidates either select corrupt methods while working or their parents demand huge dowries as their sons are engineer/doctors etc.

Every action has a reaction; it affects so many persons in different ways. Our education should be kept away from the politicians, let us give our children good education, it should be within the reach of all.

There are various definitions of education. The one as defined by the Oxford dictionary is the most satisfactory: development of character or mental powers. It is in the latter sense that today the use of the word 'education' conveys the maximum meaning. The basic validity of this concept is rooted in the very nature of man i.e. he is a learner and he has no instincts like the other animals. Thus, education is a must for man; for, it fosters development of character/mental powers. These two acquisitions enable man to field power. That is why it is often said that knowledge is power. With this power as conferred by education man manipulates and has even power over material and non-material things around. A few who have more power of education than others are more important than others. In other words, stratification of society could have come into existence based on the criterion of education power. Both in ancient Greece and ancient India the learned ranked as the highest in society. This stratification was further strengthened by the innate urge of each individual to be superior to others. In other words, there is a Lucifer in each one of us. It is this

Lucifer that was strengthened by the knowledge that education conferred. Over time as the means of disseminating education multiplied evolution of alphabet facilitating the art of writing, material on which it could be written, printing press and modern telecommunications — it has become difficult to monopolies this power of education. Locally, the distinction based on learning has come to be blurred since each individual has access to the means by which one could acquire the power conferred by education.

The mental powers that one acquires are memory, analysis, logical thinking, sense of discrimination, constructive thinking and cultivated aesthetic and spiritual sense. Human mind by itself has no mental power of its own. Man, unlike animals who are guided by instincts, is a learner. Thus whatever may be the agency that is instrumental for imparting education to new members of society contributes to the development of their mental powers. The agencies that nurture the mental powers of man are traditionally two; one family and the other society. In modern times a third agency has come into existence i.e. formal and institutionalized form of education. This agency for imparting education is becoming all-important because modern education has almost totally become utilitarian i.e. education to enable the new entrants into society find occupations for earning their livelihood.

The occupations, in turn are becoming more and more specialized or professional. In brief, the formal educational institutions that are multiplying today are primarily serving the purpose of youngsters filling the various slots that are available in society (statuses or job opportunities and professions). Apart from these three main agencies of education, today there are a few more intruders. One is the mass media, particularly exponential increase in audio-visual gadgets. On the other hand, the roles of society, family and elders are on the decline. Besides changed nature of the agencies imparting education, the content has also been transformed. In ancient times languages and scriptures constituted the primary subjects of study. In a country like India even these areas were limited to the upper most stratum of society while knowledge that was needed to pursue manual occupations were transmitted through the family channel along with the binding ethic of caste and occupation.

This pattern of education was almost totally dislodged with the introduction of western type of education by the British Raj. While educational institutions based on western pattern with English medium of instructions grew under the sponsorship of the British Raj the same tract was followed by private individuals since it came to be accepted that only in the English medium and the new kind of knowledge that was imparted that one can secure a job or pursue a profession of the time. After independence development of education became more angular because with the growing stress on specialization and professional skills. The latest figures of India show that the service sector has started making perceptible contribution to the GNP at the expense of agriculture and animal husbandry. In developed countries the percentage of contribution by the service sector occupies the top place.

The Meaning of Philosophy

So, Philosophy is "Love of Knowledge", right? Not exactly... It's "Love of Wisdom." What is the difference between Wisdom and Knowledge, one might ask? Well, Knowledge is knowing things, knowing facts, or having an accurate understanding of things as they are. Of course, there are different definitions and criteria for truth, but those don't really change the fact that we know things. The epistemic question of "how" we know is different from the question of if we have knowledge.

Science, for example, is one methodology, or "how," which helps us know facts about the physical world, and which has been quite successful. These facts are not, however, intrinsically valuable. Knowledge as a whole is not intrinsically valuable. Since value is only a result of attitudes we take toward the world—our valuations—then knowledge has only the value that it has for us. Yes, we can place a value on knowing the specific location and energy of an atom in a chair on which we are sitting, but why would we? Knowledge for the sake of knowledge (truth for the sake of truth) is misguided.

What, then, is Wisdom, and how is it not misguided in the way that a drive to Knowledge for Knowledge's sake is misguided? Wisdom, it seems, is having the ability to value appropriately, which then leads us to appropriate action ("appropriate" meaning in a manner conducive to life, health, and happiness.... oh, and ignoring our fellow beings—like Bush does—results in an emotional desensitization and disturbance antithetical to these natural, human goals). Wisdom is having the ability to discern between Knowledge that is useful and knowledge that is not, or is even destructive. Knowledge, being merely a tool to be used for the fulfilment of our natural goals, is definitely one component of wisdom, but only when properly tempered and understood within the context of it's uses. We can see quite plainly, then, that the central field of philosophy, or "first philosophy" cannot be Epistemology, Logic, or Metaphysics, but must be located within experience and is, if anything, a field such as Ethics or Aesthetics, which orient our values such that Epistemology, Logic, Metaphysics, and even Science do not drift off into meaninglessness or even become destroyers of meaning. For, after all, what each of us truly wants—deep down—is a life full of value and meaning, and the happiness which accompanies such a life even in the face of deepest suffering.

Indian Schools and Education: Vedanta

Advaita Vedanta

Advaita Vedanta was propounded by Adi Sankara and his grand-guru Gaudapada, who described Ajativada. According to this school of Vedanta, Brahman is the only reality, and the world, as it appears, is illusory. As Brahman is the sole reality, it cannot be said to possess any attributes whatsoever. An illusionary power of Brahman called Maya causes the world to arise. Ignorance of this reality is the cause of all suffering in the world and only upon true knowledge of Brahman can liberation be attained. When a person tries to know Brahman through his mind, due to the influence of Maya, Brahman appears as God (Ishvara), separate from the world and from the individual. In reality, there is no difference between the individual soul *jivatman* and Brahman. Liberation lies in knowing the reality of this non-difference (i.e. a-dvaita, "non-duality"). Thus, the path to liberation is finally only through knowledge (*jnana*).

Vishishtadvaita

Vishishtadvaita was propounded by Ramanuja and says that the *jivatman* is a part of Brahman, and hence is similar, but not identical. The main difference from Advaita is that in Visishtadvaita, the Brahman is asserted to have attributes, including the individual conscious souls and matter. Brahman, matter and the individual souls are distinct but mutually inseparable entities. This school propounds Bhakti or devotion to God visualized as Vishnu to be the path to liberation. Maya is seen as the creative power of God.

Dvaita

Dvaita was propounded by Madhvacharya. It is also referred to as tatvavada-The Philosophy of Reality. It identifies God with Brahman completely, and in turn with Vishnu or his various incarnations like Krishna, Narasimha, Srinivasa etc. In that sense it is also known as sat-vaishnava philosophy to differentiate from the Vishishtadvaita school known by sri-vaishnavism. It regards Brahman, all individual souls (*jivatmans*) and matter as eternal and mutually separate entities. This school also advocates Bhakti as the route to sattvic liberation whereas hatred (Dvesha) and indifference towards the Lord will lead to eternal hell and eternal bondage respectively. Liberation is the state of attaining maximum joy or sorrow, which is awarded to individual souls (at the end of their sadhana), based on the souls' inherent and natural disposition towards good or evil. In that way, this is the only mainstream Vedantic philosophy that provides a realist solution to the so called problem of evil. The achintya-adbhuta shakti (the immeasurable power) of Lord Vishnu is seen as the efficient cause of the universe and the primordial matter or prakrti is the material cause. Dvaita also propounds that all action is performed by the Lord energising every soul from within, awarding the results to the soul but Himself not affected in the least by the results.

Dvaitadvaita

Dvaitadvaita was propounded by Nimbarka, based upon an earlier school called Bhedabheda, which was taught by Bhaskara. According to this school, the *jivatman* is at once the same as yet different from Brahman. The jiva relation may be regarded as dvaita from one point of view and advaita from another. In this school, God is visualized as Krishna.

Shuddhadvaita

Shuddhadvaita was propounded by Vallabha. This system also identifies Bhakti as the only means of liberation, 'to go to Goloka' (lit., the world of cows; the Sankrit word 'go', 'cow', also means 'star'). The world is said to be the sport (Leela) of Krishna, who is *Sat-Chit-Ananda*.

Achintya Bhedabheda

Achintya Bhedabheda was propounded by Chaitanya Mahaprabhu (Bengal, 1486-1534). This doctrine of inconceivable and simultaneous one-ness and difference states that the soul or energy of God is both distinct and non-distinct from God, whom he identified as Krishna, Govinda, and that this, although unthinkable, may be experienced through a process of loving devotion (*bhakti*). This philosophy of "inconceivable oneness and difference" is followed by a number of modern Gaudiya Vaishnava movements, including ISKCON. Smartism/Smarta was propounded by Adi Shankara, all the other above-mentioned acharyas were strongly Vaishnavite in orientation. The Advaita, Vishishtadvaita and Mimamsa (i.e., purva-) have their epistemology in common.

Purnadvaita or Integral Advaita

According to his followers, Sri Aurobindo, in his *The Life Divine*, synthesized all the exant schools of Vedanta and gave a comprehensive resolution integrating cues from the Western metaphysics and modern science. He is said to have restored the umbilical cord of the Vedantic exegesis with the Vedas.

Modern Vedanta

The term "modern Vedanta" is sometimes used to describe the interpretation of Advaita Vedanta given by Swami

Vivekananda of the Ramakrishna order of monks. He stressed that:

- Although God is the absolute reality, the world has a relative reality. It should therefore not be completely ignored.
- Conditions of abject poverty should be removed; only then will people be able to turn their minds toward God.
- All religions are striving in their way to reach the ultimate truth. Narrow sectarian bickering should therefore be abandoned, and religious tolerance should be practiced — between different Hindu denominations, as well as Christianity, Judaism, Islam, Buddhism, etc.

Vivekananda travelled to the Parliament of the World's Religions in Chicago in 1893, and became an influential figure in synthesising Eastern and Western thought. He played a major role in the spread of Vedanta to Western nations. His travel to the West was criticised by some orthodox Hindus. His proponents claim that he made Vedanta living, by understanding how it could be applied to the modern world, and by investing it with his own spirit. For Vivekananda, Vedanta was not something dry or esoteric, but a living approach to the quest for self-knowledge.

In his interpretation of Advaita (as in Shankara's), there is still a place for Bhakti (devotion). Monks of the Ramakrishna order suggest that it is easier to begin meditation on a personal God with form and qualities, rather than the formless Absolute, of which everyone is said to be part. Saguna Brahman and Nirguna Brahman are viewed as obverse and reverse of the same coin.

List of Teachers

There have been many teachers of Vedanta in India and other countries over the centuries. Maharshi Swami Dayananda Saraswati (Arya Samaj), Hari Prasad Shastri, D. Krishna Ayyar, Bhagavan Shri Ramana Maharshi, Narayana Guru, Shri Bhausaheb Maharaj, Shri Siddharameshwar Maharaj, Shri Nisargadatta Maharaj, Sri Ranjit Maharaj, Swami Rama

Tirtha, Swami Vivekananda, Swami Sivananda, Swami Krishnananda, Swami Paramananda, Swami Chinmayananda, Swami Sri Lilashahji Maharaj, Shri Maharishi Mahesh Yogi, Sri Aurobindo, Shri Swami Tapovan Maharaj, Sengalipuram Muthannaval, Mannargudi periyaval, Paruthiyur Krishna Sastri, Anantarama Dikshitar, Kanchi Mahaswamigal, Swami Ranganathananda were great Vedanta scholars. Parthasarathy Swami Parthasarathy, Sri Swami Dayananda Saraswati, Pujya Sri Prem Siddharth, Baba Ramdev, Nithyananda Swamigal, Muralidara Swamigal, Swami Krsnapriyananda Saraswati, Nome are distinguished, traditional teacher of Vedanta of the present day.

Influence in the West

The influential philosopher Georg Wilhelm Friedrich Hegel refers to Indian thought reminiscent of Advaita-Vedanta in his introduction to his *The Phenomenology of Spirit* and in his *Science of Logic*. Arthur Schopenhauer was influenced by the Vedas and Upanishads; in his own words: "If the reader has also received the benefit of the Vedas, the access to which by means of the Upanishads is in my eyes the greatest privilege which this still young century (1818) may claim before all previous centuries, if then the reader, I say, has received his initiation in primeval Indian wisdom, and received it with an open heart, he will be prepared in the very best way for hearing what I have to tell him." (*The World as Will and Representation*) Among western figures who have been influenced by or have commented on Vedanta are Ram Dass, Friedrich Nietzsche, Max Muller, Voltaire, J.D. Salinger, Aldous Huxley, T. S. Eliot, J.B. Priestley, Christopher Isherwood, Romain Rolland, Alan Watts, Eugene Wigner, Arnold Toynbee, Joseph Campbell, Hermann Hesse, Ralph Waldo Emerson, Henry David Thoreau, Will Durant, Nikola Tesla, Erwin Schrodinger and John Dobson.

J. Robert Oppenheimer, theoretical physicist and director of the Manhattan Project, also was a professed Vedantist. In reference to the Trinity test in New Mexico, where his Los Alamos team tested the first atomic bomb, Oppenheimer famously recalled the Bhagavad Gita: "If the radiance of a thousand suns were to burst at once into the sky, that would be like the splendour of the mighty one. Now I am become Death, the destroyer of worlds."

Buddhism

Buddhism flourished in Karnataka in ancient times, along with Vedic religion and Jainism. Ashoka Maurya (274-236 B.C.), the great Indian emperor, may be considered to be the first emperor of Karnataka as well. For a long time, it was believed that the region presently called Karnataka was outside the pale of Mauryan rule and instead formed part of the *dharma-vijaya* or lands conquered through religious conquests attained by Ashoka, where he subsequently erected edifices with inscriptions expounding the teaching of Buddha, codes of conduct, and welfare-measures. However the chance discovery in 1986 of inscribed edicts and several Mauryan relics at Sannati in the Gulburga district has revealed that the Krishna river basin in northern Karnataka once came under the direct supervision and rule of Ashoka. The Sannati region enjoyed the special status of *raja-vishaya* (king's division). *Mahamatras* or supervisors were given the responsibility of creating cultural awareness, and providing education for the masses. In all the important divisions of his empire, the emperor directly appointed these *mahamatras*. Sannati boasted of a *mahamatra*. Ashokan edicts were installed at prominent places that were frequented by people and caravans, and on or near ancient highways, in order to attract the most attention. Sannati in the Mauryan age occupied a crucial position and had cultural links with Vanavasi (Banavasi in North Kanara district), with Sriparvata (presently called Nagarjunakonda, in Andhra Pradesh) and with Sri Lanka. "Sannati," according to some scholars, is the modern name of Suvarnagiri, which is mentioned in Ashokan inscriptions.

Just like Sannati, Banavasi (also called Vanavasi) was another important Buddhist cultural centre. According to Mahavamsha, an ancient Ceylonese chronicle, Ashoka sent a monk called Mahadeva to Mahishamandala (modern day Mysore) and the monk Rakshita to Banavasi, in order to propagate Buddha's teachings. Several Buddhist *acharyas* under the leadership of Chandragupta proceeded from Banavasi to Sri Lanka to attend the consecration of the great stupa (Buddhist monument) built by king Duttagamini in the 1st century B.C.E. Indications are that by this time Banavasi flourished as an important centre of Buddhism. It is frequently referred to in Sinhalese tradition as a seat of learning. Banavasi was closely linked with Nagarjunakonda, which was a resort for Buddhist *acharyas*, who helped convert residents of Kashmira, Gandhara, Banavasi and Tamralipti regions to Buddhism. Banavasi, although merely a small town today, represented a very vast region in ancient times, which was collectively called Banavasi-*nadu*. It was called thus for centuries, under different dynasties that ruled Karnataka. Buddhist relics as late as from the thirteenth century C.E. are found in the region that formed administrative division of Banavasi-nadu.

Buddhist monasteries or *viharas* were and still are centres of education; the first mention of a *vihara* in Karnataka happens to be in Banavasi. An inscription in the Brahmi script dating back to the third century C.E. indicates that a Chutu princess called Shivaskanda Nagashree donated a *vihara* in this location. Hiuen Tsang, the Chinese pilgrim who travelled in south India in about 640 C.E., wrote that Buddhism flourished in Karnataka and that there were many monasteries of both Mahayana and Hinayana sects.

Buddhist relics are found scattered throughout the state of Karnataka. Besides the six minor rock inscriptions, three each in Raichur and Chitradurga districts, there are idols of Yaksha in Haigund, and fragmentary relics and inscriptions in Babruwada, Divgi, Hiregutti (all in Uttara Kannada district), Koliwada, Dambal (Gadag district), Kundapur, Mulur, Pampalli, Kadri (South Kanara district) and Ballegavi (Shimoga district.) These indicate that there were Buddhist habitations in all these places at one time or another. Perhaps a lack of direct royal patronage made the Buddhist community, by then reduced to a minority, leave capital cities, and take shelter in smaller towns. From existing historical evidence it may be surmised that Buddhism did remain an important sect for nearly fifteen centuries in Karnataka, and that it has left a permanent mark on the native system of education and deserves special study for this reason also. In the initial years of the spread of Buddhist doctrine, itinerant monks carried the message far and wide. They literally lived the instruction, "move on, ye monks, for the welfare of the masses, their happiness and for the sake of kindness towards humanity, keep on moving!" ("*charata bhikkave, charitam, bahujanahitaya, bahujana sukhaya, lokanu kampaya...*"). Those who took the message seriously were determined to provide religious education to the masses, toured every nook and corner of the land, and at some point arrived in Kuntala desha or Karnataka (Konkanapura of Hiuen Tsang), a land of rivers, mountains and the sea.

During the rainy season, the monks had to take shelter in secluded and protected places. They also needed space for meditation, study and discussion. Cave-resorts or *layanas* thus came into existence, which eventually grew into *viharas* or places of rest, where education was also imparted. These *layanas* (also called *lenis*) were built by the royalty and the laity alike, in gratitude for the spiritual and moral guidance they received from the monks. The entire region of the Deccan plateau, from the Konkan coast to the Krishna river in the east, and down to the river Tungabhadra in the South, came under the Satavahana rule, after the decline of the Mauryas. This period of more than three hundred years saw the building of rock-cut *chetiyas* (also called *chaityas*) or places of worship and smaller *layanas* for *bhikkus* (renunciate-monks). These *viharas*, *chetiyas* and *layanas* provide valuable insight into the educational activities of those times.

All famous *guhalayas* or cave-resorts such as those of Kanheri, (near Mumbai), Karla and Bhaja near Pune, Ajanta and Ellora and also those of Nasik, were hewn out of rock in order to accommodate numerous monks, student-*bhikkus*, and also the laity on special occasions. The earlier caves, though spacious, lacked sculptural decoration. But the later ones at Karla, Ajanta and Ellora represent feats of art and engineering as well. At times, they are double storyed and contain prayer halls, meditation centres and hostels – consisting of cubicles for *bhikkus* – all in the same structure.

The *chaitya* had the main gate or porch, which led to the stupa or alternatively to an image of Buddha. Usually this area was spacious enough to hold the large teacher-student congregation. A hall was attached to every *chaitya,* at some places with stone benches and a niche in the wall (for a notice board or a writing board). This hall appeared to have been a classroom. Small cubicles or cells were often seen around the hall, which contained one or two stone bunks, space to store a pair of sandals or clothes, and an alcove for an oil lamp. These might have served as dormitory cells for student *bhikkus* (as shown in the picture no. 2). The cave-temple schools flourished for centuries as educational centres.

One of the beautifully carved cave-dwellings in Karla was constructed by Bhuta Pala Shetti of Vaijayanti or Banavasi, as declared by an inscription in the Prakrit language on a stone pillar. He may have been one of the many rich merchants who traded with Greece and Rome in the early centuries of the Christian era. The nearby towns of Kalyan and Sopara (now in Maharashtra) known to ancient Greek historians, were international ports, and continued to function as such under Chalukyan and Rashtrakuta times.

The caves at Kanheri, Karla, and Nasik received several grants from the royal and lay patrons in support of education. Irrespective of their personal religious inclinations, the kings of Karnataka patronized Buddhism for centuries, not only at home, but also in distant lands. Hiuen Tsang writes of having stayed in the *vihara* at Kapisa (in far-away Afghanistan), which was built by the Chalukya dynasty of Badami, in the 7th century C.E.! Liberal grants from the Rashtrakuta rulers, Dantidurga and Dhruva II, to the *mahavihara* at Kampilya in Saurashtra (modern-day Gujarat) are mentioned in inscriptions. These rulers had earlier defeated the Maitraka dynasty that ruled the region, but donations continued in the 7th and 8th centuries. Kampilya at the time accommodated 500 *bhikkus* in its *mahavihara*. Akkadevi, the governor of Banavasi-nadu, is described as practicing religious observances prescribed by the rituals of four deities: Jina, Buddha, Ananta (Vishnu) and Rudra, according to an inscription from 1022 C.E.

We see that commoners also were acknowledged as donors and builders of *viharas*. For instance, the people of Balligame built a *matha* (monastery) in honour of Buddha, along with one each for Hari Hara, Brahma and Jina. Bappur Nagiyakka built a temple for Tara Bhagavati, and Rupabhattayya constructed a *vihara* called Jayanti-prabha in memory of his birthplace, Banavasi. Since *viharas* were centres of learning where *bhikkus* and commoners received instruction, we may safely state that the Buddhist system of education prevailed in Karnataka until the 11th century C.E.

Unlike the age-old oral tradition of learning, wherein attentive listening, memorizing and reproduction were everything, the Buddhist system laid stress on writing and literary education. In the *viharas* children were taught the alphabet. Regardless of caste, students were allowed to attend temple-schools at the age of seven. Students in this age group were considered to be ideally suited and receptive enough to learn and obey the *guru*'s instructions.

The academic day in a typical elementary school began with the paying of obeisance to Siddha (Buddha) or the enlightened one. "*Siddham namah*" (literally, "I bow to the Siddha") became the universal invocation, and survives to this day. Members of the older generation in India inscribe these words at the top of a letter or other important document. After the ritual obeisance at the start of the day, the alphabet was taught to the students. The letters were printed in a calendar, or alternatively in an arrangement of fifty-two letters a series of twelve blocks, and called *barakhadi* (*bara* = twelve, *khadi* = block). This method of reading and writing the alphabet can be found today in Marathi, Kannada and other Indian languages. Hiuen Tsang and the renowned Arab scholar, Alberuni, who referred to it as the *siddhamatrika,* (it is prevalent even today) mention this method of learning the alphabet.

The use of vernacular languages for higher learning also began during Buddhist times. Buddha preached in Magadhi, the spoken language, rather than in Sanskrit, the language of the elite. With the spread of Buddhism, all regional languages gained importance as mediums of instruction. Ashokan inscriptions bear witness that the Prakrit language and the Brahmi script (with local variations) were used throughout the Indian subcontinent, and beyond. The growth of the written word occurred mainly for spreading Buddha's teachings, and also to teach monastic rules to monks. The written language also helped establish rules of good conduct for lay people, through inscriptions on stone – a method ingeniously devised by emperor Ashoka.

After mastering the alphabet, the student was taught grammar, arithmetic, and elements of a skilled profession such as *shilpa* or sculpture. Principles of mechanical arts, medicine, reasoning (logic), the degrees of religious attainment and the subtle doctrine of *karma* were taught gradually. Although the curriculum was originally designed to train Buddhist monks, these principles of education became applicable to lay students as well. The emphasis placed on vocational skills such as sculpting, painting, carpentry, weaving and medicine helped the populace immensely.

With the expansion of religion came the spread of literacy and education. Bigger monasteries appeared near towns and cities, with huge grants from royalty, noblemen and traders. Education became broad-based with the inclusion of comparative religions in the curriculum. Monks arrived from distant lands such as China, Japan and Korea, where Buddhism had already taken root. This is partly why we are able to obtain a vivid description of the life in Indian monasteries such as Nalanda, through the writings of Hiuen Tsang (600-664 C.E.) and Itsing (8th century C.E.). Hiuen Tsang thought that the reason for the high scholarship of Indian Buddhists was due to their relative freedom from worldly needs, and the consequent ability to focus one-pointedly on study. He was very appreciative of liberal grants made by patrons towards the promotion of education and learning.

Karnataka did not have a big university like Nalanda (of northeastern India), but there were more than a thousand *viharas* in the land of Pulikeshi, with ten thousand *bhikkus*, as noted by Hiuen Tsang. All the three important schools of Buddhism, namely Hinayana, Mahayana, and later Vajrayana flourished in Karnataka over the centuries. Although Buddhism slowly declined after the 12th century, the strong educational foundation it left behind continued to thrive. In Jaina and Vedic centres, the same curriculum prevailed at the elementary level, where the medium of instruction remained Kannada.

It is possible that the combination of literary education and vocational training imparted in *veerashaiva mathas* was similar to the system prevailing in Buddhist *viharas*. Emphasis was laid on *kayaka* or vocation, as a means of realizing God. '*Kayakave kailasa*" (or "work is worship") was the motto of Basava's teaching. Arts and crafts played a prominent role, as most *veerashaiva* saints undertook them. Among these saints were weavers, spinners, washermen, and shoemakers. The temple-schools included *Sali-mathas*, *odisuva-mathas* and *virakta-mathas,* which taught spinning, weaving, smithy, agriculture and medicine, in addition to spiritual doctrine. This vocational training provided in the *mathas* might have helped lessen social and economic differences in the society of those times. This again reminds us of the legacy of the Buddhist system, which preached a casteless society.

Buddhist monks used several artistic forms to propagate religious teaching. Jataka stories – the rebirth stories of Buddha– were represented in sculpture and paintings. Monks excelled in these arts, as evidenced by the cave paintings and sculptures of Ajanta and Ellora, which formed part of greater Karnataka in bygone days.

The original Buddhist educational system was resurfaced in this land in an unexpected way, after several centuries: Tibetans fleeing communist Chinese aggression arrived in India in 1959, in the footsteps of His Holiness, the Dalai Lama, their spiritual leader. Some batches of these refugees were comfortably accommodated in Baylakuppe near Mysore and Mundgod in North Kanara district. Nine batches of refugees were granted four thousand acres of agricultural land in Tattihalli near Mundgod. Although the climate in these southern regions of India was very different from that of the Himalayan region from which they arrived, the hard-working Tibetan community adapted very quickly to its new surroundings.

In Mundgod there are two monasteries dedicated to Buddha Avalokiteshvara, the patron deity of Tibet. In these monasteries, the places of worship, meditation and learning, namely Gomang, Sakya and Sarse, are reminiscent of the ancient *vihara* and *chaitya* prayer halls. They brim with activity, day and night. No fear of bandits or theft pesters them. The atmosphere is serene and quiet. Their *chortens* resemble *pagodas* and ancient *stupas* and are painted in pink and yellow colors, which are considered auspicious. These Tibetan *stupas* are sometimes dedicated to the memory of departed Lamas. Building these *chortens* is a continuous process, which is believed to be essential for the welfare of the community. All the residents of the monastery undertake meditation and *japa* (ritual chanting accompanied by the rosary or the prayer-wheel). Every member of the monastic community is engaged in one constructive activity or the other, including carpentry, gardening, weaving, and scores of other crafts. Youngsters are engaged in bringing water, fetching wood, etc.

Each family in the community aspires to have at least one child follow the monastic path, by becoming a *bhikku* or a *lama* (revered one). From a very young age, the chosen ones start living in the monastery, engaging themselves in studying scriptures, reading, writing and meditation, besides mastering different crafts. Prayer halls are beautifully decorated with multi-coloured flags and inlay-work in gold and other metals, and also contain elaborately carved wooden pedestals to support statues of Buddha and other deities. The blowing of conches and the beating of drums alert students to times for prayer and study. Reading, writing and arithmetic (the three Rs) predominate in their course of study for young acolytes. Traditionally, students write the Tibetan alphabet on a slate placed on wooden blocks, using black ink and a bamboo pen. Sacred writing is copied on birch leaves (*bhurjapatra*) as was the practice in ancient *viharas*. Monks also recite various scriptures that are appropriate for the specific training they undergo. They learn drawing, painting and sculpting as well. In some ways, the scene in Gomang takes one back two thousand years, when life in the Buddhist *viharas* of Karnataka might have been similar!

Early Buddhist Schools

The Early Buddhist Schools were the various schools in which pre-sectarian Buddhism split in the first few centuries after the passing away of the Buddha (in about the fifth century BC). These schools have in common an attitude to the scriptures, that doesn't accept the inclusion of the Mahayana Sutras as valid teachings of Gautama Buddha. It accepts the Tipitaka as the final recension of the teachings of the Buddha.

- Theravada is the single remaining representative of the Early Buddhist Schools of Indian Buddhism. Theravada is now practiced mainly in Sri Lanka, Myanmar, Thailand, Cambodia, and Laos.
- Another prominent Nikaya school was the Sarvastivada, and much of its doctrine was incorporated into Tibetan Buddhism. It included one of the main branches of Indian *Abhidharma* that was instrumental in the creation of the Yogacara doctrine. Its system of monastic rules *Vinaya* is still used in Tibetan Buddhism and has also been influential in monastic Chinese Buddhism.

Contributions to Indian Philosophy

Jainism had a major influence in developing a system of philosophy and ethics that had a major impact on all aspects of Indian culture in all ages : from Upanishads to Mahatma Gandhi. The scholarly research and evidences have shown that philosophical concepts that are considered typically Indian – Karma, Ahimsa, Moksa, reincarnation and like-either have their origins in the sramana school of thought or were propagated and developed by the Jaina teachers. These concepts were later assimilated in Hinduism and other religions, often in a different form and sometimes having a different meaning. The sramanic ideal of mendicancy and renunciation, that the worldly life was full of suffering and that emancipation required giving up of desires and withdrawal into a lonely and contemplative life, was in stark contrast with the brahmanical ideal of an active and ritually punctuated life based on sacrifices, household duties and chants to deities. Sramanas developed and laid emphasis on Ahimsa, Karma, moksa and renunciation.

Early Upanishad thinkers like Yajnavalkya were acquainted with the sramanic thinking and tried to incorporate these ideals into the vedic thought implying a disparagement of the vedic ritualism and recognising the mendicancy as an ideal.

Schools and Traditions

Jain philosophy arose from the Sramana philosophy. In its 2,500 years post-Mahavira history, Jain philosophy remained, more or less, fundamentally the same as preached by Mahavira, who preached essentially the same religion as the previous Tirthankaras. However, he modified the four vows of Parsva by adding a fifth vow of celibacy. Jain texts like Uttaradhyana Sutra speak of parallel existence the order of Parsva which was ultimately merged into Mahaviras order. For a few centuries after Mahavira, the Jain religion remained united. The schisms into Uvetambara and Digambara traditions arose mainly on account of differences in question of practice of nudity amongst monks and liberation of women. Apart from these minor differences in practices, there are no major philosophical differences between the different sects of Jainism. Tattvarthasutra which encapsulates the major philosophical doctrine of Jainism is accepted by all traditions of Jainism. This coherence in philosophical doctrine and consistency across different schools has led many scholars like Jaini to remark that in the course of history of Jainism no heretical movements like Mahayana, tantric or bhakti movement developed outside mainstream Jainism. Thus, we have many traditions within the Jainism, but basically the same philosophy that is at the core of all the sects and sub-sects.

Earlier Traditions

As per the tradition, Jain Sangh was divided into two major sects, a few centuries after the nirvana of Mahavira :

- Uvetambara – Svetambaras believe that women can attain liberation and that nudity is optional. Uvetambara scriptures support both *acelakatva*, nudity in monks and *sacelakatva*, the wearing of white clothes by ascetics. They also hold that Jain canon were not lost.

- Digambara-Digambaras hold that nudity is necessary for liberation and only men can attain the final stage of non-attachment to the body by remaining nude. They also hold that the canonical literature was eventually lost.

The now defunct, Yapaniya sect followed Digambara nudity and eating from the hands while standing up; along with several Uvetambara beliefs and texts. They are now believed to have been absorbed in the Digambara community during the medieval period.

Medieval Traditions

The period of 16th to 18th century was a period of reforms in Jainism. The later schools arose against certain practices and belief that were perceived as corrupting and not sanctioned by scriptures. The following schools arose during this period :

- Sthanakvasi – Sthanakvasi arising from Svetambara tradition rejected idol worship as not sanctioned by scriptures.
- Terapanthi (Digambara) – Digambara Terapantha movement arose in protest against the institution of Bhattarakas (Jain priestly class), usage of flowers and offerings in Jain temples, and worship of minor gods.
- Terapanthi (Uvetambara) – Terapanthi, also a non-iconic sect, arose from Sthanakvasi on account of differences in religious practices and beliefs.

Recent Developments

Dissatisfaction with the monkhood and its related emphasis on austerities saw rising of two new sects within Jainism in 20th Century.

These were essentially led by laity rather than ascetics and soon became a major force to be reckoned with. The non-sectarian cult of Srimad Rajcandra, who was one of the major influences on Mahatma Gandhi is now one of the most popular cults amongst the Jains. Another cult founded by Kanjisvami laying stress on determinism and "knowledge of self" has gained a large following among Jains.

Jainism

Jainism is much more ancient faith than Buddhism. Jinas or Tirthankars are founders of Jainism. There were twenty-three *teerthankaras* before Mahaveera, who was a contemporary of Gautama Buddha (6th century BCE) and is credited with formulation of a sect known as Jainism. Jainas laid great stress on right knowledge and right conduct for self-realization. It was a full-fledged sect with well-organized sanghas in north before arriving in Karnataka.

Scholars differ in their opinions on identity, date and time of the entry of first Jaina preceptors in the south. Jaina traditional accounts and literature state that the great ascetic Bhadrabahu was foretold about a calamity and famine of twelve years in the north and migrated with his disciple Chandragupta and the entire sangha or community of ascetics to Shravanabelagola in the fourth century BCE . Chandragupta, the disciple is identified with Chandragupta Maurya, grandfather of Emperor Ashoka who ruled from 322 B.C. – 298 B.C. Another theory is that Chandragupta was a grandson of Ashoka, who was Jaina by faith. However, it is generally believed that arrival of sage Bhadrabahu in the third century before the Christian era laid the foundation of Jainism in Karnataka. Shravanabelagola (Hassan District) became a great centre of pilgrimage and learning. It has retained this unique honour for more than twenty-three centuries now! Very few places in the world can claim this long uninterrupted tradition of learning and imparting religious education.

Most of the education in ancient times was imparted orally and the students had to listen attentively. *Sravana* or *samana* (listening) came to be identified with student ascetics who were supposed to be ardent listeners of a guru's teaching. Belgola means white and pure lake. The great lake between two hills is so clean and sparkling that the surroundings are clearly reflected in the water. Shravanabelagola and its surroundings teem with monuments and inscriptions and epitaphs. The latter are erected in memory of great gurus and preceptors, who provided life-long spiritual guidance to monks and masses. Similarly a number of epigraphs on the hillocks of Chikkabetta and Doddabetta bear witness to the continuous tradition of unflinching devotion of the Jaina disciples towards their gurus.

The fifty-seven feet-tall statue of Gommata at Shravanabelagola is the very embodiment of teachings of Mahaveera, which stresses compassion, renunciation, non-violence and readiness to undergo any suffering to achieve the three goals. The life story of Gommata or Bahubali, who outshone in valour, intelligence and good looks, but who sacrificed everything including the huge empire he inherited, is ever-enchanting and enlightening.

Shravanabelagola boasts of self-inscribed letters or signature of the great Kannada poet Ranna. Ranna might have engraved it when he visited the sacred place as a devotee. Several well-known Kannada poets like Mallishena, Boppana, Mallinatha, and Nagavarma have composed writings on stone, attesting thereby that the place was renowned for academic excellence and a testing place for seasoned as well as budding poets for centuries.

Great ascetic teacher of Jainism like Kondakunda, Samantabhadra, Pujyapada, Jinasena, Puspadanta and Somadeva etc. hailed from Karnataka and their works in Sanskrit and Prakrit are studied throughout India. Jainism, unlike Buddhism continues to flourish over centuries in this land.

Jainism is divided into two sects of Swetambara and Digambara. The Swetambara monks wear white and Digambara ascetics who practice extreme renunciation have to discard even the last piece of cloth or the barest necessity of life, to overcome worldly binding. Similarly *sallekhana* or death by observing religious injunction of fast unto death is not only permitted in Jainism , but also held in high esteem. Individuals who have died observing *sallekhana* are remembered in special epitaphs known as *nishidi* or *nisadi* stones.

The Jaina contribution to Karnataka has been tremendous and manifold. Most of the distinguished early poets like Pampa, Ponna, Ranna, and Janna were Jains. So were the early lexicographers and grammarians of the Kannada language. In the field of architecture, sculpture and painting Jaina element outshines all others. All this was possible due to the liberal patronage of royal dynasties, rich merchants and traders and munificent householders. Jaina faith lays stress on charity as a path towards self-realization. This charity is fourfold, consisting of food, shelter, medicine, and donating of books. This aspect of charity has helped the spread of education and learning in a great measure. *Granthadana* or giving of religious books was common to all faiths but among Jains it took an institutionalized form and helped masses a good deal to acquire knowledge.

As in the case of Buddhistic system, *layanas* or *lenas* (caves) were constructed in early centuries for temporary residence of the Jaina monks, around *jinalayas* or temples with *teerthankara* idols. These *jinalayas* were basically places of worship and meditation, and grew into centres of learning. Basadi or originally residential quarter came to denote a building consisting of a shrine, place for group worship, and became a shelter for wandering monks as also residence for teachers, scholars and students. The inscriptions registering grants to *basadis* run into hundreds throughout the state of Karnataka providing huge amount and land..

All activities in *jinalayas* or *basadis* were concentrated around five revered great persons, called Panchaparamesthis. Among these, the Arhats or Siddhas were equivalent to Jinas and *teerthankaras*. *Acharyas* or the learned were peripatetic gurus as well as heads of the *basadis* . A group of *sadhus* or monks accompanied an Acharya while touring and they were termed *gachchas*. Several such gachchas are mentioned in inscriptions.

Next in the educational hierarchy came *upadhyayas*. They were subject-teachers. *Sadhus* were also known as *sramanas* who were always on the move and had close contact with the masses. A Jaina nun was known as *sadhvi* or *kanti* or *ganti* and this class of *sadhus* and *sadhvis* have contributed a good deal of towards propagation and spread of Jaina learning.

The local people administered *jinalayas*. Their total involvement in the maintenance helped organization of religious ceremonies, festivals, and arrangement of lectures and discourses of moving *acharyas*. Jaina mathas also came up, which were bigger establishments and catered to religious and spiritual requirements of the community. All the Jaina Preceptors, *acharyas*, *upadhyas* and *sadhus* or *shramanas* were recluses and did not have a family or place of their own. They belonged to the whole humanity. To avoid attachment to worldly things, they kept on moving. Jaina mathas and *basadis* that existed throughout the country made provisions for the stay, food and religious discourses of ascetics. These mathas provided shelter and education to students of other faiths as well.

The *sadhus* and student ascetics used to live together in the mathas and *jinalayas*. *Ajjis* or *aryakas* or *gantis* also had a place there. With the arrival of *Acharyas*, the place buzzed with activity. The village community accorded warm hospitality and arrangements were made for the address of the acharya attended by the whole congregation. The acharyas in assembly solved religious issues, and provided direction.

There was provision for education from primary level to highest education in a Jaina *matha*. Education of youngsters began at the age of five years. The Acharya or Upadhyaya initiated the young boys. Drawing letters of *siddhamatraka* or table started with Siddham Namah. The boys wrote on fine sand, spread on a board with their fingers. After mastering *siddhamatraka* they wrote on folding blackboards (*kadata*) with chalk (*balapa*) and finally wont on to write on palm leaves. Ratnakarandashravakachara or code of conduct for householders was studied by heart by boys and girls alike. This handbook of 150 verses was written by sage Samantabhadra in Sanskrit but was translated in all Indian languages and studied in *Pathasalas* or schools attached to the *basadis* and *mathas*. Stress was laid on learning through regional language. In northern parts of India it was Ardhamagadhi or variation of Prakrit, and in Karnataka it was Kannada. Many works in Sanskrit and Prakrit got translated into Kannada.

However, learning at a higher level had to be in Sanskrit only. All existing sects deemed knowledge as whole and study of Vedas, Upanishads, different darsanas (schools of philosophy), *shastras* (science) and puranas were studied by Buddhists, Jains, Tantriks, Shaktas, Shaivas and Vaishnavas . Tradition mentions sixty-four arts a person had to learn and Jains added eight more to the list . Special mention may be made of chemistry, science (*vijnana*) and manufacture of small machines. Perhaps the merchant class — the main patrons of Jainism — encouraged the study of these for the promotion of different arts and crafts.

The method of learning various subjects was traditional, i.e., memorizing repeating, and reproducing. Vada or discussion formed the main platform in Jaina system and training was given in oratory. Most of the famous preceptors were great orators and established supremacy of Jainism over other sects by arguing, disputing, and discussing logically. Tarkasasatra or science of logic occupied prominent place in Jaina syllabus. Titles like Vadikolahala (who causes confusion among arguers) Prativadi bhayankara ("terror to counter arguers") Vadi-raja (king among disputers) Vadibha simha (lion to elephant-like arguers) were given by the king to the scholars in the assembly of the learned. Later, such titles were conferred to established disputants of other faiths as well.

A Jaina guru was the most respected in the Jaina community and we have a good deal of pictorial evidence. Sculptures depicting teachers imparting lesson are several. Stools (*tavanekolu*) to keep the palm-book ready are depicted in numerous sculptures. Self-study was given due importance and a student is shown as reading a palm-leaf book with great attention. In one sculpture, a mendicant is studying palm-leaf books under a tiled roof with oil lamp.

Sallekhana samadhis or *nishadi* stone memorials erected for the departed revered, illustrate the teachers in preaching pose with palm-leaf texts in hand. The Jaina monasteries invariably had libraries of palm-leaf books and these included treatises on many secular subjects besides Jaina *agamas* or holy texts. There were texts of other languages and regions as well. When we realize that a manuscript of Bilhana's Vikramankadevacharita depicting life and achievements of Chalukya king Vikramaditya of Karnataka was found in a

Jaina library of Jaisalmer (Rajasthan) and a copy of Pampa's Adipurana in Ara (Bihar), we could visualize the length and breadth of the country these books traveled in ancient times. They are also witness to the care and attention they received for preservation over centuries. Perhaps many more old and rare manuscripts are stored in the libraries of well-known Jaina monasteries. But these are not easily available to scholars who are of non-Jaina faith.

The Jaina monastic life was well organized and an officer known as *pravajyadayaka* selected student-ascetics after careful examination. Family backgrounds, educational and religious leanings were considered. After getting admission, a supervisor, known as the *niryapaka* kept a watch on the behaviour of each and every student. Wrongdoers were admonished in time and waywardness punished. Rigorous training and study awaited the incumbents. They had to make their own arrangements for day-to-day needs and beg for food. Spicy food was to be avoided. Training was given to restrain basic instincts like anger, joy, and sorrow and show equanimity to all creatures under all circumstances.

Besides food and shelter, books were distributed free at *jinalaya*s and it is likely that medical instruction was also imparted at the free hospitals attached. Hospitals big and small were attached to Jaina *mathas* where sick cattle and birds were also treated besides human beings. Jainism stood for compassion towards all living beings (*sarvajeevidayapara*), and youngsters developed this trait early in life.

The role of the merchant community in the promotion and spread of Jainism is significant. They toured the entire subcontinent and beyond, in caravans (*sarthavaha*) built hospices along trade routes. They provided transport and protection to *sadhus* and *sadhvis* and received religious instruction gratefully. They patronized several shrines and mathas and gave hefty donations of land and cash for the upkeep and maintenance of basadis, orchards, tanks, inns and wells. All passersby folk benefited by these charitable deeds, irrespective of caste or creed. The trading class knew several languages and scripts and mastered accounting. Their grants helped the Jaina system of education and there was no dearth of funds at anytime.

The *basadis* and *mathas* of Karnataka attracted ascetics from all over. Mudabidri, Karkala, Venuru, Barkuru (all in South Kanara district) Haduvalli, Gerasoppa Banavasi (North Kanara district) Ballegavi, Humcha (Shimoga district) Koppal, Bankapur (Dharwad district), Kogali, (Bellary district), and Terdal (Belgaum district) were well-known centres of Jaina learning. Sholapur and Kolhapur, now in Maharashtra, attracted scholars from far and wide.

Reference has been already made to Shravanabelagola as age-old centre of religion and learning. Banavasi being centre of Buddhism in early centuries also shone as a Jaina centre. Jaina erudition and teachings of Mahaveera were compiled, scripted and propagated in book-form from Banavasi for the first time. Shatkhandagama, an anthology of tenets of Jainism in Prakrit language took shape in Banavasi. Sage Pushpadanta who authored it lived in 2nd century CE It is the most ancient anthology on Jainism.

Special mention has to be made regarding the instruction available for women in Jaina system. It is well known that Buddha welcomed women to sangha or monastic organization after initial reluctance and hesitation. The Jaina order had no such dithering.

From the times prior to Mahaveera, Jaina nunneries existed. *Dharmadana* or imparting religious education was a mission with this class. Wandering nuns created cultural awareness through discourses, which were attended by all classes and without gender discrimination.

We come across grants to *ajjis* in inscriptions. This term is similar to *arye* or *aryake*, a learned nun. An *ajji* or *kanti* was entitled to initiate disciples into renunciation. Ajjis with several male disciples (*gudda*) figure in inscriptions and literature . These were well versed in Jaina cannon and religious practices, since they had to initiate various disciples of different caliber and attainment, they had to remember and practice elaborate injunctions and rites.

As late as 14th century C.E., the Tapogachha University in Gujarat conferred various degrees on learned women. They were 1) *Ganini* (leader of *gana*), 2) *Pravarthini* (Propagator), and 3) *Mahattara* (The great or superior) . The first and second category of female ascetics seems to have traveled across the country, providing spiritual guidance.

Mahattara was a leader of nuns. We know one Mahattara par excellence by the name of Yakini. Haribhadrasuri is a great name in Indian literature. He wrote books on Jaina ethics, yoga, logic, rituals and commentaries on *shastras*, besides stories. He calls himself Yakini-Mahattara-sunu or son of great nun Yakini! This suggests that she must have been a genius and a great influence on his scholastic life.

Many *sadhvis* and *kantis* mastered and preached Jaina *Agamas* or holy texts. Some of them have erected monuments in memory of their gurus. The *kantis* were employed as instructors to princesses, to teach reading, writing and various arts. There were nuns who specialized in astrology and logic. Administrators like Jakkiabbe who administered a division, and several queens who ruled provinces, towns and religious establishments were of Jaina faith.

The legendary queen Shantala excelled in music, dance and drama. Undoubtedly they all availed the facilities of education in Jaina system of those times.

We have to go back to Shravanabelagola to have pictorial evidence of *sadhvis* who moved from place to place. In the wall-murals of the Jaina matha is a scene of instruction wherein a senior nun is engaged in reading out and explaining to juniors who are intently listening with folded hands. Another scene depicts a nun addressing an assembly. From the dress of the instructor we can guess that she is a visiting *sadhvi* from north or west India. This only proves that wandering and preaching nuns were quite common.

The basadis continued to impart popular education where *shravaka-goshtis* or listening assemblies were held. Women learnt to read and recite Jinagamas, participated in community singing and listened to the stories of great men in Jainism.

Kannada classics speak of housewives attending such sessions and their men folk encouraging it.

Jaina devotees undertook copying out sacred texts and donating them to basadis and individuals. Attimabbe's grant of a thousand copies of Shantipurana was a landmark. Those who could not arrange donation on such a large scale engaged copyists on a moderate scale. Others undertook it upon themselves.

Basadis in Kolhapur are in possession of such manuscripts of copies of holy texts made by nuns and commoners. These holy texts and classics were read out to the conglomeration on special days and weeks. The *ajjis* used to conduct story-sessions and recitals. In the days when education could not be separated from religion, both mingled to motivate individuals with character-building and leading a pious life.

Unit–II

Western Philosophy and Education

Western philosophy is a term that refers to philosophical thinking in the Western or Occidental world, as distinct from Eastern or Oriental philosophies and the varieties of indigenous philosophies. Historically, the term was recently invented to refer to the philosophical thinking of Western civilization, beginning with Greek philosophy in ancient Greece, and eventually covering a large area of the globe, including North America and Australia. There is some debate of whether to include areas such as Northern Africa, some parts of the Middle East, Russia, and so on. The word *philosophy* itself originated in ancient Greece: *philosophia*, literally, "the love of wisdom" (philein = "to love" + sophia = wisdom, in the sense of knowledge).

In contemporary terms, *Western Philosophy* refers to the two main traditions of contemporary philosophy: Analytic philosophy and Continental philosophy.

Western Schools of Philosophy and Education

Origins

The scope of philosophy in the ancient understanding, and the writings of (at least some of) the ancient philosophers, was *all* intellectual endeavors. This included the problems of philosophy as they are understood today; but it also included many other disciplines, such as pure mathematics and natural sciences such as physics, astronomy, and biology. (Aristotle, for example, wrote on all of these topics; and as late as the 17th century, these fields were still referred to as branches of "natural philosophy"). Over time, academic specialization and the rapid technical advance of the special sciences led to the development of distinct disciplines for these sciences, and their separation from philosophy: mathematics became a specialized science in the ancient world, and "natural philosophy" developed into the disciplines of the natural sciences over the course of the scientific revolution. Today, philosophical questions are usually explicitly distinguished from the questions of the special sciences, and characterized by the fact that (unlike those of the sciences) they are the sort of questions which are foundational and abstract in nature, and which are not amenable to being answered by experimental means.

The origins of the idea of "Western philosophy" in terms of geopolitical boundaries started in the 1800s and 1900s. Prior to this, most people would have thoughts about different nations, languages, individuals, and geographical regions, but with no idea of "Western" nations, philosophy, and culture as some of us think today. Many world maps were so crude, inaccurate, and not well known before the 1800s that specific geographical and political differences would be hard to measure. Few had access to precise maps and even fewer had access to accurate descriptions of who lived in far away lands. Western philosophy as some people think of it, is recently shaped by ideas originating mainly in Europe. What we think of as Western philosophy today is generally defined as Greco-Roman and Judeo-Christian culture, the Renaissance, the Enlightenment, and ideas about colonialism. As a consequence the term "Western philosophy" is at times unhelpful and vague, since the definition involves a vast variety of distinct traditions, political groups, religious groups, and individual writers over thousands of years.

Western Philosophical Subdisciplines

Western philosophers have often divided into several major branches based on the questions typically addressed by people working in different parts of the field. In the ancient world, the most influential division of the subject was the Stoics' division of philosophy into Logic, Ethics, and **Physics** (conceived as the study of the nature of the world, and including both natural science and metaphysics). In contemporary philosophy, specialties within the field are more commonly divided into metaphysics, epistemology, ethics and aesthetics (which together comprise axiology). Logic is sometimes included as another main branch of philosophy, sometimes as a separate science which philosophers often happen to work on, and sometimes just as a characteristically philosophical method applying to all branches of philosophy.

Within these broad branches there are now numerous sub-disciplines of philosophy. At the broadest level there is the division between Analytic and Continental Philosophy. For Continental Philosophy subdividing philosophy between "experts" is problematic for the very nature of the unifying task of philosophy itself; however, for most of Analytic Philosophy further divisions simplify the task for philosophers in each area.

The interest in particular sub-disciplines waxes and wanes over time; sometimes sub-disciplines become particularly hot topics and can occupy so much space in the literature that they almost seem like major branches in their own right. (Over the past 40 years or so philosophy of mind — which is, strictly speaking, mainly a sub-discipline of metaphysics — has taken on this position within Analytic philosophy, and has attracted so much attention that some suggest philosophy of mind as *the* paradigm for what contemporary Analytic philosophers do.)

Philosophy Contrasted with Other Disciplines

Natural Science

Originally the term "philosophy" was applied to *all* intellectual endeavours. Aristotle studied what would now be called biology, meteorology, physics, and cosmology, alongside his metaphysics and ethics. Even in the eighteenth century physics and chemistry were still classified as "natural philosophy", that is, the philosophical study of nature. Today these latter subjects are popularly referred to as sciences, and as separate from philosophy.

More recently, psychology, economics, sociology, and linguistics were once the domain of philosophers insofar as they were studied at all, but now have only a weaker connection with the field. In the late twentieth century cognitive science and artificial intelligence could be seen as being forged in part out of "philosophy of mind."

Philosophy is done primarily through reflection. It does not tend to rely on experiment. However, in some ways philosophy is close to science in its character and method; some Analytic philosophers have suggested that the method of philosophical analysis allows philosophers to emulate the methods of natural science; Quine holds that philosist in any more than clarifying the arguments and claims of other sciences. This suggests that philosophy might be the study of meaning and reasoning generally; but some still would claim either that this is not a science, or that if it is it ought not to be pursued by philosophers.

All these views have something in common: whatever philosophy essentially is or is concerned with, it tends on the whole to proceed more "abstractly" than most (or most other) natural sciences. It does not depend as much on experience and experiment, and does not contribute as directly to technology. It clearly would be a mistake to identify philosophy with any one natural science; whether it can be identified with science very broadly construed is still an open question.

Philosophy of Science

This is an active discipline pursued by both trained philosophers and scientists. Philosophers often *refer to*, and interpret, experimental work of various kinds (as in philosophy of physics and philosophy of psychology). But this is not surprising: such branches of philosophy aim at philosophical understanding *of* experimental work. It is not the philosophers in their capacity *as* philosophers, who perform the experiments and formulate the scientific theories under study. Philosophy of science should not be confused with science it studies any more than biology should be confused with plants and animals.

Theology and Religious Studies

Like philosophy, most religious studies are not experimental. Parts of theology, including questions about the existence and nature of gods, clearly overlap with philosophy of religion. Aristotle considered theology a branch of metaphysics, the central field of philosophy, and most philosophers prior to the twentieth century have devoted significant effort to theological questions. So the two are not unrelated. But other part of religious studies, such as the comparison of different world religions, can be easily distinguished from philosophy in just the way that any other social science can be distinguished from philosophy. These are closer to history and sociology, and involve specific observations of particular phenomena, here particular religious practices.

The Empiricist tradition in modern philosophy often held that religious questions are beyond the scope of human knowledge, and many have claimed that religious language is literally meaningless: there are not even questions to be answered. Some philosophers have felt that these difficulties in evidence were irrelevant, and have argued for, against, or just about religious beliefs on moral or other grounds. Nonetheless, in the main stream of twentieth century philosophy there were very few philosophers who give serious consideration to religious questions.

Mathematics

Mathematics uses very specific, rigorous methods of proof that philosophers sometimes (only rarely) try to emulate. Most philosophy is written in ordinary prose, and while it strives to be precise it does not usually attain anything like mathematical clarity. As a result, mathematicians hardly ever disagree about results, while philosophers of course do disagree about their results, as well as their methods.

The philosophy of mathematics is a branch of philosophy of science; but in many ways mathematics has a special relationship to philosophy. This is because the study of logic is a central branch of philosophy, and mathematics is a paradigm example of logic. In the late nineteenth and twentieth centuries logic made great advances, and mathematics has been proven to be reducible to logic (at least, to first-order logic with some set theory). The use of formal, mathematical logic in philosophy now resembles the use of math in science, although it is not as frequent.

Idealism

Idealism is defined as the view that the existence of objects depends wholly or in part on the minds of those perceiving them. This definition is not complete by any means, in fact those who truly explore Idealistic concepts often come to the point where physical reality is nothing more than symbolism for the workings of the mind. This might sound strange and a little far-fetched but that is only because we are used to one particular view of the world, to explore another view would require a great deal of courage and the acceptance that You are not simply an accumulation of your beliefs.

Natualism-Pragmatism

Pragmatism, philosophical movement that has had a major impact on American culture from the late 19th century to the present. Pragmatism calls for ideas and theories to be tested in practice, by assessing whether acting upon the idea or theory produces desirable or undesirable results. According to pragmatists, all claims about truth, knowledge, morality, and politics must be tested in this way. Pragmatism has been critical of traditional Western philosophy, especially the notion that there are absolute truths and absolute values. Although pragmatism was popular for a time in France, England, and Italy, most observers believe that it encapsulates an American faith in know-how and practicality and an equally American distrust of abstract theories and ideologies.

Characteristics of Pragmatism

Pragmatists regard all theories and institutions as tentative hypotheses and solutions. For this reason they believed that efforts to improve society, through such means as education or politics, must be geared toward problem solving and must be ongoing. Through their emphasis on connecting theory to practice, pragmatist thinkers attempted to transform all areas of philosophy, from metaphysics to ethics and political philosophy.

Pragmatism sought a middle ground between traditional ideas about the nature of reality and radical theories of nihilism and irrationalism, which had become popular in Europe in the late 19th century. Traditional metaphysics assumed that the world has a fixed, intelligible structure and that human beings can know absolute or objective truths about the world and about what constitutes moral behaviour. Nihilism and irrationalism, on the other hand, denied those very assumptions and their certitude. Pragmatists today still try to steer a middle course between contemporary offshoots of these two extremes.

The ideas of the pragmatists were considered revolutionary when they first appeared. To some critics, pragmatism's refusal to affirm any absolutes carried negative implications for society. For example, pragmatists do not believe that a single absolute idea of goodness or justice exists, but rather that these concepts are changeable and depend on the context in which they are being discussed. The absence of these absolutes, critics feared, could result in a decline in moral standards. The pragmatists' denial of absolutes, moreover, challenged the foundations of religion, government, and schools of thought. As a result, pragmatism influenced developments in psychology, sociology, education, semiotics (the study of signs and symbols), and scientific method, as well as philosophy, cultural criticism, and social reform movements. Various political groups have also drawn on the assumptions of pragmatism, from the progressive movements of the early 20th century to later experiments in social reform.

History

Pragmatism is best understood in its historical and cultural context. It arose during the late 19th century, a period of rapid scientific advancement typified by the theories of British biologist Charles Darwin, whose theories suggested to many thinkers that humanity and society are in a perpetual state of progress. During this same period a decline in traditional religious beliefs and values accompanied the industrialization and material progress of the time. In consequence it became necessary to rethink fundamental ideas about values, religion, science, community, and individuality.

The three most important pragmatists are American philosophers Charles Sanders Peirce, William James, and John Dewey. Peirce was primarily interested in scientific method and mathematics; his objective was to infuse scientific thinking into philosophy and society, and he believed that human comprehension of reality was becoming ever greater and that human communities were becoming increasingly progressive. Peirce developed pragmatism as a theory of meaning—in particular, the meaning of concepts used in science. The meaning of the concept "brittle," for example, is given by the observed consequences or properties that objects called "brittle" exhibit. For Peirce, the only rational way to increase knowledge was to form mental habits that would test ideas through observation, experimentation, or what he called inquiry. Many philosophers known as logical positivists, a group of philosophers who have been influenced by Peirce, believed that our evolving species was fated to get ever closer to Truth. Logical positivists emphasize the importance of scientific verification, rejecting the assertion of positivism that personal experience is the basis of true knowledge.

James moved pragmatism in directions that Peirce strongly disliked. He generalized Peirce's doctrines to encompass all concepts, beliefs, and actions; he also applied pragmatist ideas to truth as well as to meaning. James was primarily interested in showing how systems of morality, religion, and faith could be defended in a scientific civilization. He argued that sentiment, as well as logic, is crucial to rationality and that the great issues of life—morality and religious belief, for example—are leaps of faith. As such, they depend upon what he called "the will to believe" and not merely on scientific evidence, which can never tell us what to do or what is worthwhile. Critics charged James with *relativism* (the belief that values depend on specific situations) and with crass expediency for proposing that if an idea or action works the way one intends, it must be right. But James can more accurately be described as a pluralist—someone who believes the world to be far too complex for any one philosophy to explain everything. Dewey's philosophy can be described as a version of philosophical naturalism, which regards human experience, intelligence, and communities as ever-evolving mechanisms. Using their experience and intelligence, Dewey believed, human beings can solve problems, including social problems, through inquiry. For Dewey, naturalism led to the idea of a democratic society that allows all members to acquire social intelligence and progress both as individuals and as communities. Dewey held that traditional ideas about knowledge, truth, and values, in which absolutes are assumed, are incompatible with a broadly Darwinian worldview in which individuals and society are progressing. In consequence, he felt that these traditional ideas must be discarded or revised. Indeed, for pragmatists, everything people know and do depends on a historical context and is thus tentative rather than absolute.

Many followers and critics of Dewey believe he advocated elitism and social engineering in his philosophical stance. Others think of him as a kind of romantic humanist. Both tendencies are evident in Dewey's writings, although he aspired to synthesize the two realms.

The pragmatist tradition was revitalized in the 1980s by American philosopher Richard Rorty, who has faced similar charges of elitism for his belief in the relativism of values and his emphasis on the role of the individual in attaining knowledge. Interest has renewed in the classic pragmatists—Pierce, James, and Dewey—as an alternative to Rorty's interpretation of the tradition.

In an ever changing world, pragmatism has many benefits. It defends social experimentation as a means of improving society, accepts pluralism, and rejects dead dogmas. But a philosophy that offers no final answers or absolutes and that appears vague as a result of trying to harmonize opposites may also be unsatisfactory to some.

Realism

Contemporary **philosophical realism**, also referred to as **metaphysical realism**, is the belief in a reality that is completely ontologically independent of our conceptual schemes, linguistic practices, beliefs, etc. Philosophers who profess realism also typically believe that truth consists in a belief's correspondence to reality. However, some realist philosophers prefer deflationary theories of truth to more traditional correspondence accounts. In recent times, debates concerning realism have become quite contentious due mostly in part to the influence of postmodernism. Reality in everyday usage means the state of things as they actually exist.... A common dictionary definition of truth is agreement with fact or reality. There is no single definition of truth about which the majority of philosophers agree.... The correspondence theory of truth states that something (for example, a proposition or statement or sentence) is rendered true by the existence of a fact with corresponding elements and a similar structure.... The deflationary theory of truth is a family of theories which all have in common the belief that assertions that predicate truth of a statement do not provide any substantive information or insight into the nature of truth.... The term Postmodernism (sometimes abbreviated Pomo) was coined in 1949 to describe a dissatisfaction with modern architecture, founding the postmodern architecture....

Realists tend to believe that whatever we believe now is only an approximation of reality and that every new observation brings us closer to understanding reality.

Debates about Realism

Despite the seeming straightforwardness of the realist position, in the history of philosophy there has been continuous debate about what is real. In addition, there has been significant evolution in what is meant by the term "real".

The oldest use of the term comes from medieval interpretations and adaptations of Greek philosophy. In this medieval "scholastic" philosophy, however, "realism" meant something different — indeed, in some ways almost opposite— from what it means today. In medieval philosophy, realism is contrasted with "conceptualism" and "nominalism". The opposition of realism and nominalism developed out of debates over the problem of universals. Universals are terms or properties that can be applied to many things, rather than denoting a single specific individual—for example, red, beauty, five, or dog, as opposed to "Socrates" or "Athens". Realism in this context holds that universals really exist, independently and somehow prior to the world; it is associated with Plato. Conceptualism holds that they exist, but only insofar as they are instantiated in specific things; they do not exist *separately*. Nominalism holds that universals do not "exist" at all; they are no more than words we use to describe specific objects, they do not name anything. This particular dispute over realism is largely moot in contemporary philosophy, and has been for centuries. Philosophy seated between the seven liberal arts â€" Picture from the Hortus deliciarum of Herrad von Landsberg (12th century) Medieval philosophy is the philosophy of Europe and the Middle East in the era now known as medieval or the Middle Ages, the period roughly extending from the fall of the Roman... Greek philosophy focused on the role of reason and inquiry.... Conceptualism is a doctrine in philosophy intermediate between nominalism and realism, that universals exist only within the mind and have no external or substantial reality.... In philosophy, nominalism is the theory that abstract terms, general terms, or universals do not represent objective real existents, but are merely names, words, or vocal utterances (flatus vocis).... This article or section is in need of attention from an expert on the subject.... Universals (used as a noun) are either properties, relations, or types, but not classes.... Platonic realism is a philosophical term usually used to refer to the idea of realism regarding the existence of universals after the Greek philosopher Plato who lived between c....

In its modern sense, *realism* is contrasted with both *idealism* and *materialism*, and is considered synonymous with *weak dualism*. In still a third, and very contemporary sense, *realism* is contrasted with *anti-realism*, primarily in the philosophy of science. This section may require cleanup to meet Wikipedias quality standards.... In philosophy, materialism is that form of physicalism which holds that the only thing that can truly be said to exist is matter; that fundamentally, all things are composed of material and all phenomena are the result of material interactions.... Rena Descartes illustration of dualism.... In philosophy, the term anti-realism is used to describe any position involving either the denial of the objective reality of entities of a certain type or the insistence that we should be agnostic about their real existence.... Philosophy of science is the study of assumptions, foundations, and implications of science, especially in the natural sciences and social sciences.... Both these disputes are often carried out relative to some specific area: one might, for example, be a realist about physical matter but an anti-realist about ethics. The high necessity of specifying the area in which the claim is made has been increasingly acknowledged in recent years.

Increasingly these last disputes, too, are rejected as misleading, and some philosophers prefer to call the kind of realism espoused there "metaphysical realism," and eschew the whole debate in favour of simple "naturalism" or "natural realism", which is not so much a theory as the position that these debates are ill-conceived if not incoherent, and that there is no more to deciding what is *really real* than simply taking our words at face value. Naturalism is any of several philosophical stances, typically those descended from materialism and pragmatism, that do not distinguish the supernatural (including strange entities like non-natural values, and universals as they are commonly conceived) from nature....

Realism in Physics

Realism in physics refers to the fact that Bell's theorem proves that every quantum theory must either violate local realism or counterfactual definiteness. Physics up to the 19th century was always implicitly and sometimes explicitly taken to be based on philosophical realism. With the advent of quantum mechanics in the 20th century, it was noted that it is no longer possible to adhere local realism — that is, to both the principle of locality (that distant objects cannot affect local objects), and a form of ontological realism implicit in classical physics. This has given rise to a contentious debate of the interpretation of quantum mechanics. Although locality and 'realism' are jointly false, it is possible to retain one of them. The majority of working physicists discard 'realism' in favour of locality, since non-locality is held to be contrary to relativity. The implications of this stance are rarely discussed outside of the microscopic domain.

Realism as a Philosophy of Education

What is admirable about realism as a philosophy of education – and I speak here of classical realism – is that it revolted against the idealist confinement of what is ultimately real to the world of ideas. This revolutionary viewpoint alone has important educative implications, the first being that of putting man in a position of primacy in relation with instead of supremacy in condescending rule over the rest of the universe. Since what is outside man as perceived through sensation is real, since what I see is what I get, then I have the responsibility of knowing these things in order that I may use them well. I resist the utopian belittling of the material as mere, poor copies of what they truly are in an other-world without illusions, but instead care for my world knowing that it is the only one I have and realizing that it is ultimately not mine, but that of many more who would be in it long after my time is past. Whether I am there to perceive the world or not, the world exists. I would be selfish and callous if I do not revere this world that is independent of me: that is not a product of my conception, but an independent reality, for, to paraphrase Max Ehrmann, with all its sham, drudgery, and broken dreams, it is still a beautiful world. If I am educated in such a way as to not reject this world as a mere specter, then I would be equipped with the knowledge of being responsible for it. I need not look forward exclusively to looking forward to a better world, but I endeavour with all of myself as well to make this world a better place.

The Christianization of classical realism courtesy of St. Thomas Aquinas is in my assessment a most venerable culmination of this educational philosophy. While Aristotle's realism placed man in relation with his world, Aquinas' realism philosophically fortified man in relation with God. In doing so he tied up the final chain of the triad that forms the subjects or objects of man's philosophical inquiries across the ages: God, the world, and himself. God being pure reason and man being made in the image and likeness of this pure reason becomes more and more identified with the deity the better and the more he exercises reason through thinking In our secularized setting, Christian-classical realism is considered quaint, if not prehistoric. But in truth it is only when educators are aware of a Divine Teacher who will one day judge their own teachings that they will be inspired to perform their tasks with excellence. Hence they will impart not just knowledge per se but education geared towards the common good, education guided by a God who seeks the salvation of all in a re-creation that is not only spiritual but holistic, thus converting too the temporal realm and not just the unseen. The educational philosophy prevails today in Catholic academic circles under the language of "stewardship" whereby the end of knowledge is sustainable development – the use of creation and human time, treasure and talent in a way that enhances but neither depletes nor oppresses the gifts placed under our care.

The secular-minded among us tend to warn against the danger of knowledge being made subservient to religion in sectarian institutions. In my view, the continuing dialogue between culture and faith has ensured that the academe and magisterium intertwined in say, Catholic educational institutions remain at the service of truth, so that culture does not succumb to ideology and religion does not give way to bigotry. Concretely, the Vatican has a Pontifical Academy for Sciences, while many universities across the world have study centres for faith and ecumenism. Such marriage of classical and religious realist trains of thought is a guarantee of hope amid the many problems besetting society today, not least among them the problem of keeping education well-grounded and well-used.

Francis Bacon responded to this problem by proposing the tearing down of the idols that according to him limited the scope, depth, and veracity of human knowledge. I have no problems with the seed of modern realism that Bacon planted. Indeed, limited experience, linguistic disparity, philosophical dogmatism and religious bigotry, and go-with-the-flow, bend-or-break mentality are ingredients for educational darkness. Yet educational iconoclasm should not be wholesale but restrained, for otherwise it risks chaos and at worst, nihilism. Many philosophical currents decried as dogmatic never became dogmas as such without the test of time and validation via human experience. We cannot, to cite a few examples, do away with marriage as union between a man and a woman just because it has been libelled a dogma, undo the results of an election just because it springs from a tribal majority vote, ignore the hunger in a corner of the world just because food is abundant in Europe and therefore incidents of hunger are isolated Third World maladies, or view "truth is subjectivity" as a mere philosophical fad.

It is well and good to restart from particulars before making generalizations vis-a-vis gaining knowledge, and indeed, where possible, to make qualifications to generalizations, exemptions to rules. Nonetheless there undeniably are things best left unsullied. The right to life for example, or the dignities of man as stipulated in the Universal Declaration of Human Rights are not conclusions drawn from inductive studies but expressions of a clear vision of what constituted a dignified life based on a knowledge of it before it was ravaged by war. We do not need a long and winding inductive study to know that poverty is a scourge on mankind and that neither band-aid solutions or material redress suffice to compensate for it because we know deep within that the poor need not mere philanthropy but compassionate solidarity. Thus the realist iconoclasm of Francis Bacon should be tempered by human compassion lest it aid an educational system that ends up treating mankind, the world and God with a heartless, laboratory precision that is but another name for irreverence towards reality.

The sensation and reflection espoused by John Locke as an apparent development of Bacon's ideas are useful in very particular fields of human endeavour. However, as it reduces philosophy into a hard science it cannot stand on its own as a philosophy for holistic human education. What he classifies as abstract idealisms – real but beyond verification by reflection and sensation may be what he calls them but they are indispensable for human life to be called at least decent. Imagine if such realities as love and heroism, saintliness and dedication, service and the invisible rewards of an embrace have to be subjected to the rigours of empiricism in order to be accepted as real. Such would lose their vitality. It would be as dissecting the rose and losing the entire flower, indeed missing the forest for the trees. I couldn't care less if it was by refraction or reflection or whatsoever cosmic and celestial phenomenon the sun grandly paints the western horizon every twilight time. What matters is that I am able to drink in this rare everyday beauty, so much the better with people held dear sharing the scenery with me.

As for my views on logical positivism and linguistic analysis which are concrete manifestations of contemporary realism, I say that these bode well for the communion of peoples and the purification of philosophies and belief systems from superstition, yet educators should be careful not to promote its discoveries as summits of knowledge, for these ought to be but instruments for achieving the greater hopes of man, instruments that are not necessarily helpful in achieving his greatest hope that is love.

Eclecticism

Eclecticism is a conceptual approach that does not hold rigidly to a single paradigm or set of assumptions, but instead draws upon multiple theories, styles, or ideas to gain complementary insights into a subject, or applies different theories in particular cases.

It can sometimes seem inelegant or lacking in simplicity, and eclectics are sometimes criticized for lack of consistency in their thinking. It is, however, common in many fields of study. For example, most psychologists accept certain aspects of behaviourism, but do not attempt to use the theory to explain all aspects of human behaviour. A statistician may use frequentist techniques on one occasion and Bayesian ones on another.

Unit-III

Eastern and Western Thinkers on Education

Swami Vivekananda

Swami Vivekananda (January 12, 1863–July 4, 1902), born **Narendranath Dutta** is the chief disciple of the 19th century mystic Ramakrishna and the founder of Ramakrishna Mission. He is considered a key figure in the introduction of Vedanta and Yoga in Europe and America and is also credited with raising interfaith awareness, bringing Hinduism to the status of a world religion during the end of the 19th Century. Vivekananda is considered to be a major force in the revival of Hinduism in modern India. He is best known for his inspiring speech beginning with "sisters and brothers of America", through which he introduced Hinduism at the Parliament of the World's Religions at Chicago in 1893.

Swami Vivekananda was born in an aristocratic family of Calcutta in 1863. His parents influenced the Swami's thinking—the father by his rational mind and the mother by her religious temperament. From his childhood, he showed inclination towards spirituality and God realization. While searching for a man who could directly demonstrate the reality of God, he came to Ramakrishna and became his disciple. As a guru Ramakrishna taught him *Advaita Vedanta* and that all religions are true, and service to man was the most effective worship of God. After the death of his Guru, he became a wandering monk touring the Indian subcontinent and getting a first hand account of India's condition. He later sailed to Chicago and represented India as a delegate in the 1893 Parliament of World religions. An eloquent speaker, Vivekananda was invited to several forums in United States and spoke at universities and clubs. He conducted several public and private lectures, disseminating Vedanta, Yoga and Hinduism in America, England and few other countries in Europe. He also established Vedanta societies in America and England. He later sailed back to India and in 1897 he founded the Ramakrishna Math and Mission, a philanthropic and spiritual organization. The Swami is regarded as one of India's foremost nation-builders. His teachings influenced the thinking of other national leaders and philosophers, like Mahatma Gandhi, Jawaharlal Nehru, Subhas Chandra Bose, Aurobindo Ghosh, Radhakrishnan.

Biography

College and Brahmo Samaj

Narendranath entered the first year Arts class of Presidency College, Calcutta in January 1880 and the next year he shifted to Scottish Church College, Calcutta. During the course, he studied western logic, western philosophy and history of European nations. In 1881 he passed the Fine Arts examination and in 1884 he passed the Bachelor of Arts.

According to his professors, student Narendranath was a prodigy. Dr. William Hastie, the principal of Scottish Church College, where he studied during 1881-84, wrote, "Narendra is really a genius. I have travelled far and wide but I have never come across a lad of his talents and possibilities, even in German universities, among philosophical students." He was regarded as a *srutidhara*—a man with prodigious memory. After a discussion with Narendranath, Dr. Mahendralal Sarkar reportedly said, "I could never have thought that such a young boy had read so much!"

From his childhood, he showed inclination towards spirituality, God realisation and realizing the highest spiritual truths. He studied different religious and philosophical systems of East and the West; he met different religious leaders. He came under the influence of the Brahmo Samaj, an important socio-religious organization of that time. His initial beliefs were shaped by Brahmo Samaj, which believed in formless God, deprecated the worship of idols and devoted itself to socio-religious reforms. He met the leaders of Brahmo Samaj—Devendranath Tagore and Keshub Chandra Sen, questioning them about the existence of God, but he could not get convincing answers.

Narendranath is said to have studied the writings of David Hume, Immanuel Kant, Johann Gottlieb Fichte, Baruch Spinoza, Georg W. F. Hegel, Arthur Schopenhauer, Auguste Comte, Herbert Spencer, John Stuart Mill, and Charles Darwin. Narendra became fascinated with the Evolutionism of Herbert Spencer, and translated Spencer's book on *Education* into Bengali for Gurudas Chattopadhyaya, his publisher. Narendra also had correspondence with Herbert Spencer for some time. Alongside his study of Western philosophers, he was thoroughly acquainted with Indian Sanskrit scriptures and many Bengali works. His first introduction to Ramakrishna occurred in a literature class, when he heard Principal Hastie lecturing on William Wordsworth's poem *The Excursion* and the poet's nature-mysticism. In the course of explaining the word *trance* in the poem, Hastie told his students that if they wanted to know the real meaning of it, they should go to Ramakrishna of Dakshineswar. This prompted some of his students, including Narendranath to visit Ramakrishna.

With Ramakrishna

His meeting with Ramakrishna Paramahamsa in November 1881 proved to be a turning point in his life. About this meeting, Narendranath said, "He [Ramakrishna] looked just like an ordinary man, with nothing remarkable about him. He used the most simple language and I thought 'Can this man be a great teacher?'– I crept near to him and asked him the question which I had been asking others all my life: 'Do you believe in God, Sir?' 'Yes,' he replied. 'Can you prove it, Sir?' 'Yes.' 'How?' 'Because I see Him just as I see you here, only in a much intenser sense.' That impressed me at once. [...] I began to go to that man, day after day, and I actually saw that religion could be given. One touch, one glance, can change a whole life."

Even though Narendra did not accept Ramakrishna as his guru initially and revolted against his ideas, he was attracted by his personality and visited him frequently. He initially looked upon on Ramakrishna's ecstasies and visions as, "mere figments of imagination", "mere hallucinations". As a member of Brahmo samaj, he revolted against idol worship and polytheism, and Ramakrishna's worship of Kali. He even rejected the *Advaitist Vedantism* of identity with absolute as blasphemy and madness, and often made fun of the concept

Though Narendra could not accept Ramakrishna and his visions, he could not neglect him either. It had always been in Narendra's nature to test something thoroughly before he would accept it. He tested Ramakrishna, who never asked Narendra to abandon reason, and faced all of Narendra's arguments and examinations with patience—"Try to see the truth from all angles" was his reply. During the course of five years of his training under Ramakrishna, Narendra was transformed from a restless, puzzled, impatient youth to a mature man who was ready to renounce everything for the sake of God-realization. In time, Narendra accepted Ramakrishna, and when he accepted, his acceptance was whole-hearted.

In 1885 Ramakrishna suffered from throat cancer and he was shifted to Calcutta and later to Cossipore. Vivekananda and his brother disciples took care of Ramakrishna during this final days. His spiritual education under Ramakrishna continued here. At Cossipore, Vivekananda reportedly experienced *Nirvikalpa Samadhi*. During the last days of Ramakrishna, Vivekananda and some of the other disciples received the ochre monastic robes from Ramakrishna, which formed the first monastic order of Ramakrishna. Vivekananda was taught that service to men was the most effective worship of God. It is reported that when Vivekananda, doubted Ramakrishna's claim of *avatara*, Ramakrishna reportedly said, "He who was Rama, He who was Krishna, He himself is now Ramakrishna in this body." During his final days, Ramakrishna asked Vivekananda to take care of other monastic disciples and in turn asked them to look upon Vivekananda as their leader. Ramakrishna's condition worsened gradually and he expired in the early morning hours of August 16, 1886 at the Cossipore garden house. According to his disciples, this was *Mahasamadhi*.

Baranagore Monastery

After the death of their master, the monastic disciples led by Vivekananda formed a fellowship at a half-ruined house at Baranagar near the river Ganga, with the financial assistance of the householder disciples. This became the first Math or monastery of the disciples who constituted the first Ramakrishna Order.

The dilapidated house at Baranagore was chosen because of its low rent and proximity to the Cossipore burning-ghat, where Ramakrishna was cremated. Narendra and other members of the Math often spent their time in meditation, discussing about different philosophies and teachings of spiritual teachers including Ramakrishna, Shankaracharya, Ramanuja, and Jesus Christ. Narendra reminisced about the early days in the monastery as follows, "We underwent a lot of religious practice at Baranagore Math. We used to get up at 3:00 am and become absorbed in *japam* and meditation. What a strong spirit of dispassion we had in those days! We had no thought even as to whether the world existed or not" In the early part of 1887, Narendra and eight other disciples took formal monastic vows. Narendra took the name of Swami Vividishananda.

First visit to the West

His journey to America took him through China, Japan, Canada and he arrived at Chicago in July 1893. But to his disappointment he learnt that no one without credentials from a *bona fide* organization would be accepted as a delegate. He came in contact with Professor John Henry Wright of Harvard University. After inviting him to speak at Harvard and on learning of his not having credential to speak at the Parliament, Wright is quoted as having said, "To ask for your credentials is like asking the sun to state its right to shine in the heavens." Wright then addressed a letter to the Chairman in charge of delegates writing, "Here is a man who is more learned than all of our learned professors put together." On the Professor Vivekananda himself writes, "He urged upon me the necessity of going to the Parliament of Religions, which he thought would give an introduction to the nation."

Parliament of World's Religions

The Parliament of Religions opened on 11 September 1893 at the Art Institute of Chicago. On this day Vivekananda gave his first brief address. He represented India and Hinduism. Though initially nervous, he bowed to *Saraswati*, the goddess of learning and began his speech with, "Sisters and brothers of America!". To these words he got a standing ovation from a crowd of seven thousand, which lasted for two minutes. When silence was restored he began his address. He greeted the youngest of the nations in the name of "the most ancient order of monks in the world, the Vedic order of sannyasins, a religion which has taught the world both tolerance and universal acceptance." And he quoted two illustrative passages in this relation, from the *Bhagavad Gita*—"As the different streams having their sources in different places all mingle their water in the sea, so, O Lord, the different paths which men take, through different tendencies, various though they appear, crooked or straight, all lead to Thee!" and "Whosoever comes to Me, through whatsoever form, I reach him; all men are struggling through paths that in the end lead to Me." Despite being a short speech, it voiced the spirit of the Parliament and its sense of universality.

Dr. Barrows, the president of the Parliament said, "India, the Mother of religions was represented by Swami Vivekananda, the Orange-monk who exercised the most wonderful influence over his auditors." He attracted widespread attention in the press, which dubbed him as the "Cyclonic monk from India". The *New York Critique* wrote, "He is an orator by divine right, and his strong, intelligent face in its picturesque setting of yellow and orange was hardly less interesting than those earnest words, and the rich, rhythmical utterance he gave them." The *New York Herald* wrote, "Vivekananda is undoubtedly the greatest figure in the Parliament of Religions. After hearing him we feel how foolish it is to send missionaries to this learned nation." Swami Vivekananda was regarded as, "undoubtedly the greatest figure in the parliament of religions", "beyond question, the most popular and influential man in the parliament."

He spoke several more times at the Parliament on topics related to Hinduism and Buddhism. The parliament ended on 27 September 1893. All his speeches at the Parliament had one common theme—Universality and stressed religious tolerance.

Lecturing tours in America, England

After the Parliament of Religions, held in Sept. 1893 at The Art Institute of Chicago, Vivekananda spent nearly two whole years lecturing in various parts of eastern and central United States, appearing chiefly in Chicago, Detroit, Boston, and New York. By the spring of 1895, he was weary and in poor health, because of his continuous exertion. After suspending his lecture tour, the Swami started giving free and private classes on Vedanta and Yoga. In June 1895, for two months he conducted private lectures to a dozen of his disciples at the Thousand Island Park. Vivekananda considered this to the happiest part of his first visit to America. He later founded the "Vedanta Society of New York".

During his first visit to America, he travelled to England twice—in 1895 and 1896. His lectures were successful there. Here he met Miss Margaret Noble an Irish lady, who later became Sister Nivedita. During his second visit in May 1896, the Swami met Max Muller a renowned Indologist at Oxford University who wrote Ramakrishna's first biography in the West. From England, he also visited other European countries. In Germany he met Paul Deussen, another famous Indologist.

He also received two academic offers, the chair of Eastern Philosophy at Harvard University and a similar position at Columbia University. He declined both, saying that, as a wandering monk, he could not settle down to work of this kind.

He attracted several sincere followers. Among his other followers were, Josephine MacLeod, Miss Muller, Miss Noble, E.T. Sturdy, Captain and Mrs. Sevier—who played an important role in the founding of Advaita Ashrama and J.J.Goodwin—who became his stenographer and recorded his teachings and lectures. The Hale family became one of his warmest hosts in

America. His disciples—Madame Louise, a French woman, became Swami Abhayananda, and Mr. Leon Landsberg, became Swami Kripananda. He initiated several other followers into Brahmacharya.

Swami Vivekananda's ideas were admired by several scholars and famous thinkers—William James, Josiah Royce, C. C. Everett, Dean of the Harvard School of Divinity, Robert G. Ingersoll, Nikola Tesla, Lord Kelvin, and Professor Hermann Ludwig Ferdinand von Helmholtz. Other personalities who were attracted by his talks were Harriet Monroe and Ella Wheeler Wilcox—two famous American poets, Professor William James of Harvard University; Dr. Lewis G. Janes, president of Brooklyn Ethical Association; Sara C. Bull wife of Ole Bull, the Norwegian violinist; Sarah Bernhardt, the French actress and Madame Emma Calve, the French opera singer.

From West, he also set his Indian work in motion. Vivekananda wrote a stream of letters to India, giving advice and sending money to his followers and brother monks. His letters from the West in these days laid down the motive of his campaign for social service. He constantly tried to inspire his close disciples in India to do something big. His letters to them contain some of his strongest words. In one such letter, he wrote to Swami Akhandananda, "Go from door to door amongst the poor and lower classes of the town of Khetri and teach them religion. Also, let them have oral lessons on geography and such other subjects. No good will come of sitting idle and having princely dishes, and saying "Ramakrishna, O Lord!"—unless you can do some good to the poor." Eventually in 1895, the periodical called *Brahmavadin* was started in Madras, with the money supplied by Vivekananda, for the purpose of teaching the Vedanta. Subsequenly, Vivekananda's translation of first six chapters of *The Imitation of Christ* was published in *Brahmavadin* (1889).

Vivekananda left for India on 16 December 1896 from England with disciples, Capitan and Mrs. Sevier, and J.J.Goodwin. On the way they visited France, Italy, seeing Leonardo Da Vinci's *The Last Supper*, and set sail for India from the Port of Naples on December 30, 1896. Later, he was followed to India by Miss Muller and Sister Nivedita. Sister Nivedita devoted the rest of her life to the education of Indian women and the cause of India's independence.

Founding of Ramakrishna Math and Mission

On 1 May 1897 at Calcutta, Vivekananda founded the "Ramakrishna Math"—the organ for propagating religion and "Ramakrishna Mission"—the organ for social service. This was the beginning of an organized socio-religious movement to help the masses through educational, cultural, medical and relief work. The ideals of the Ramakrishna Mission are based on *Karma Yoga*. Two monasteries were founded by him, one at Belur, near Calcutta, which became the Headquarters of Ramakrishna Math and Mission and the other at Mayavati on the Himalayas, near Almora called the *Advaita Ashrama* and later a third monastery was established at Madras. Two journals were started, *Prabuddha Bharata* in English and *Udbhodan* in Bengali. The same year, the famine relief work was started by Swami Akhandananda at Murshidabad district.

Vivekananda had inspired Sir Jamshetji Tata to set up a research and educational institution when they had travelled together from Yokohama to Chicago on the Swami's first visit to the West in 1893. About this time the Swami received a letter from Tata, requesting him to head the Research Institute of Science that Tata had set up. But Vivekananda declined the offor saying that it conflicted with his spiritual interests.

He later visited Punjab, in Pakistan with the mission of establishing harmony between the *Arya Samaj* which stood for reinterpreted Hinduism and the *Sanatanaists* who stood for orthodox Hinduism. At Rawalpindi, he suggested methods for rooting out antagonism between Arya Samajists and Muslims. His visit to Lahore is memorable for his famous speeches and his inspiring association with Tirtha Ram Goswami, then a brilliant professor of Mathematics, who later graced monasticism as Swami Rama Tirtha and preached *Vedanta* in India and America. He also visited other places, including Delhi and Khetri and returned to Calcutta in January 1896. He spent the next few months consolidating the work of the *Math* and training the disciples. During this period he composed the famous *arati* song, *Khandana Bhava Bandhana* during the event of consecration of Ramakrishna's temple at a devotees' house.

Teachings and Philosophy

Vivekananda was a renowned thinker in his own right. One of his most important contributions was to demonstrate how Advaitin thinking is not merely philosophically far-reaching, but how it also has social, even political, consequences. According to Vivekananda, a important lesson he received from Ramakrishna was that "Jiva is Shiva" (each individual is divinity itself). This became his Mantra, and he coined the concept of *daridra narayana seva*-the service of God in and through (poor) human beings. *If there truly is the unity of Brahman underlying all phenomena, then on what basis do we regard ourselves as better or worse, or even as better-off or worse-off, than others?*- This was the question he posed to himself. Ultimately, he concluded that these distinctions fade into nothingness in the light of the oneness that the devotee experiences in Moksha. What arises then is compassion for those "individuals" who remain unaware of this oneness and a determination to help them.

Swami Vivekananda belonged to that branch of Vedanta that held that no one can be truly free until all of us are. Even the desire for personal salvation has to be given up, and only tireless work for the salvation of others is the true mark of the enlightened person. He founded the Sri Ramakrishna Math and Mission on the principle of **Atmano Mokshartham Jagat-hitaya cha** (for one's own salvation and for the welfare of the World).

However, Vivekananda also pleaded for a strict separation between religion and government ("church and state") a value found in Freemasonry which as a Freemason he had been exposed to. Although social customs had been formed in the past with religious sanction, it was not now the business of religion to interfere with matters such as marriage, inheritance and so on. The ideal society would be a mixture of Brahmin knowledge, Kshatriya culture, Vaisya efficiency and the egalitarian Shudra ethos. Domination by any one led to different sorts of lopsided societies. Vivekananda did not feel that religion, nor, any force for that matter, should be used forcefully to bring about an ideal society, since this was something that would evolve naturally by individualistic change when the conditions were right.

Vivekananda made a strict demarcation between the two classes of Hindu scriptures : the *Sruti* and the *Smritis*. The Sruti, by which is meant the Vedas, consist of eternally and universally valid spiritual truths. The Smritis on the other hand, are the dos and donts of religions, applicable to society and subject to revision from time to time. Vivekananda felt that existing Hindu smritis had to be revised for modern times. But the Srutis of course are eternal-they may only be re-interpreted.

Vivekananda advised his followers to be holy, unselfish and have shraddha (faith). He encouraged the practice of Brahmacharya (Celibacy). In one of the conversations with his childhood friend Priya Nath Sinha he attributes his physical and mental strengths, eloquence to the practice of Brahmacharya.

Vivekananda didn't advocate the emerging area of parapsychology, astrology (one instance can be found in his speech *Man the Maker of his Destiny*, *Complete-Works,*

Influence

Several leaders of 20th Century India and philosophers have acknowledged Vivekananda's influence. The first governor general of independent India, Chakravarti Rajagopalachari, once observed that "Vivekananda saved Hinduism, saved India." According to Subhas Chandra Bose, Vivekananda "is the maker of modern India" and for Mohandas Gandhi, Vivekananda's influence increased his "love for his country a thousandfold." National Youth Day in India is held on his birthday, January 12, to commemorate him. This was a most fitting gesture as much of Swami Vivekananda's writings concerned the Indian youth and how they should strive to uphold their ancient values whilst fully participating in the modern world.

Swami Vivekananda is widely considered to have inspired India's freedom struggle movement. His writings inspired a whole generation of freedom fighters including Aurobindo Ghose and Bagha Jatin. Vivekananda was the brother of the extremist revolutionary, Bhupendranath Dutta. Subhash Chandra Bose one of the most prominent figures in Indian independence movement said,

I cannot write about Vivekananda without going into raptures. Few indeed could comprehend or fathom him even among those who had the privilege of becoming intimate with him. His personality was rich, profound and complex... Reckless in his sacrifice, unceasing in his activity, boundless in his love, profound and versatile in his wisdom, exuberant in his emotions, merciless in his attacks but yet simple as a child, he was a rare personality in this world of ours

Aurobindo Ghosh considered Vivekananda as his spiritual mentor.

Vivekananda was a soul of puissance if ever there was one, a very lion among men, but the definitive work he has left behind is quite incommensurate with our impression of his creative might and energy. We perceive his influence still working gigantically, we know not well how, we know not well where, in something that is not yet formed, something leonine, grand, intuitive, upheaving that has entered the soul of India and we say, "Behold, Vivekananda still lives in the soul of his Mother and in the souls of her children. —*Sri Aurobindo in Vedic Magazine (1915)*

The French Nobel Laureate, Romain Rolland writes, "His words are great music, phrases in the style of Beethoven, stirring rhythms like the march of Handel choruses. I cannot touch these sayings of his, scattered as they are through the pages of books, at thirty years' distance, without receiving a thrill through my body like an electric shock. And what shocks, what transports, must have been produced when in burning words they issued from the lips of the hero!

Vivekananda inspired Jamshedji Tata to set up Indian Institute of Science, one of India's finest Institutions. Abroad, he had some interactions with Max Mueller. Nikola Tesla was one of those influenced by the Vedic philosophy teachings of the Swami Vivekananda.

Above all Swami Vivekananda helped restore a sense of pride amongst the Hindus, presenting the ancient teachings of India in its purest form to a Western audience, free from the propaganda spread by British colonial administrators and Christian missionaries, of Hinduism being a caste-ridden, misogynistic idolatrous faith. Indeed his early foray into the West would set the path for subsequent Indian religious teachers to make their own marks on the world, as well herald the entry of Hindus and their religious traditions into the Western world.

Swami Vivekananda's ideas have had a great influence on the Indian youth. In many institutes, students have come together and formed organizations meant for promoting discussion of spiritual ideas and the practice of such high principles. Many of such organizations have adopted the name Vivekananda Study Circle. One such group also exists at IIT Madras and is popularly known as (VSC). Additionally, Swami Vivekananda's ideas and teachings have carried on globally, being practiced in institutions all over the world.

Mahatma Gandhi said, "Swami Vivekananda's writings need no introduction from anybody. They make their own irresistible appeal." Many years after Vivekananda's death, Rabindranath Tagore a Nobel Poet Laureate had said, "If you want to know India, study Vivekananda. In him everything is positive and nothing negative."

Works

Vivekananda left a body of philosophical works which Vedic scholar Frank Parlato has called, "the greatest comprehensive work in philosophy ever published." His books (compiled from lectures given around the world) on the four Yogas (Raja Yoga, Karma Yoga, Bhakti Yoga, Jnana Yoga) are very influential and still seen as fundamental texts for anyone interested in the Hindu practice of Yoga. His letters are of great literary and spiritual value. He was also considered a very good singer and a poet. By He had composed many songs including his favourite

Kali the Mother. He used humour for his teachings and was also an excellent cook. His language is very free flowing. His own Bengali writings stand testimony to the fact that he believed that words-spoken or written should be for making things easier to understand rather than show off the speaker or writer's knowledge.

Mahatma Gandhi

Mohandas Karamchand Gandhi (2 October 1869 – 30 January 1948) was a prominent political and spiritual leader of India and the Indian independence movement. He was the pioneer of *satyagraha*—resistance to tyranny through mass civil disobedience, firmly founded upon *ahimsa* or total non-violence—which led India to independence and inspired movements for civil rights and freedom across the world. He is commonly known around the world as **Mahatma Gandhi** ("Great Soul", an honorific first applied to him by Rabindranath Tagore) and in India also as *Bapu*. He is officially honoured in India as the *Father of the Nation*; his birthday, 2 October, is commemorated there as *Gandhi Jayanti*, a national holiday, and worldwide as the International Day of Non-Violence.

Gandhi first employed non-violent civil disobedience as an expatriate lawyer in South Africa, in the resident Indian community's struggle for civil rights. After his return to India in 1915, he set about organising peasants, farmers, and urban labourers in protesting excessive land-tax and discrimination. Assuming leadership of the Indian National Congress in 1921, Gandhi led nationwide campaigns for easing poverty, expanding women's rights, building religious and ethnic amity, ending untouchability, increasing economic self-reliance, but above all achieving *Swaraj*—the independence of India from foreign domination. Gandhi famously led Indians in the Non-cooperation movement in 1922 and in protesting the British-imposed salt tax with the 400 km (249 mi) Dandi Salt March in 1930, and later in calling for the British to *Quit India* in 1942. He was imprisoned for many years, on numerous occasions, in both South Africa and India. As a practitioner of Ahimsa Gandhi swore to speak the truth. and advocated that others do the same. He lived modestly in a self-sufficient residential community and wore the traditional Indian *dhoti* and shawl, woven with yarn he had hand spun on a *charkha*. He ate simple vegetarian food, and also undertook long fasts as means of both self-purification and social protest.

Early Life and Background

Mohandas Karamchand Gandhi was born in Porbandar, a coastal town in present-day Gujarat, India, on 2 October 1869. His father, Karamchand Gandhi (1822-1885), who belonged to the Hindu Modh community, was the *diwan* (Prime Minister) of the eponymous Porbander state, a small princely state in the Kathiawar Agency of British India. His mother, Putlibai, who came from the Hindu Pranami Vaishnava community, was Karamchand's fourth wife, the first three wives having apparently died in childbirth. Growing up with a devout mother and the Jain traditions of the region, the young Mohandas absorbed early the influences that would play an important role in his adult life; these included compassion to sentient beings, vegetarianism, fasting for self-purification, and mutual tolerance between individuals of different creeds.

In May 1883, the 13-year old Mohandas was married to 14-year old Kasturbai Makhanji (her first name was usually shortened to "Kasturba," and affectionately to "Ba") in an arranged child marriage, as was the custom in the region. However, as was also the custom of the region, the adolescent bride was to spend much time at her parents' house, and away from her husband. In 1885, when Gandhi was 15, the couple's first child was born, but survived only a few days; Gandhi's father, Karamchand Gandhi, had died earlier that year. Mohandas and Kasturbai had four more children, all sons: Harilal, born in 1888; Manilal, born in 1892; Ramdas, born in 1897; and Devdas, born in 1900. At his middle school in Porbandar and high school in Rajkot, Gandhi remained an average student academically. He passed the matriculation exam for Samaldas College at Bhavnagar, Gujarat with some difficulty. While there, he was unhappy, in part because his family wanted him to become a barrister.

On 4 September 1888, less than a month shy of his nineteenth birthday, Gandhi travelled to London, England, to study law at University College London and to train as a barrister. His time in London, the Imperial capital, was influenced by a vow he had made to his mother in the presence of the Jain monk Becharji, upon leaving India, to observe the Hindu precepts of abstinence from meat, alcohol, and promiscuity. Although Gandhi experimented with adopting "English" customs—taking dancing lessons for example—he could not stomach his landlady's mutton and cabbage. She pointed him towards one of London's few vegetarian restaurants. Rather than simply go along with his mother's wishes, he read about, and intellectually embraced vegetarianism. He joined the Vegetarian Society, was elected to its executive committee, and founded a local chapter. He later credited this with giving him valuable experience in organizing institutions. Some of the vegetarians he met were members of the Theosophical Society, which had been founded in 1875 to further universal brotherhood, and which was devoted to the study of Buddhist and Hindu literature. They encouraged Gandhi to read the *Bhagavad Gita*. Not having shown a particular interest in religion before, he read works of and about Hinduism, Christianity, Buddhism, Islam and other religions. He returned to India after being called to the bar of England and Wales by the Inner Temple but had limited success establishing a law practice in Mumbai. Later, after applying and being turned down for a part-time job as a high school teacher, he ended up returning to Rajkot to make a modest living drafting petitions for litigants, a business he was forced to close when he ran afoul of a British officer. In his autobiography, he refers to this incident as an unsuccessful attempt to lobby on behalf of his older brother. It was in this climate that, in 1893, he accepted a year-long contract from an Indian firm to a post in Natal, South Africa, then part of the British Empire.

Gandhi's Principles

Truth

Gandhi dedicated his life to the wider purpose of discovering truth, or *Satya*. He tried to achieve this by learning from his own mistakes and conducting experiments on himself. He called his autobiography *The Story of My Experiments with Truth.*

Gandhi stated that the most important battle to fight was overcoming his own demons, fears, and insecurities. Gandhi summarized his beliefs first when he said "God is Truth". He would later change this statement to "Truth is God". Thus, *Satya* (Truth) in Gandhi's philosophy is "God".

Nonviolence

Although Mahatama Gandhi was in no way the originator of the principle of non-violence, he was the first to apply it in the political field on a huge scale. The concept of nonviolence (*ahimsa*) and nonresistance has a long history in Indian religious thought and has had many revivals in Hindu, Buddhist, Jain, Jewish and Christian contexts. Gandhi explains his philosophy and way of life in his autobiography *The Story of My Experiments with Truth.* He was quoted as saying:

> *"When I despair, I remember that all through history the way of truth and love has always won. There have been tyrants and murderers and for a time they seem invincible, but in the end, they always fall — think of it, always."*
>
> *"What difference does it make to the dead, the orphans, and the homeless, whether the mad destruction is wrought under the name of totalitarianism or the holy name of liberty and democracy?"*
>
> *"An eye for an eye makes the whole world blind."*
>
> *"There are many causes that I am prepared to die for but no causes that I am prepared to kill for."*

In applying these principles, Gandhi did not balk from taking them to their most logical extremes in envisioning a world where even government, police and armies were nonviolent.

The science of war leads one to dictatorship, pure and simple. The science of non-violence alone can lead one to pure democracy...Power based on love is thousand times more effective and permanent than power derived from fear of punishment....It is a blasphemy to say non-violence can be practiced only by individuals and never by nations which are composed of individuals...The nearest approach to purest anarchy would be a democracy based on non-violence...A society organized and run on the basis of complete non-violence would be the purest anarchy

I have conceded that even in a non-violent state a police force may be necessary...Police ranks will be composed of believers in non-violence. The people will instinctively render them every help and through mutual cooperation they will easily deal with the ever decreasing disturbances...Violent quarrels between labour and capital and strikes will be few and far between in a non-violent state because the influence of the non-violent majority will be great as to respect the principle elements in society. Similarly, there will be no room for communal disturbances....

A non-violent army acts unlike armed men, as well in times of peace as in times of disturbances. Theirs will be the duty of bringing warring communities together, carrying peace propaganda, engaging in activities that would bring and keep them in touch with every single person in their parish or division. Such an army should be ready to cope with any emergency, and in order to still the frenzy of mobs should risk their lives in numbers sufficient for that purpose....Satyagraha (truth-force) brigades can be organized in every village and every block of buildings in the cities. [If the non-violent society is attacked from without] there are two ways open to non-violence. To yield possession, but non-cooperate with the aggressor...prefer death to submission. The second way would be non-violent resistance by the people who have been trained in the non-violent way...The unexpected spectacle of endless rows upon rows of men and women simply dying rather than surrender to the will of an aggressor must ultimately melt him and his soldiery...A nation or group which has made non-violence its final policy cannot be subjected to slavery even by the atom bomb.... The level of non-violence in that nation, if that even happily comes to pass, will naturally have risen so high as to command universal respect.

In accordance with these views, in 1940, when invasion of the British Isles by Nazi Germany looked imminent, Gandhi offered the following advice to the British people (*Non-Violence in Peace and War*):

> *"I would like you to lay down the arms you have as being useless for saving you or humanity. You will invite Herr Hitler and Signor Mussolini to take what they want of the countries you call your possessions...If these gentlemen choose to occupy your homes, you will vacate them. If they do not give you free passage out, you will allow yourselves, man, woman, and child, to be slaughtered, but you will refuse to owe allegiance to them."*

In a post-war interview in 1946, he offered a view at an even further extreme:

> *"The Jews should have offered themselves to the butcher's knife. They should have thrown themselves into the sea from cliffs."*

However, Gandhi was aware that this level of nonviolence required incredible faith and courage, which he realized not everyone possessed. He therefore advised that everyone need not keep to nonviolence, especially if it were used as a cover for cowardice:

> *"Gandhi guarded against attracting to his* satyagraha *movement those who feared to take up arms or felt themselves incapable of resistance. 'I do believe,' he wrote, 'that where there is only a choice between cowardice and violence, I would advise violence.'"*

> *"At every meeting I repeated the warning that unless they felt that in non-violence they had come into possession of a force infinitely superior to the one they had and in the use of which they were adept, they should have nothing to do with non-violence and resume the arms they possessed before. It must never be said of the Khudai Khidmatgars that once so brave, they had become or been made cowards under Badshah Khan's influence. Their bravery consisted not in being good*

marksmen but in defying death and being ever ready to bare their breasts to the bullets."

Vegetarianism

As a young child, Gandhi experimented with meat-eating. This was due partially to his inherent curiosity as well as his rather persuasive peer and friend Sheikh Mehtab. The idea of vegetarianism is deeply ingrained in Hindu and Jain traditions in India, and, in his native land of Gujarat, most Hindus were vegetarian and so are almost all Jains. The Gandhi family was no exception. Before leaving for his studies in London, Gandhi made a promise to his mother, Putlibai and his uncle, Becharji Swami that he would abstain from eating meat, taking alcohol, and engaging in promiscuity. He held fast to his promise and gained more than a diet: he gained a basis for his life-long philosophies. As Gandhi grew into adulthood, he became a strict vegetarian. He wrote the book *The Moral Basis of Vegetarianism* and several articles on the subject, some of which were published in the London Vegetarian Society's publication, *The Vegetarian*. During this period, the young Gandhi became inspired by many great minds and was befriended by the chairman of the London Vegetarian Society, Dr. Josiah Oldfield.

Having also read and admired the work of Henry Stephens Salt, the young Mohandas met and often corresponded with the vegetarian campaigner. Gandhi spent much time advocating vegetarianism during and after his time in London. To Gandhi, a vegetarian diet would not only satisfy the requirements of the body, it would also serve an economic purpose as meat was, and still is, generally more expensive than grains, vegetables, and fruits. Also, many Indians of the time struggled with low income, thus vegetarianism was seen not only as a spiritual practice but also a practical one. He abstained from eating for long periods, using fasting as a form of political protest. He refused to eat until his death or his demands were met. It was noted in his autobiography that vegetarianism was the beginning of his deep commitment to Brahmacharya; without total control of the palate, his success in Bramacharya would likely falter.

Gandhi had been a fruitarian, but started taking goat's milk on the advice of his doctor. He never took dairy products obtained from cows because of his view initially that milk is not the natural diet of man, disgust for cow blowing, and, specifically, because of a vow to his late mother.

Brahmacharya

When Gandhi was 16 his father became very ill. Being very devoted to his parents, he attended to his father at all times during his illness. However, one night, Gandhi's uncle came to relieve Gandhi for a while. He retired to his bedroom where carnal desires overcame him and he made love to his wife. Shortly afterward a servant came to report that Gandhi's father had just died. Gandhi felt tremendous guilt and never could forgive himself. He came to refer to this event as "double shame." The incident had significant influence in Gandhi becoming celibate at the age of 36, while still married. This decision was deeply influenced by the philosophy of Brahmacharya — spiritual and practical purity — largely associated with celibacy and asceticism. Gandhi saw Brahmacharya as a means of becoming close with God and as a primary foundation for self realization. In his autobiography he tells of his battle against lustful urges and fits of jealousy with his childhood bride, Kasturba. He felt it his personal obligation to remain celibate so that he could learn to love, rather than lust. For Gandhi, Brahmacharya meant "control of the senses in thought, word and deed."

Simplicity

Gandhi earnestly believed that a person involved in social service should lead a simple life which he thought could lead to Brahmacharya. His simplicity began by renouncing the western lifestyle he was leading in South Africa. He called it "reducing himself to zero," which entailed giving up unnecessary expenditure, embracing a simple lifestyle and washing his own clothes. On one occasion he returned the gifts bestowed to him from the natals for his diligent service to the community.

Gandhi spent one day of each week in silence. He believed that abstaining from speaking brought him inner peace. This influence was drawn from the Hindu principles of *mauna*. On such days he communicated with others by writing on paper. For three and a half years, from the age of 37, Gandhi refused to read newspapers, claiming that the tumultuous state of world affairs caused him more confusion than his own inner unrest. After reading John Ruskin's *Unto This Last*, he decided to change his lifestyle and create a commune called *Phoenix Settlement*. Upon returning to India from South Africa, where he had enjoyed a successful legal practice, he gave up wearing Western-style clothing, which he associated with wealth and success. He dressed to be accepted by the poorest person in India, advocating the use of homespun cloth (*khadi*).

Gandhi and his followers adopted the practice of weaving their own clothes from thread they themselves spun, and encouraged others to do so. While Indian workers were often idle due to unemployment, they had often bought their clothing from industrial manufacturers owned by British interests. It was Gandhi's view that if Indians made their own clothes, it would deal an economic blow to the British establishment in India. Consequently, the spinning wheel was later incorporated into the flag of the Indian National Congress. He subsequently wore a dhoti for the rest of his life to express the simplicity of his life.

Faith

Gandhi was born a Hindu and practised Hinduism all his life, deriving most of his principles from Hinduism. As a common Hindu, he believed all religions to be equal, and rejected all efforts to convert him to a different faith. He was an avid theologian and read extensively about all major religions. He had the following to say about Hinduism:

> *"Hinduism as I know it entirely satisfies my soul, fills my whole being...When doubts haunt me, when disappointments stare me in the face, and when I see not one ray of light on the horizon, I turn to the* Bhagavad Gita, *and find a verse to comfort me; and I immediately begin to smile in the midst of overwhelming sorrow. My life has been full of tragedies and if they have not left*

any visible and indelible effect on me, I owe it to the teachings of the Bhagavad Gita."

Gandhi wrote a commentary on the *Bhagavad Gita* in Gujarati. The Gujarati manuscript was translated into English by Mahadev Desai, who provided an additional introduction and commentary. It was published with a Foreword by Gandhi in 1946.

Gandhi believed that at the core of every religion was truth and love (compassion, nonviolence and the Golden Rule). He also questioned what he saw as hypocrisy, malpractices, and dogma in all religions, including his own, and he was a tireless advocate for social reform in religion. Some of his comments on various religions are:

"Thus if I could not accept Christianity either as a perfect, or the greatest religion, neither was I then convinced of Hinduism being such. Hindu defects were pressingly visible to me. If untouchability could be a part of Hinduism, it could but be a rotten part or an excrescence. I could not understand the raison d'etre *of a multitude of sects and castes. What was the meaning of saying that the Vedas were the inspired Word of God? If they were inspired, why not also the Bible and the Koran? As Christian friends were endeavouring to convert me, so were Muslim friends. Abdullah Seth had kept on inducing me to study Islam, and of course he had always something to say regarding its beauty."*

"As soon as we lose the moral basis, we cease to be religious. There is no such thing as religion overriding morality. Man, for instance, cannot be untruthful, cruel or incontinent and claim to have God on his side."

"The sayings of Muhammad are a treasure of wisdom, not only for Muslims but for all of mankind."

"I like your Christ, I do not like your Christians."

Later in his life when he was asked whether he was a Hindu, he replied:

"Yes I am. I am also a Christian, a Muslim, a Buddhist and a Jew."

In spite of their deep reverence to each other, Gandhi and Rabindranath Tagore engaged in protracted debates more than once. These debates exemplify the philosophical differences between the two most famous Indians at the time. On 15 January 1934, an earthquake hit Bihar and caused extensive damage and loss of life. Gandhi maintained this was because of the sin committed by upper caste Hindus by not letting untouchables in their temples (Gandhi was committed to the cause of improving the fate of untouchables, referring to them as Harijans, people of Krishna). Tagore vehemently opposed Gandhi's stance, maintaining that an earthquake can only be caused by natural forces, not moral reasons, however repugnant the practice of untouchability may be.

Writings

Gandhi was a prolific writer. For decades he edited several newspapers including *Harijan* in Gujarati, Hindi and English; *Indian Opinion* while in South Africa and, *Young India*, in English, and Navajivan, a Gujarati monthly, on his return to India. Later Navajivan was also published in Hindi. In addition, he wrote letters almost every day to individuals and newspapers.

Gandhi also wrote a few books including his autobiography, *An Autobiography of My Experiments with Truth*, *Satyagraha in South Africa* about his struggle there, *Hind Swaraj or Indian Home Rule*, a political pamphlet, and a paraphrase in Gujarati of John Ruskin's *Unto This Last*. This last essay can be considered his program on economics. He also wrote extensively on vegetarianism, diet and health, religion, social reforms, etc. Gandhi usually wrote in Gujarati, though he also revised the Hindi and English translations of his books.

Gandhi's complete works were published by the Indian government under the name *The Collected Works of Mahatma Gandhi* in the 1960s. The writings comprise about 50,000 pages published in about a hundred volumes. In 2000, a revised edition of the complete works sparked a controversy, as Gandhian followers argue that the government incorporated the changes for political purposes. The Indian government later withdrew the revised edition.

Tagore

Rabindranath Tagore (7 May 1861 – 7 August 1941), also known by the sobriquet **Gurudev**, was a Bengali polymath. He was a poet, visual artist, playwright, novelist, educationist, social reformer, nationalist, business-manager and composer whose works reshaped Bengali literature and music in the late 19th and early 20th centuries. He became Asia's first Nobel laureate when he won the 1913 Nobel Prize in Literature. A Pirali Brahmin from Calcutta, India, Tagore first wrote poems at the age of eight. At the age of sixteen, he published his first substantial poetry under the pseudonym *Bhanushingho* ("Sun Lion") and wrote his first short stories and dramas in 1877. In later life Tagore protested strongly against the British Raj and gave his support to the Indian Independence Movement. Tagore's life work endures, in the form of his poetry and the institution he founded, Visva-Bharati University. Tagore wrote novels, short stories, songs, dance-dramas, and essays on political and personal topics. *Gitanjali* (*Song Offerings*), *Gora* (*Fair-Faced*), and *Ghare-Baire* (*The Home and the World*) are among his best-known works. His verse, short stories, and novels, which often exhibited rhythmic lyricism, colloquial language, meditative naturalism, and philosophical contemplation, received worldwide acclaim. Tagore was also a cultural reformer and polymath who modernised Bengali art by rejecting strictures binding it to classical Indian forms. Two songs from his canon are now the national anthems of Bangladesh and India: the *Amar Shonar Bangla* and the *Jana Gana Mana* respectively.

Works

Tagore's literary reputation is disproportionately influenced by regard for his poetry; however, he also wrote novels, essays, short stories, travelogues, dramas, and thousands of songs. Of Tagore's prose, his short stories are perhaps most highly regarded; indeed, he is credited with originating the Bengali-language version of the genre. His works are frequently noted for their rhythmic, optimistic, and lyrical nature. Such stories mostly borrow from deceptively simple subject matter: the lives of ordinary people.

Novels and Non-fiction

Tagore wrote eight novels and four novellas, including *Chaturanga*, *Shesher Kobita*, *Char Odhay*, and *Noukadubi*. *Ghare Baire* (*The Home and the World*)—through the lens of the idealistic *zamindar* protagonist Nikhil—excoriates rising Indian nationalism, terrorism, and religious zeal in the *Swadeshi* movement; a frank expression of Tagore's conflicted sentiments, it emerged out of a 1914 bout of depression. Indeed, the novel bleakly ends with Hindu-Muslim sectarian violence and Nikhil's being (probably mortally) wounded. In some sense, *Gora* shares the same theme, raising controversial questions regarding the Indian identity. As with *Ghore Baire*, matters of self-identity (*jati*), personal freedom, and religion are developed in the context of a family story and love triangle. Another powerful story is *Jogajog* (*Relationships*), where the heroine Kumudini—bound by the ideals of *Shiva-Sati*, exemplified by Dakshayani—is torn between her pity for the sinking fortunes of her progressive and compassionate elder brother and his foil: her exploitative, rakish, and patriarchical husband. In it, Tagore demonstrates his feminist leanings, using *pathos* to depict the plight and ultimate demise of Bengali women trapped by pregnancy, duty, and family honour; simultaneously, he treats the decline of Bengal's landed oligarchy.

Other novels were more uplifting: *Shesher Kobita* (translated twice—*Last Poem* and *Farewell Song*) is his most lyrical novel, with poems and rhythmic passages written by the main character (a poet). It also contains elements of satire and postmodernism; stock characters gleefully attack the reputation of an old, outmoded, oppressively renowned poet who, incidentally, goes by the name of Rabindranath Tagore. Though his novels remain among the least-appreciated of his works, they have been given renewed attention via film adaptations by such directors as Satyajit Ray; these include *Chokher Bali* and *Ghare Baire*; many have soundtracks featuring selections from Tagore's own *Rabindra sangeet*. Tagore wrote many non-fiction books, writing on topics ranging from Indian history to linguistics. Aside from autobiographical works, his travelogues, essays, and lectures were compiled into several volumes, including *Europe Jatrir Patro* (*Letters from Europe*) and *Manusher Dhormo* (*The Religion of Man*).

Music and Artwork

Tagore was a prolific musician and painter, writing around 2,230 songs. They comprise *rabindrasangit*, now an integral part of Bengali culture. Tagore's music is inseparable from his literature, most of which—poems or parts of novels, stories, or plays alike—became lyrics for his songs. Primarily influenced by the *thumri* style of Hindustani classical music, they ran the entire gamut of human emotion, ranging from his early dirge-like Brahmo devotional hymns to quasi-erotic compositions. They emulated the tonal colour of classical *ragas* to varying extents. Though at times his songs mimicked a given raga's melody and rhythm faithfully, he also blended elements of different ragas to create innovative works.

For Bengalis, their appeal, stemming from the combination of emotive strength and beauty described as surpassing even Tagore's poetry, was such that the *Modern Review* observed that "[t]here is in Bengal no cultured home where Rabindranath's songs are not sung or at least attempted to be sung... Even illiterate villagers sing his songs". Music critic Arthur Strangways of *The Observer* first introduced non-Bengalis to *rabindrasangeet* with his book *The Music of Hindostan*, which described it as a "vehicle of a personality... [that] go behind this or that system of music to that beauty of sound which all systems put out their hands to seize." Among them are Bangladesh's national anthem *Amar Shonar Bangla* and India's national anthem *Jana Gana Mana*; Tagore thus became the only person ever to have written the national anthems of two nations. In turn, *rabindrasangeet* influenced the styles of such musicians as sitar maestro Vilayat Khan, and the *sarodiyas* Buddhadev Dasgupta and Amjad Ali Khan.

At age sixty, Tagore took up drawing and painting; successful exhibitions of his many works—which made a debut appearance in Paris upon encouragement by artists he met in the south of France—were held throughout Europe. Tagore—who likely exhibited protanopia ("colour blindness"), or partial lack of (red-green, in Tagore's case) colour discernment—painted in a style characterised by peculiarities in aesthetics and colouring schemes. Nevertheless, Tagore took to emulating numerous styles, including that of craftwork by the Malanggan people of northern New Ireland, Haida carvings from the west coast of Canada (British Columbia), and woodcuts by Max Pechstein. Tagore also had an artist's eye for his own handwriting, embellishing the scribbles, cross-outs, and word layouts in his manuscripts with simple artistic leitmotifs, including simple rhythmic designs.

Theatrical Pieces

Tagore's experience in theatre began at age sixteen, when he played the leading role in his brother Jyotirindranath's adaptation of Moliere's *Le Bourgeois Gentilhomme*. At age twenty, he wrote his first drama-opera—*Valmiki Pratibha* (*The Genius of Valmiki*)—which describes how the bandit Valmiki reforms his ethos, is blessed by Saraswati, and composes the *Ramayana*. Through it, Tagore vigorously explores a wide range of dramatic styles and emotions, including usage of revamped *kirtans* and adaptation of traditional English and Irish folk melodies as drinking songs. Another notable play, *Dak Ghar* (*The Post Office*), describes how a child—striving to escape his stuffy confines—ultimately "fall[s] asleep" (which suggests his physical death). A story with worldwide appeal (it received rave reviews in Europe), *Dak Ghar* dealt with death as, in Tagore's words, "spiritual freedom" from "the world of hoarded wealth and certified creeds". During World War II, Polish doctor and educator Janusz Korczak selected "The Post Office" as the play the orphans in his care in the Warsaw Ghetto would perform. This occurred on July 18, 1942, less than three weeks before they were to be deported to the Treblinka death camp. According to his main English-language biographer, Betty Jean Lifton, in her book *The King of Children*, Dr. Korszak thought a great deal about whether one should be able to determine when and how to die. He may have been trying to find a way for the children in his orphanage to accept death.

His other works—emphasizing fusion of lyrical flow and emotional rhythm tightly focused on a core idea—were unlike previous Bengali dramas. His works sought to articulate, in Tagore's words, "the play of feeling and not of action". In 1890 he wrote *Visarjan* (*Sacrifice*), regarded as his finest drama. The Bengali-language originals included intricate subplots and extended monologues. Later, his dramas probed more philosophical and allegorical themes; these included *Dak Ghar*. Another is Tagore's *Chandalika* (*Untouchable Girl*), which was modelled on an ancient Buddhist legend describing how Ananda—the Gautama Buddha's disciple—asks water of an *Adivasi* ("untouchable") girl. Lastly, among his most famous dramas is *Raktakaravi* (*Red Oleanders*), which tells of a kleptocratic king who enriches himself by forcing his subjects to mine. The heroine, Nandini, eventually rallies the common people to destroy these symbols of subjugation. Tagore's other plays include *Chitrangada*, *Raja*, and *Mayar Khela*. Dance dramas based on Tagore's plays are commonly referred to as *rabindra nritya natyas*.

Short Stories

Tagore's "Sadhana" period, comprising the four years from 1891 to 1895, was named for one of Tagore's magazines. This period was among Tagore's most fecund, yielding more than half the stories contained in the three-volume *Galpaguchchha*, which itself is a collection of eighty-four stories. Such stories usually showcase Tagore's reflections upon his surroundings, on modern and fashionable ideas, and on interesting mind puzzles (which Tagore was fond of testing his intellect with). Tagore typically associated his earliest stories (such as those of the "*Sadhana*" period) with an exuberance of vitality and spontaneity; these characteristics were intimately connected with Tagore's life in the common villages of, among others, Patisar, Shajadpur, and Shilaida while managing the Tagore family's vast landholdings. There, he beheld the lives of India's poor and common people; Tagore thereby took to examining their lives with a penetrative depth and feeling that was singular in Indian literature up to that point.

In "The Fruitseller from Kabul", Tagore speaks in first person as town-dweller and novelist who chances upon the Afghani seller. He attempts to distil the sense of longing felt by those long trapped in the mundane and hardscrabble confines of Indian urban life, giving play to dreams of a different existence in the distant and wild mountains: "There were autumn mornings, the time of year when kings of old went forth to conquest; and I, never stirring from my little corner in Calcutta, would let my mind wander over the whole world. At the very name of another country, my heart would go out to it... I would fall to weaving a network of dreams: the mountains, the glens, the forest.... ". Many of the other *Galpaguchchha* stories were written in Tagore's *Sabuj Patra* period (1914–1917; also named for one of Tagore's magazines).

Tagore's *Golpoguchchho* (*Bunch of Stories*) remains among Bengali literature's most popular fictional works, providing subject matter for many successful films and theatrical plays. Satyajit Ray's film *Charulata* was based upon Tagore's controversial novella, *Nastanirh* (*The Broken Nest*). In *Atithi* (also made into a film), the young Brahmin boy Tarapada shares a boat ride with a village zamindar. The boy reveals that he has run away from home, only to wander around ever since. Taking pity, the zamindar adopts him and ultimately arranges his marriage to the zamindar's own daughter. However, the night before the wedding, Tarapada runs off—again. *Strir Patra* (*The Letter from the Wife*) is among Bengali literature's earliest depictions of the bold emancipation of women. The heroine Mrinal, the wife of a typical patriarchical Bengali middle class man, writes a letter while she is travelling (which constitutes the whole story). It details the pettiness of her life and struggles; she finally declares that she will not return to her husband's home with the statement *Amio bachbo. Ei bachlum* ("And I shall live. Here, I live").

In *Haimanti*, Tagore takes on the institution of Hindu marriage, describing the dismal lifelessness of married Bengali women, hypocrisies plaguing the Indian middle classes, and how Haimanti, a sensitive young woman, must—due to her sensitiveness and free spirit—sacrifice her life. In the last passage, Tagore directly attacks the Hindu custom of glorifying Sita's attempted self-immolation as a means of appeasing her husband Rama's doubts. Tagore also examines Hindu-Muslim tensions in *Musalmani Didi*, which in many ways embodies the essence of Tagore's humanism. On the other hand, *Darpaharan* exhibits Tagore's self-consciousness, describing a young man harbouring literary ambitions. Though he loves his wife, he wishes to stifle her own literary career, deeming it unfeminine. Tagore himself, in his youth, seems to have harboured similar ideas about women. *Darpaharan* depicts the final humbling of the man via his acceptance of his wife's talents. As many other Tagore stories, *Jibito o Mrito* provides the Bengalis with one of their more widely used epigrams: *Kadombini moriya proman korilo she more nai* ("Kadombini died, thereby proved that she hadn't").

Poetry

Tagore's poetry—which varied in style from classical formalism to the comic, visionary, and ecstatic—proceeds out a lineage established by 15th-and 16th-century Vaicgava poets. Tagore was also influenced by the mysticism of the *rishi*-authors who—including Vyasa—wrote the Upanishads, the Bhakta-Sufi mystic Kabir, and Ramprasad. Yet Tagore's poetry became most innovative and mature after his exposure to rural Bengal's folk music, which included ballads sung by Baul folk singers—especially the bard Lalan Uah. These—which were rediscovered and popularised by Tagore—resemble 19th-century Kartabhaja hymns that emphasize inward divinity and rebellion against religious and social orthodoxy. During his Shilaidaha years, his poems took on a lyrical quality, speaking via thc *maner manus* (the Bauls' "man within the heart") or meditating upon the *jivan devata* ("living God within"). This figure thus sought connection with divinity through appeal to nature and the emotional interplay of human drama. Tagore used such techniques in his Bhanusigha poems (which chronicle the romance between Radha and Krishna), which he repeatedly revised over the course of seventy years.

Later, Tagore responded to the (mostly) crude emergence of modernism and realism in Bengali literature by writing experimental works in the 1930s. Examples works include *Africa* and *Camalia*, which are among the better known of his latter poems. He also occasionally wrote poems using *Shadhu*

Bhasha (a Sanskritised dialect of Bengali); later, he began using *Cholti Bhasha* (a more popular dialect). Other notable works include *Manasi*, *Sonar Tori* (*Golden Boat*), *Balaka* (*Wild Geese*—the title being a metaphor for migrating souls), and *Purobi*. *Sonar Tori*'s most famous poem—dealing with the ephemeral nature of life and achievement—goes by the same name; it ends with the haunting phrase. Internationally, *Gitanjali* is Tagore's best-known collection, winning him his Nobel Prize. Song VII of *Gitanjali*:

Amar e gan chheoechhe tar shokol olongkar
Tomar kachhe rakhe ni ar shajer ohongkar
Olongkar je majhe pooe milonete aoal kore,
Tomar kotha ohake je tar mukhoro jhongkar.
Tomar kachhe khape na mor kobir gorbo kora,
Mohakobi, tomar paee dite chai je dhora.
Jibon loe joton kori jodi shorol bashi gooi,
Apon shure dibe bhori sokol chhidro tar.

Free-verse translation by Tagore (*Gitanjali*, verse VII):

"My song has put off her adornments. She has no pride of dress and decoration. Ornaments would mar our union; they would come between thee and me; their jingling would drown thy whispers."

"My poet's vanity dies in shame before thy sight. O master poet, I have sat down at thy feet. Only let me make my life simple and straight, like a flute of reed for thee to fill with music."

"Klanti", the sixth poem in *Gitali*, reads:

Klanti amar khoma koro, probhu
Pothe jodi pichhie pooi kobhu
Ei je hia thoro thoro kape aji emontoro,
Ei bedona khoma koro, khoma koro probhu.
Ei dinota khoma koro, probhu,
Pichhon-pane takai jodi kobhu.
Diner tape roudrojalae shukae mala pujar thalae,
Shei mlanota khoma koro, khoma koro, probhu.

Tagore's poetry has been set to music by various composers, among them classical composer Arthur Shepherd's triptych for soprano and string quartet, as well as composer Garry Schyman's "Praan," an adaptation of Tagore's poem "Stream of Life" from Gitanjali. The latter was composed and recorded with vocals by Palbasha Siddique to accompany Internet celebrity Matt Harding's 2008 viral video.

Impact and Legacy

Tagore's legacy can be felt through the many festivals held worldwide in his honour—examples include the annual Bengali festival/celebration of *Kabipranam* (Tagore's birthday anniversary), the annual Tagore Festival held in Urbana, Illinois in the United States, the *Rabindra Path Parikrama* walking pilgrimages leading from Calcutta to Shantiniketan, and ceremonial recitals of Tagore's poetry held on important anniversaries. This legacy is most palpable in Bengali culture, ranging from language and arts to history and politics; indeed, Nobel laureate Amartya Sen noted that even for modern Bengalis, Tagore was a "towering figure", being a "deeply relevant and many-sided contemporary thinker". Tagore's collected Bengali-language writings—the 1939 *Rabindra Racanavali*—is also canonized as one of Bengal's greatest cultural treasures, while Tagore himself has been proclaimed "the greatest poet India has produced".

Tagore was famed throughout much of Europe, North America, and East Asia. He was key in founding Dartington Hall School, a progressive coeducational institution; in Japan, he influenced such figures as Nobel laureate Yasunari Kawabata. Tagore's works were widely translated into English, Dutch, German, Spanish, and other European languages by Czech indologist Vincenc Lesny, French Nobel laureate Andre Gide, Russian poet Anna Akhmatova, former Turkish Prime Minister Bulent Ecevit and others. In the United States, Tagore's popular lecturing circuits (especially those between 1916–1917) were widely attended and acclaimed. Nevertheless, several controversies involving Tagore resulted in a decline in his popularity in Japan and North America after the late 1920s, contributing to his "near total eclipse" outside of Bengal.

Tagore, through Spanish translations of his works, also influenced leading figures of Spanish literature, including Chileans Pablo Neruda and Gabriela Mistral, Mexican writer Octavio Paz, and Spaniards Jose Ortega - Gasset, Zenobia Camprubi, and Juan Ramón Jimenez.

Between 1914 and 1922, the Jimenez-Camprubi spouses translated no less than twenty-two of Tagore's books from English into Spanish. Jimenez, as part of this work, also extensively revised and adapted such works as Tagore's *The Crescent Moon*. Indeed, during this time, Jimenez developed the now-heralded innovation of "naked poetry".

Ortega – Gasset wrote that "Tagore's wide appeal [may stem from the fact that] he speaks of longings for perfection that we all have... Tagore awakens a dormant sense of childish wonder, and he saturates the air with all kinds of enchanting promises for the reader, who... pays little attention to the deeper import of Oriental mysticism". Tagore's works were published in free editions around 1920 alongside works by Dante Alighieri, Miguel de Cervantes, Johann Wolfgang von Goethe, Plato, and Leo Tolstoy.

Tagore's talents came to be regarded as overrated by several Westerners, none of whom had read his poetry in the original Bengali. Graham Greene doubted that "anyone but Mr. Yeats can still take his poems very seriously." Modern remnants of a once widespread Latin American reverence of Tagore were discovered, for example, by an astonished Salman Rushdie during a trip to Nicaragua.

Sri Aurobindo

Sri Aurobindo (August 15, 1872–December 5, 1950) was an Indian nationalist, scholar, poet, mystic, evolutionary philosopher, Yogi and spiritual master. After a short political career in which he became one of the leaders of the early movement for Indian independence from British rule, Sri Aurobindo turned to the exploration of the subtle realms of human existence and, as a consequence, developed his own vision and philosophy of human progress and a spiritual path which he termed *Integral Yoga*.

The *Times Literary Supplement* wrote of Aurobindo:

"In fact, he is a new type of thinker, one who combines in his vision the alacrity of the West with the illumination of the East. To study his writings is to enlarge the boundaries of one's knowledge... He is a yogi who writes as though he were standing among the stars, with the constellations for his companions".

The central theme of Sri Aurobindo's vision is the evolution of life into a "life divine". In his own words:

"Man is a transitional being. He is not final. The step from man to superman is the next approaching achievement in the earth's evolution. It is inevitable because it is at once the intention of the inner spirit and the logic of Nature's process".

The principal writings of Sri Aurobindo include, in prose, *The Life Divine*, *The Synthesis of Yoga*, *Secrets of the Vedas*, *Essays on the Gita*, *The Human Cycle*, *The Ideal of Human Unity*, *Renaissance in India and other essays*, *Supramental Manifestation upon Earth*, *The Future Poetry*, *Thoughts and Aphorisms* and several volumes of letters. In poetry, his principal work is "Savitri-a Legend and a Symbol" in blank verse.

Conversion from Politics to Spirituality

His conversion from political action to spirituality occurred gradually, first at Vadodara (then Baroda) under the spiritual instruction of a Maharashtrian Yogi called **Vishnu Bhaskar Lele**, and second, while awaiting trial as a prisoner in Alipore Central Jail (in Kolkata in the province of Bengal). Here his study and practice of the teachings of the Bhagavad Gita led to a number of mystical experiences. Sri Aurobindo claimed to have been visited in his meditations by the renowned Swami Vivekananda, a Hindu philosopher of great importance to Advaita Vedanta, who guided Sri Aurobindo in an important aspect of his spiritual practice or yoga. Sri Aurobindo later said that while imprisoned he saw the convicts, jailers, policemen, the prison bars, the trees, the judge, the lawyers as different forms of Vishnu in the spiritual experience of Vasudeva. The subsequent trial involving Aurobindo was one of the defining moments in the Indian nationalist movement. There were 49 accused and 206 witnesses, 400 documents were filed and 5000 exhibits produced—including bombs, handguns and acid. The English judge, C.P. Beachcroft, turned out to have been a student with Sri Aurobindo at Cambridge. The Chief Prosecutor Eardley Norton displayed a loaded revolver on his briefcase during the trial. The case for Sri Aurobindo was taken up by Chittaranjan Das who said in his conclusion to the Judge:

> *My appeal to you is this, that long after the controversy will be hushed in silence, long after this turmoil, this agitation will have ceased, long after he (Sri Aurobindo) is dead and gone, he will be looked upon as the poet of patriotism, as the prophet of nationalism and lover of humanity. Long after he is dead and gone, his words will be echoed and re-echoed, not only in India, but across distant seas and lands. Therefore, I say that the man in his position is not only standing before the bar of this Court, but before the bar of the High Court of History.*
>
> *The trial ("Alipore Bomb Case, 1908") lasted for one full year, but eventually Sri Aurobindo was acquitted. Afterwards Aurobindo started two new weekly papers: the* Karmayogin *in English and the* Dharma *in Bengali. However, it appeared that the British government would not tolerate his nationalist program as Lord Minto wrote about him:* "I can only repeat that he is the most dangerous man we have to reckon with."

Sought again by the Indian police, he was guided to the French settlements, and on April 4, 1910 he finally found refuge with other nationalists in the French colony of Pondicherry.

Philosophical and Spiritual Writings

In 1914, after four years of concentrated yoga at Pondicherry (now Puducherry), Sri Aurobindo launched *Arya*, a 64 page monthly review. For the next six and a half years this became the vehicle for most of his most important writings, which appeared in serialised form. These included *The Life Divine*,

The Synthesis of Yoga, Essays on The Gita, The Secret of The Veda, Hymns to the Mystic Fire, The Upanishads, The Foundations of Indian Culture, War and Self-determination, The Human Cycle, The Ideal of Human Unity, and *The Future Poetry*. Sri Aurobindo however revised some of these works before they were published in book form.

Somewhat later, he wrote an essay *The Mother* which was published in 1928 in booklet form. It also included passages from his letters that could provide essentails of the Integral Yoga. In the main essay, Sri Aurobindo wrote about the Divine Mother, the consciousness and force of the Supreme, and about the "Four great Aspects of the Mother, four of her leading Powers and Personalities (which) have stood in front in her guidance of the Universe and her dealings with the terrestrial play..." He also wrote about the conditions to be fulfilled by the "Sadhaka" or practitioner of the yoga in order to be receptive to the Mother's Grace. He explained his view of money and wealth: "Money is a sign of universal force, and this force in its manifestation on earth works on the vital and physical planes and is indispensable to the fullness of outer life. In its origin and its true action it belongs to the Divine. But like other powers of the Divine it is delegated here and in the ignorance of the lower Nature can be usurped for the uses of the ego or held by Asuric influences and perverted to their purpose."

For some time afterwards, Sri Aurobindo's main literary output was his voluminous correspondence with his disciples. His letters, most of which were written in the 1930s, numbered in the several thousands. Many were brief comments made in the margins of his disciple's notebooks in answer to their questions and reports of their spiritual practice—others extended to several page carefully composed explanations of practical aspects of his teachings. These were later collected and published in book form in three volumes of *Letters on Yoga*. In the late 1930s, Sri Aurobindo resumed work on a poem he had started earlier—he continued to expand and revise this poem for the rest of his life. It became perhaps his greatest literary achievement, *Savitri*, an epic spiritual poem in blank verse of approximately 24,000 lines.

Although Sri Aurobindo wrote most of his material in English, his major works were later translated into a number of languages, including the Indian languages Hindi, Bengali, Oriya, Gujarati, Marathi, Sanskrit, Tamil, Telugu, Kannada, and Malayalam, as well as French, German, Italian, Dutch, Spanish, Chinese, Portuguese, Slovene and Russian. A large amount of his work in Russian translation is also available online.

Evolutionary Philosophy

Sri Aurobindo argues that humankind as an entity is not the last rung in the evolutionary scale, but can evolve spiritually beyond its current limitations associated with an essential ignorance to a future state of supramental existence. This further evolutionary step would lead to a divine life on Earth characterized by a supramental or truth-consciousness, and a transformed and divinised life and material form. There are parallels between Sri Aurobindo's vision and that of Teilhard de Chardin.

The Triple Transformation of the Individual

One of the key aspects of Sri Aurobindo's philosophy is how Man is born an Ignorant divided being since he is a product of the original inconscience of Matter. He does not know who he is, nor the parts of his being, what purpose he serves, what the universe and the Reality is made up of, what the purpose of life is, etc. In addition he sees all life in division and duality, as his limited Mind can only know the part, not the integral truth (i.e. the many parts, the whole and essence) of any matter or of life; or of the true integral nature of the relationship of the Unmanifest and the Manifest in making up the omnipresent Reality.

To overcome these, as explained above, Man must embark on a process of self-discovery in which he uncovers his Divine nature. Aside from perfecting the limited parts of his psychological nature, he makes a double movement (1) above mind to intuitive mind and above, and (2) a movement within, inside to his true self and evolving soul (the Psychic Being). The latter enables him to overcome his ego sense that supports the limited and divided nature and knowledge that is his Ignorance. These two movements allow him to move beyond the divisions and dualities of life and see instead them as harmonies and complementary aspect, including that which exists between Spirit and Matter. As he goes deeper within, he also opens to the spiritual Force that is descending in the atmosphere, which enables him to make the decisive change.

Eventually the spirit works to overcome his limited nature, which is followed by the (ultimate) supramental transformation. Thus, we see three stages through which man emerges from his original Ignorance nature: the Psychic, the Spiritual, and the Supramental change. This is Sri Aurobindo's Triple Transformation. At that point, his essential Ignorance born of creation is turned into an Integral Knowledge, and his vital, psychological and physical parts are transformed, ushering a new supramental individual (Gnostic being), and in tandem with others, a supramental social existence (i.e. a Divine life on earth).

The Evolving Soul (Psychic Being)

Sri Aurobindo indicated that his greatest discovery was the existence of a Psychic Being (i.e. an Evolving Soul) within that is the essence of our spiritual selves. If we forge our way into the deepest parts of our being the Subliminal realm, we will come upon a Personal Evolving Soul. From this Psychic Being we can overcome the limits of consciousness of the individual human. From there we perceive our true nature and essence; we become more aware of our surroundings; we become one with others and life; we experience an inner Guide that influences to move in the right direction and catches our negative propensities as they arise on the surface; we come in touch with our universal nature; we come in touch with the transcendent reality and spiritual Force; we overcome the limits of time, bringing timelessness into time; and evoke the powers of the Infinite into this finite existence, to name several. Also when we plunge within and touch the evolving soul, we move up in consciousness above mind to spiritual mind of illumination, intuition, revelation, and (supramental) truth consciousness. It should also be noted that this psychic entity is itself evolving, as it enters the person's whose experience it believes it can benefit from, extracts the essence of that person's experience, and then moves on to the next birth until it is fulfilled in its journey through space and time. The connection to the evolving soul is thus the key to the evolution from this the human side, as from there we overcome the inherent Ignorance, division, dualities, and suffering of Man, enabling him to fulfil his human aspiration of God, freedom, joy, and immortality. (From the spiritual side, it is the descending Supramental Force that enables the progress of life to its ultimate capacity. The two together, the connection to the Psychic Being and the surrender to the descending (supramental) Force are the keys to the evolution and transformation of the individual, humanity, and life in the universe.)

Supramental Existence

Sri Aurobindo's vision of the future includes the appearance of what we may a call a new species, the supramental being, a divine being which would be as different and superior to present humanity as humanity is to the animal. It would have a consciousness different in kind than the mind of the human, a different status and quality and functioning. Even the physical form of this being would be different, more luminous and flexible and adaptable, entirely conscious and harmonious. Between this supramental being and humanity, there would be transitional beings, who would be human in birth and form, but whose consciousness would approach that of the supramental being. These transitional beings would appear prior to that of the full supramental being, and would constitute an intermediate stage in the earth evolution, through which the soul would pass in its growth towards its divine manifestation as the supramental being in the earth nature.

Thus, an important part of Sri Aurobindo's future vision is the elucidation of the transitional being and the supramental being. Although it is frequently mentioned in his writings that the supramental consciousness is impossible to describe in mental terms, he has nevertheless provided clear indications of its general nature and capacities. These have been described at length in Sri Aurobindo's books *The Life Divine*, *The Synthesis of Yoga*, *The Supramental Manifestation Upon Earth*, and *Savitri*. *Mother's Agenda*, which is a 13 volume edited transcription of the Mother's conversations with a disciple called Satprem between the years 1951 and 1973, also has much information on the nature of the new species and its emergence. The descriptions made of the nature of the transitional and supramental beings are dazzling, above ordinary conceptions of human possibility. We may give as an example, which touches upon a defining characteristic, this sentence from Sri Aurobindo's chapter "The Gnostic Being" in *The Life Divine*: "A complete self-knowledge in all things and at all moments is the gift of the supramental gnosis and with it a complete self-mastery, not merely in the sense of control of Nature but in the sense of a power of perfect self-expression in Nature."

Another interesting aspect of the vision is the manner and sequence of processes through which the supramental being will make its appearance in the earth nature. Again, these processes were not specified in exact detail, and in many cases they were presented as possibilities or probabilities rather than as certainties, but Sri Aurobindo and the Mother have been given very interesting suggestions and outlines of the scenario. Sri Aurobindo indicates that "there will be established on earth a gnostic Consciousness and Power which will shape a race of gnostic spiritual beings and take up into itself all of earth-nature that is ready for this new transformation. It will also receive into itself from above, progressively, from its own domain of perfect light and power and beauty all that is ready to descend from that domain into the terrestrial being." He further indicates that "The creation of a supramental being, nature, life on earth, will not be the sole result of this evolution; it will also carry with it the consummation of the steps that have led up to it; for it will confirm in possession of terrestrial birth the Overmind, the Intuition and the other gradations of the spiritual nature-force and establish a race of gnostic beings and a hierarchy, a shining ladder of ascending degrees and successive constituent formations of the gnostic light and power in earth nature." In other words, there would be established ascending levels of transitional beings, manifesting the levels of consciousness and expressive nature intermediate between the ordinary human and the supramental levels.

Sri Aurobindo indicates that even all of nature might be affected by the appearance of the supramental light and force:

> *"A dominant principle of harmony would impose itself on the life of the Ignorance; the discord, the blind seeking, the clash of struggle, the abnormal vicissitudes of exaggeration and depression and unsteady balance of the unseeing forces at work in their mixture and conflict, would feel the influence and yield place to a more orderly pace and harmonic steps of the development of being, a more revealing arrangement of progressing life and consciousness, a better life-order. A freer play of intuition and sympathy and understanding would enter into human life, a clearer sense of the truth of self and things and a more enlightened dealing with the opportunities and difficulties of existence.".*

The development of human society and world culture is another important aspect of Sri Aurobindo's future vision. In his book *The Human Cycle*, Sri Aurobindo described the various stages of the development of human society which have led to the present subjective age that is beginning, and the possibilities of a future spiritual age. This spiritual age would be characterized by the dominance of a spiritual ideal and trend in world culture.

It is in the acceptance of the spiritual ideal and a sincere turning of the being towards its manifestation—first by individuals, then by "a great number of individuals," and finally by the community—that marks the advent of the spiritual age. This turn must start with individuals, only afterwards can it become established more generally in the social order. But this turn towards the spirit and soul as the effective leader and master of the mind, life, and physical existence must be true and sincere, there must be a genuine shift from the mental and vital ego to the divine. This true change of standpoint from the ego to the spirit is difficult to establish even in the individual; for the society, for the mass of humanity, it is an even greater difficulty. As this change becomes effectively realised first in individuals, through them it must be powerfully communicated to the society as a whole as an uplifting ideal, not as something that is imposed. Then gradually it will become accepted and assimilated into segments of the society, and from there permeate throughout the society and become generalized. The signs of this turning in the society would become evident in all its aims and activities and institutions. It "would make the revealing and finding of the divine Self in man the whole first aim of all its activities, its education, its knowledge, its science, its ethics, its art, its economical and political structure... It would embrace all knowledge in its scope, but would make the whole trend and aim and the permeating spirit not mere worldly efficiency, but this self-developing and self-finding."

Sri Aurobindo's Integral Yoga

In *The Synthesis of Yoga*, and in his voluminous correspondence with his disciples collected under the title *Letters on Yoga*, Sri Aurobindo laid out the psychological principles and practices of the Integral Yoga or Poorna Yoga. The aim of the yoga is to enable the individual who undertakes it to attain conscious identity with the Divine, the true Self, and to transform the mind, life, and body so they would become fit instruments for a divine life on earth. Practitioners believe achieving the ultimate aims of Integral Yoga requires an entire devotion.

The Integral Yoga utilizes various yogic practices of India's cultural heritage and synthesizes them with its own unique methods, however, there is no one set method or practice that its practitioners follow. Certain broad guidelines have been provided, several basic approaches have been described, and many specific practices and techniques have been suggested. But for each individual who undertakes this discipline, the specific path will differ. The reasons for this are twofold. The first is that, according to Sri Aurobindo, the goals of this yoga can be achieved only through the guidance and power and action of the Divine.. The Divine uses many methods and the circumstances of life flexibly with a wisdom and subtle precision impossible in a rigid programme. The second reason is that each individual presents unique characteristics, possibilities, and obstacles that can only be taken into account by the Divine that sees and holds all things in its total regard.

The central guiding principle of this yoga is a complete surrender to the Divine. It is the Divine alone who can transform and divinise human consciousness and life. Elaborating on this central principle, Sri Aurobindo has characterized the discipline to be followed as a "triple labour of aspiration, rejection, and surrender." Aspiration means the sustained call of the individual to the Divine to take possession of the ego-centred and limited surface being. Rejection involves separating oneself and withdrawing from all wrong movements that contradict or conflict with the aims of the yoga. Together, the force of aspiration and the rejection of the obstacles in the nature work to effect a sincere and true surrender of all the parts of the being to the Divine. In proportion to the completeness of this surrender, the individual will feel the Divine taking up the being and working in it, substituting and pouring into it its own higher powers of peace, wisdom, harmony, force, beauty, and delight.

There are several basic approaches within which these three practices may be embedded or with which they may be harmonized. The first of these approaches is the yoga of works, and here works has a broad significance that includes all one's actions external and internal. Its central character is that all one's actions are to be done as an offering to the Divine and no longer for the personal satisfaction of the ego or even for the benefit of a greater social purpose. Through this offering—which progressively must expand to the extent that this remembrance of the Divine and inner self-offering become the constant state of the being—the inner contact with the Divine grows increasingly close and entire. As this inner communion develops, one's actions begin to be felt as being originated, guided, inspired, and even executed by the Divine, eventually one feels oneself simply to be a pure channel for the outflow of a divine action.

The second approach is the yoga of knowledge. Here the central process is a drawing back of the true divine Self from its false identification with the limited personal ego, as well as a drawing back from identification with the superficial movements of mind, and life, and body. Here Sri Aurobindo capitalizes on a fundamental distinction in our conscious existence, that between the conscious, witnessing being or spirit, the Purusha, and the workings of the nature, Prakriti In this approach, the Purusha disengages itself first from the body, observing its workings silently as a witness but not identifying with them. Subsequently, the Purusha separates itself in a similar manner from the action of the life-energy and the mind. After this separation of the Purusha from the Prakriti has been achieved, there remains a vague, elusive sense of "I," an essential ego-sense. This sense of "I" also must be eliminated through a constant denial of its fundamental reality, and through a "constant fixing of the thought on the idea of the One and Infinite in itself or the One and Infinite everywhere.". These processes change first the mental outlook on oneself, which in turn deepens into a spiritual realisation in the substance of the being.

A third approach to the Divine is through the yoga of love and devotion. Here it is the emotional nature that is to be turned entirely towards the Divine Being in a movement of devotion, love, and self-giving. According to Sri Aurobindo, the Divine is not only an impersonal abstraction or state of existence, but is capable of varied relations with its conscious individualities manifested in the infinity of its being. The Divine can be viewed and approached as the Master of our existence, as our Father, Mother, Friend, Guide, Lover. The heart of this approach is the progressive development of a personal relation or relations with the Divine, in which the Divine is brought into close and frequent relation, gradually developing into a constant and increasingly intense and intimate relation. The crown of this movement is the delight of conscious union with the Divine.

A fourth approach is through what Sri Aurobindo has called the yoga of self-perfection. This approach has elements in common with the others, because to perfect the nature it is necessary to disengage the Self from the ego and the outer nature, and to become receptive to the action of the Divine who alone can effect this change. The first need is to purify the various parts of the mental, vital, and physical nature. Each part has a particular function in the overall expression of the spirit in the outer nature. Ordinarily, however, the various parts of the nature do not keep to their proper role, but become intermixed and confused with the others. Purification is to become aware of the complex elements of the nature, and to put this confused action into order. In addition, the various elements of the being must be developed and uplifted beyond their ordinary action and abilities and raised to their highest possibilities. As part of this elevation, the yoga of self-perfection includes in its scope the development of the higher reaches of the mind beyond the intellect—the higher mind, illumined mind, intuition, and Overmind. As the consciousness successively ascends to each higher level, their greater lights and powers are brought down to enlighten and change the lower nature. Ascending beyond even the Overmind, one enters the supramental consciousness, an entirely divine consciousness and omnipotent force, which Sri Aurobindo argues alone can entirely transform and perfect the outer nature.

These four basic approaches constitute the main lines of spiritual discipline of the Integral Yoga. Each of the four feeds into the others and assists in their development and perfection. Depending on the individual, one or another approach may be emphasized in the beginning, but eventually all are developed sc as to include all the parts of the nature in the inner realisation and the outer transformation of the being. For the principle of the Integral Yoga is that all the parts of the nature participate in the Divine Consciousness and Delight and express this divinity in a transformed outer life.

Philosophy of Social Evolution

Sri Aurobindo's spiritual vision extends beyond the perfection and transformation of the individual; it includes in its scope the evolution and transformation of human society. In both the individual and in the society, the soul and spirit is at first hidden and occult, influencing the direction and course of development from behind, but allowing nature to follow its gradual, zigzagging, and conflict-ridden course. Afterwards, as mind develops and becomes more and more dominant over the obscure impulses and ego-centred drives of the vital nature, a clearer, more objective and enlightened perception and approach towards human existence and development become possible. At some highest stage of mental development, there comes into view a greater possibility and principle that is spiritual and supramental in nature, and it is at this point that a true solution to humanity's persistent problems becomes visible in the context of a greater and more radical transformation of human life into a divine living.

In *The Human Cycle*, Sri Aurobindo describes the stages of development of human society, illustrating with a perceptive analysis of historical and political developments and trends, and outlining a future ideal society towards which he says it is moving. Starting from Lamprecht's theory that societies pass through several distinct psychological stages of development—symbolic, typal and conventional, individualist, and subjective—Sri Aurobindo expresses his view of historical and sociological development in the light of his own theory of spiritual evolution. After taking a passing glance at the symbolic, typal, and conventional stages in Indian and European history, Sri Aurobindo focuses on the individualistic and the beginning subjective stages of modern societies. He then presents a more detailed picture of a future spiritual stage in which he indicates all the others will find their meaning and towards which they unconsciously move.

The symbolic stage is illustrated by the ancient Vedic age, in which "the religious institution of sacrifice governs the whole society and all its hours and moments, and the ritual of the sacrifice is at every turn and in every detail, as even a cursory study of the Brahmanas and Upanishads ought to show us, mystically symbolic." The typal stage is characterized by a dominance of psychological and ethical concerns and motives; all else, including spiritual and religious concerns, are subordinate to these. In Indian society, it was best expressed in the ideal and concept of Dharma, the upholding of tradition and the fulfilment of one's social position and responsibility. In the conventional stage, the outward expressions of the ideal overshadow the ideal itself, such that customs, outward signs and symbols become ends in themselves, and their inner spirit and significance becomes eclipsed. In its early phase, the spirit and inner significance of the social institutions still live and thrive within well-developed structures, but afterwards the institutions become more and more formalized and artificial, and their inner purpose and significance become obscured. In Indian society, this is illustrated with the growing rigidity of the caste system in which the society was organized, with its increasing emphasis on custom, heredity, and ritual.

Sri Aurobindo explains that "the individualistic age of human society comes as a result of the corruption and failure of the conventional, as a revolt against the reign of the petrified typal figure." He illustrates the occurrence of this stage in Europe beginning with its revolt of reason against the Church and fixed authority and its continuation and blossoming with the growth of scientific inquiry. Through science, a new basis of principles and laws could be discovered and established that were open to scrutiny and logical analysis and reasoning. There were also established the democratic ideals that all individuals had the right to develop to the full stature of their capabilities, and that the individual was not simply a social unit with a social function, but also had unique individual needs, possibilities, and tendencies which should be allowed freedom and opportunity for development. As a part of the revolt against traditional authority, there developed in some regions another intellectual philosophy and political movement, apparently in contradiction to individualism, of the supremacy of the society as a whole over the individual. Sri Aurobindo also analyses the strengths and limitations of this viewpoint, and its relations and opposition to the democratic ideal.

The subjective age comes as an outgrowth of the individualistic and rational questioning of the conventional institutions and structures of society. The individualistic age culminates in a new intellectual foundation and development in all the spheres of life, but this rational view of the world and the self can only go so far, it cannot reach into the depths of the being. Nevertheless, its questioning spirit, its search for truth leads it beyond its own capabilities, leads it to search for a deeper foundation and a more complete understanding of the mysteries and subtleties of self and world. The subjective age begins when society begins to search for the deeper truths of its existence below the surfaces which the reason has explored and explained in an ordered, but limited sense. He explains that examples of this tendency are already apparent. In education, there is the trend to understand the psychology of the growing child and to base systems of teaching upon this basis. In criminal justice, there is an effort to understand the psychology of the criminal, and to strive to educate and rehabilitate rather than simply punish or isolate. In societies and groupings of people, there is a growing tendency to regard them as living and growing organisms with their own soul and inner tendencies, which must be fostered, developed, and perfected.

According to Sri Aurobindo, the present subjective age, with its inward turn towards the essential truth of the self and of things, opens the possibility of a true spiritual age. He explains that the subjective age could conceivably stop short of becoming spiritual. He says that a true spiritual age will come only if the idea becomes strong in the intellectual life of humanity that the Spirit is the true Reality standing behind our physical existence, and that to realise the Spirit and express it outwardly in mental, vital, and physical terms is the real meaning and aim of human existence. Sri Aurobindo argues that there is a deeper spiritual Reality that is the true Self of both the individual and the society, and it is only by identifying ourselves with it, rather than the limited and superficial individual or social ego, that the individual and social existence find their true centre and their proper relation with one another. In a spiritual age, therefore, he says that society would "make the revealing and finding of the divine Self in man the whole first aim of all its activities, its education, its knowledge, its science, its ethics, its art, its economical and political structure."

J.J. Rousseau

Jean-Jacques Rousseau (Geneva, 28 June 1712 – Ermenonville, 2 July 1778) was a major philosopher, writer, and composer of the eighteenth century Enlightenment, whose political philosophy influenced the French Revolution and the development of modern political and educational thought. His novel, *Emile: or, On Education*, which he considered his most important work, is a seminal treatise on the education of the whole person for citizenship. His sentimental novel, *Julie, ou la nouvelle Heloise*, was of great importance to the development of pre-Romanticism and romanticism in fiction. Rousseau's autobiographical writings: his *Confessions*, which initiated the modern autobiography, and his *Reveries of a Solitary Walker* (along with the works of Lessing and Goethe in Germany, and Richardson and Sterne in England), were among the pre-eminent examples of the late eighteenth century movement known as the "Age of Sensibility", featuring an increasing focus on subjectivity and introspection that has characterized the modern age. Rousseau also wrote a play and two operas, and made important contributions to music as a theorist. During the period of the French Revolution, Rousseau was the most popular of the *philosophes* among members of the Jacobin Club. He was interred as a national hero in the Pantheon in Paris, in 1794, sixteen years after his death.

Biography

Rousseau was born in 1712 in Geneva, since 1536 a (Huguenot) republic and the seat of Calvinism (now part of Switzerland). Rousseau was proud that his family, of the *moyen* (or middle-class) order, had voting rights in that city and throughout his life he described himself as a citizen of Geneva. In theory Geneva was governed democratically by its male voting citizens (who were a minority of the population). In fact, a secretive executive committee, called the Little Council (made up of 25 members of its wealthiest families), ruled the city. In 1707 a patriot called Pierre Fatio protested at this situation and the Little Council had him shot. Jean-Jacques Rousseau's father Isaac was not in the city at this time, but Jean-Jacques's grandfather supported Fatio and was penalized for it. Rousseau's father, Isaac Rousseau, was a watchmaker who, notwithstanding his artisan status, was well educated and a lover of music. "A Genevan watchmaker," Rousseau wrote, "is a man who can be introduced anywhere; a Parisian watchmaker is only fit to talk about watches." Rousseau's mother, Suzanne Bernard Rousseau, the daughter of a Calvinist preacher, died of birth complications nine days after his birth. He and his older brother Francois were brought up by their father and a paternal aunt, also named Suzanne. Jean-Jacques had no recollection of learning to read, but he remembered how when he was five or six his father encouraged his love of reading:

> *Every night, after supper, we read some part of a small collection of romances [i.e., adventure stories], which had been my mother's. My father's design was only to improve me in reading, and he thought these entertaining works were calculated to give me a fondness for it; but we soon found ourselves so interested in the adventures they contained, that we alternately read whole nights together and could not bear to give over until at the conclusion of a volume. Sometimes, in the morning, on hearing the swallows at our window, my father, quite ashamed of this weakness, would cry, "Come, come, let us go to bed; I am more a child than thou art."* — Confessions, Book 1

Not long afterwards, Rousseau abandoned his taste for escapist stories in favour of the antiquity of Plutarch's *Lives of the Noble Greeks and Romans*, which he would read to his father while he made watches.

When his older brother Francois got into trouble, Rousseau recounts how he deflected punishment onto himself in a bid for Francois's approval and affection. Later, Francois ran away, disappearing for good Some scholars have connected this event to Rousseau's lifelong tendency to masochism and his martyrdom complex. Survivors' guilt associated with causing his mother's death in childbirth may have played a part, as well.

When Jean Jacques Rousseau was ten, his father, an avid hunter, got into a legal quarrel with a wealthy landowner on whose lands he had been caught trespassing. To avoid certain defeat in the courts, he moved away to Nyon in the territory of Bern, taking Rousseau's aunt Suzanne with him. He remarried, and from that point Jean-Jacques saw little of him.

Jean-Jacques was left in with his maternal uncle, who packed him, along with his own son, Abraham Bernard, away to board for two years with a Calvinist minister in a hamlet outside of Geneva. Here the boys picked up the elements of mathematics and drawing. Rousseau, who was always deeply moved by religious services, for a time even dreamed of becoming a Protestant minister.

Virtually all our information about Rousseau's first youth has come from his posthumously published *Confessions*, in which the chronology is somewhat confused, though recent scholars have combed the archives for confirming evidence to fill in the blanks. At age 13 Rousseau was apprenticed first to a notary and then to an engraver who beat him. At fifteen he ran away from Geneva (on 14 March 1728) after returning to the city and finding the city gates locked due to the curfew. In adjoining Savoy he took shelter with a Catholic priest, who introduced him to Francoise-Louise de Warens, age 29. She was a noblewoman of Protestant background who was separated from her husband. As professional lay proselytizer, she was paid by the King of Piedmont to help bring Protestants to Catholicism. They sent the boy to Turin, the capital of Savoy (which included Piedmont, in what is now Italy), to complete his conversion. This resulted in his having to give up his Genevan citizenship, although he would later revert back to Calvinism in order to regain it.

In converting to Catholicism, both De Warens and Rousseau were likely reacting to the severity of Calvinism's insistence on the total depravity of man. Leo Damrosch writes, "an eighteenth century Genevan liturgy still required believers to declare 'that we are miserable sinners, born in corruption, inclined to evil, incapable by ourselves of doing good'." De Warens, a deist by inclination, was attracted to Catholicism's doctrine of forgiveness of sins.

Finding himself on his own, since his father and uncle had more or less disowned him, the teenaged Rousseau supported himself for a time as a servant, secretary, and tutor, wandering in Italy (Piedmont and Savoy) and France. During this time, he lived on and off with De Warens, whom he idolized and called his "*maman*". Flattered by his devotion, De Warens tried to get him started in a profession, and arranged formal music lessons for him. At one point, he briefly attended a seminary with the idea of becoming a priest. When he reached 20 she took him as her lover, notwithstanding her ongoing relationship with the steward of her house. The sexual aspect of their relationship (in fact a *menage a trois*) confused Rousseau and made him uncomfortable, but he always considered De Warens the greatest love of his life. A rather profligate spender, she had a large library and loved to entertain and listen to music. She and her circle, comprising educated members of the Catholic clergy, introduced Rousseau to the world of letters and ideas. Rousseau had been an indifferent student, but during his twenties, which were marked by long bouts of hypochondria, he applied himself in earnest to the study of philosophy, mathematics, and music. At twenty-five, he came into a small inheritance from his mother and used a portion of it to repay De Warens for her financial support of him. At twenty-seven he took a job as a tutor in Lyon.

In 1742 Rousseau moved to Paris in order to present the Academie des Sciences with a new system of numbered musical notation he believed would make his fortune. His system, intended to be compatible with typography, is based on a single line, displaying numbers representing intervals between notes and dots and commas indicating rhythmic values. Believing the system was impractical, the Academy rejected it, though they praised his mastery of the subject, and urged him to try again.

From 1743 to 1744 Rousseau had an honourable but ill-paying post as a secretary to the Comte de Montaigue, the French ambassador to Venice. This awoke in him a life-long love for Italian music, particularly opera:

> *I had brought with me from Paris the prejudice of that city against Italian music; but I had also received from nature a sensibility and niceness of distinction which prejudice cannot withstand. I soon contracted that passion for Italian music with which it inspires all those who are capable of feeling its excellence. In listening*

to barcaroles, I found I had not yet known what singing was... —Confessions

Rousseau's employer routinely received his stipend as much a year late and paid his staff irregularly. After eleven months Rousseau quit, taking from the experience a profound distrust of government bureaucracy.

Returning to Paris, the penniless Rousseau befriended and became the lover of Therese Levasseur, a pretty seamstress who was the sole support of her termagant mother and numerous ne'er-do-well siblings. At first they did not live together, though later Rousseau took Therese and her mother in to live with him as his servants, and himself assumed the burden of supporting her large family. According to his *Confessions*, before she moved in with him, Therese bore him a son and as many as four other children (there is no independent corroboration for this number). Rousseau wrote that he persuaded Therese to give each of the newborns up to a foundling hospital, for the sake of her "honour". "Her mother, who feared the inconvenience of a brat, came to my aid, and she [Therese] allowed herself to be overcome" (*Confessions*). The foundling hospitals had been started as a reform to save the numerous infants who were being abandoned in the streets of Paris. Infant mortality at that date was extremely high — some fifty percent, in large part because families sent their infants to be wet nursed. The mortality rate in the foundling hospitals, which also sent the babies out to be wet nursed, proved worse, however, and most of the infants sent there likely perished. Ten years later Rousseau, made inquiries about the fate of his son, but no record could be found. When Rousseau subsequently became celebrated as a theorist of education and child-rearing, his abandonment of his children was used by his critics, including Voltaire and Edmund Burke, as the basis for *ad hominem* attacks. In an irony of fate, Rousseau's later injunction to women to breastfeed their own babies (as had previously been recommended by the French natural scientist Buffon), probably saved the lives of thousands of infants.

While in Paris, Rousseau became a close friend of French philosopher Diderot and, beginning with some articles on music in 1749, contributed numerous articles to Diderot and D'Alambert's great Encyclopedie, the most famous of which was an article on political economy written in 1755.

Rousseau's ideas were the result of an almost obsessive dialogue with writers of the past, filtered in many cases through conversations with Diderot. His genius lay in his strikingly original way of putting things rather than in the originality, *per se*, of his thinking. In 1749 Rousseau was paying daily visits to Diderot, who had been thrown into the fortress of Vincennes under a *lettre de cachet* for opinions in his "*Lettre sur les aveugles*," that hinted at materialism, a belief in atoms, and natural selection. Rousseau had read about an essay competition sponsored by the Academie de Dijon to be published in the *Mercure de France* on the theme of whether the development of the arts and sciences had been morally beneficial. He wrote that while walking to Vincennes (about three miles from Paris), he had a revelation that the arts and sciences were responsible for the moral degeneration of mankind, who were basically good by nature. According to Diderot, writing much later, Rousseau had originally intended to answer this in the conventional way, but his discussions with Diderot convinced him to propose the paradoxical negative answer that catapulted him into the public eye. Whatever the case, it was the great French naturalist Buffon had previously suggested that man's moral decline arose from his acquisition of property and culture. Both Rousseau and Diderot would have been aware of Buffon's speculations. Rousseau's 1750 "Discourse on the Arts and Sciences", in which he made that argument, was awarded the first prize and gained him significant fame.

Rousseau continued his interest in music, and his opera *Le Devin du Village* (*The Village Soothsayer*) was performed for King Louis XV in 1752. The king was so pleased by the work that he offered Rousseau a life-long pension. To the exasperation of his friends, Rousseau turned down the great honour, bringing him notoriety as "the man who had refused a king's pension." He also turned down several other advantageous offers, sometimes with a brusqueness bordering on truculence that gave offense and caused him problems. The same year, the visit of a troupe of Italian musicians to Paris, and their performance of Giovanni Battista Pergolesi's *La Serva Padrona*, prompted the Querelle des Bouffons, which pitted protagonists of French music against supporters of the Italian style. Rousseau as noted above, was an enthusiastic supporter of the Italians against Jean-Philippe Rameau and others, making an important contribution with his *Letter on French Music*.

On returning to Geneva in 1754, Rousseau reconverted to Calvinism and regained his official Genevan citizenship. In 1755, Rousseau completed his second major work, the *Discourse on the Origin and Basis of Inequality Among Men* (the Discourse on Inequality), which elaborated on the arguments of the *Discourse on the Arts and Sciences*.

He also pursued an unconsummated romantic attachment with the twenty-five-year old Sophie d'Houdetot, which partly inspired his epistolary novel, *Julie, ou la nouvelle Heloise* (also based on memories of his idyllic youthful relationship with Mme de Warens). Sophie was the cousin and house guest of Rousseau's patroness and landlady Madame d'Epinay, whom he treated rather high highhandedly. He resented being at Mme d'Epinay's beck and call and detested the insincere conversation and shallow atheism of the *Encyclopedistes* whom he met at her table. Wounded feelings gave rise to a bitter three-way quarrel between Rousseau and Madame d'Epinay; her lover, the philologist Grimm; and their mutual friend, Diderot, who took their side against Rousseau. Diderot later described Rousseau as being, "false, vain as Satan, ungrateful, cruel, hypocritical, and wicked... He sucked ideas from me, used them himself, and then affected to despise me".

Rousseau's break with the *Encyclopedistes* coincided with the composition of his three major works, in all of which he emphasized his fervent belief in a spiritual origin of man's soul and the universe, in contradistinction to the materialism of Diderot, La Mettrie, and d'Holbach. During this period Rousseau enjoyed the support and patronage of the Duc de Luxembourg, and the Prince de Conti, two of the richest and most powerful nobles in France. These men truly liked Rousseau and enjoyed his ability to converse on any subject, but they also used him as a way of getting back at Louis XV and the political faction surrounding his mistress, Mme de Pompadour. Even with them, however, Rousseau went too far, courting rejection when he criticized the practice of tax farming, in which some of them engaged.

Rousseau's 800-page novel of sentiment, *Julie, ou la nouvelle Heloise*, was published in (1761) to immense success. The book's rhapsodic descriptions of the natural beauty of the Swiss countryside struck a chord in the public and may have helped spark the subsequent nineteenth century craze for Alpine scenery. In 1762, Rousseau published *Du Contrat Social, Principes du droit politique* (in English, literally *Of the Social Contract, Principles of Political Right*) in April and then *Emile: or, On Education* in May. The final section of *Emile*, "The Profession of Faith of a Savoyard Vicar," was intended to be a defense of religious belief. Rousseau's choice of a Catholic vicar of humble peasant background (plausibly based on a kindly prelate he had met as a teenager) as a spokesman for the defense of religion was in itself a daring innovation for the time. The vicar's creed was that of Socinianism (or Unitarism as it is called today). Because it rejected original sin and divine Revelation, both Protestant and Catholic authorities took offense. Moreover, Rousseau advocated the opinion that, insofar as they lead people to virtue, all religions are equally worthy, and that people should therefore conform to the religion in which they had been brought up. This religious indifferentism caused Rousseau and his books to be banned from France and Geneva. He was condemned from the pulpit by the Archbishop of Paris, his books were burned, and warrants were issued for his arrest.

A sympathetic observer, British philosopher David Hume, "professed no surprise when he learned that Rousseau's books were banned in Geneva and elsewhere. Rousseau, he wrote, 'has not had the precaution to throw any veil over his sentiments; and, as he scorns to dissemble his contempt for established opinions, he could not wonder that all the zealots were in arms against him. The liberty of the press is not so secured in any country ... as not to render such an open attack on popular prejudice somewhat dangerous.'" Rousseau, who thought he had been defending religion, was crushed. Forced to flee arrest he made his way, with the help of the Duc of Luxembourg and Prince de Conti, to Neuchatel, a Canton of the Swiss Confederation that was a protectorate of the Prussian crown. His powerful protectors discretely assisted him in his flight and they helped to get his banned books (published in Holland) distributed in France disguised as other works using false covers and title pages. In the town of Motiers, he sought and found protection under Lord Keith, who was the local representative of the free-thinking Frederick the Great of Prussia. While in Motiers, Rousseau wrote the *Constitutional Project for Corsica* (*Projet de Constitution pour la Corse*, 1765).

After his house in Motiers was stoned on the night of 6 September 1765, Rousseau took refuge with in Great Britain with Hume, who found lodgings for him at a friend's country estate in Wootton in Staffordshire. Neither Therese nor Rousseau were able to learn English or make friends. Isolated, Rousseau, never emotionally very stable, suffered a serious decline in his mental health and began to experience paranoid fantasies about plots against him involving Hume and others. "He is plainly mad, after having long been maddish", Hume wrote to a friend. Rousseau's letter to Hume, in which he articulates the perceived misconduct, sparked an exchange which was published in and received with great interest in contemporary Paris.

Although officially barred from entering France before 1770, Rousseau returned in 1767 under a false name. In 1768 he went through a marriage of sorts to Therese (marriages between Catholics and Protestants were illegal), whom he had always hitherto referred to as his "housekeeper". She was illiterate, she had become a remarkably good cook, a hobby her husband shared. In 1770 they were allowed to return to Paris. As a condition of his return he was not allowed to publish any books, but after completing his *Confessions*, Rousseau began private readings in 1771. At the request of Madame d'Epinay, who was anxious to protect her privacy, however, the police ordered him to stop, and the *Confessions* was only partially published in

1782, four years after his death. All his subsequent works were to appear posthumously.

In 1772, Rousseau was invited to present recommendations for a new constitution for the Polish-Lithuanian Commonwealth, resulting in the *Considerations on the Government of Poland*, which was to be his last major political work. In 1776 he completed *Dialogues: Rousseau Judge of Jean-Jacques* and began work on the *Reveries of the Solitary Walker*. In order to support himself, he returned to copying music, spending his leisure time in the study of botany.

Although a celebrity, Rousseau's mental health did not permit him to enjoy his fame. His final years were largely spent in deliberate withdrawal; however, he did respond favourably to an approach from the composer Gluck, whom he met in 1774. One of Rousseau's last pieces of writing was a critical yet enthusiastic analysis of Gluck's opera Alceste. While taking a morning walk on the estate of the marquis Rene Louis de Girardin at Ermenonville (28 miles northeast of Paris), Rousseau suffered a hemorrhage and died on 2 July 1778. He was sixty-six.

Rousseau was initially buried at Ermenonville on the Ile des Peupliers, which became a place of pilgrimage for his many admirers. His remains were moved to the Pantheon in Paris in 1794, sixteen years after his death, where they are located directly across from those of his contemporary Voltaire. His tomb, in the shape of a rustic temple, on which, in bas relief an arm reaches out, bearing the torch of liberty, evokes Rousseau's deep love of nature and of classical antiquity. In 1834, the Genevan government somewhat reluctantly erected a statue in his honour on the tiny Ile Rousseau in Lake Geneva. Today he is proudly claimed as their most celebrated native son. In 2002, the Espace Rousseau was established at 40 Grand-Rue, Geneva, Rousseau's birthplace.

Philosophy

Theory of Natural Man

> *"The first man who, having fenced in a piece of land, said "This is mine," and found people naive enough to*

believe him, that man was the true founder of civil society. From how many crimes, wars, and murders, from how many horrors and misfortunes might not any one have saved mankind, by pulling up the stakes, or filling up the ditch, and crying to his fellows: Beware of listening to this impostor; you are undone if you once forget that the fruits of the earth belong to us all, and the earth itself to nobody." — Jean-Jacques Rousseau, Discourse on Inequality, 1754

In common with other philosophers of the day, Rousseau looked to a hypothetical State of Nature as a normative guide. Rousseau deplores Hobbes for asserting that since man in the "state of nature... has no idea of goodness he must be naturally wicked; that he is vicious because he does not know virtue". On the contrary, Rousseau holds that "uncorrupted morals" prevail in the "state of nature" and he especially praised the admirable moderation of the Caribbeans in expressing the sexual urge despite the fact that they live in a hot climate, which "always seems to inflame the passions". This has led Anglophone critics to erroneously attribute to Rousseau the invention of idea of the noble savage, an oxymoronic expression that was never used in France and which grossly misrepresents Rousseau's thought. (The expression, "the noble savage" was first used in 1672 by British poet John Dryden in his play *The Conquest of Granada*. The French word "*sauvage*" means "wild", as in "a wild flower", and does not have the connotations of fierceness or brutality that the word "savage" does in English, though in the eighteenth century the English word was closer in connotation to the French one.) Rousseau did deny that morality is a construct or creation of society. He considered it as "natural" in the sense of "innate", an outgrowth of man's instinctive disinclination to witness suffering, from which arise the emotions of compassion or empathy, sentiments whose existence even Hobbes acknowledged, and which are shared with animals.

Contrary to what his many detractors have claimed on the basis of casual readings, Rousseau never suggests that humans in the state of nature act morally; in fact, terms such as "justice" or "wickedness" are inapplicable to pre-political society as Rousseau understands it. Morality proper, i.e., self restraint, can only develop through careful education in a civil state. Humans "in a state of Nature" may act with all of the ferocity of an animal. They are good only in a negative sense, insofar as they are self-sufficient and thus not subject to the vices of political society. In fact, Rousseau's natural man is virtually identical to a solitary chimpanzee or other ape, such as the orangutan as described by Buffon; and the "natural" goodness of humanity is thus the goodness of an animal, which is neither good nor bad. Rousseau, a deteriorationist, proposed that, except perhaps for brief moments of balance, at or near its inception, when a relative equality among men prevailed, human civilization has always been artificial, creating inequality, envy, and unnatural desires.

In Rousseau's philosophy, society's negative influence on men centres on its transformation of *amour de soi*, a positive self-love, into *amour-propre*, or pride. *Amour de soi* represents the instinctive human desire for self-preservation, combined with the human power of reason. In contrast, *amour-propre* is artificial and encourages man to compare himself to others, thus creating unwarranted fear and allowing men to take pleasure in the pain or weakness of others. Rousseau was not the first to make this distinction; it had been invoked by, among others, Vauvenargues.

In *Discourse on the Arts and Sciences* Rousseau argues that the arts and sciences have not been beneficial to humankind, because they arose not from authentic human needs but rather as a result of pride and vanity. Moreover, the opportunities they create for idleness and luxury have contributed to the corruption of man. He proposed that the progress of knowledge had made governments more powerful and had crushed individual liberty; and he concluded that material progress had actually undermined the possibility of true friendship by replacing it with jealousy, fear, and suspicion.

In contrast to the optimistic view of other Enlightenment figures, for Rousseau, progress has been inimical to the well-being of humanity, *that is,* unless it can be counteracted by the cultivation of civic morality and duty. Only in Civil Society, can man be ennobled — through the use of reason:

> *The passage from the state of nature to the civil state produces a very remarkable change in man, by substituting justice for instinct in his conduct, and giving his actions the morality they had formerly lacked. Then only, when the voice of duty takes the place of physical impulses and right of appetite, does man, who so far had considered only himself, find that he is forced to act on different principles, and to consult his reason before listening to his inclinations. Although, in this state, he deprives himself of some advantages which he got from nature, he gains in return others so great, his faculties are so stimulated and developed, his ideas so extended, his feelings so ennobled, and his whole soul so uplifted, that, did not the abuses of this new condition often degrade him below that which he left, he would be bound to bless continually the happy moment which took him from it for ever, and, instead of a stupid and unimaginative animal, made him an intelligent being and a man.*

Society corrupts men only insofar as the Social Contract has not *de facto* succeeded, as we see in contemporary society as described in the *Discourse on Inequality* (1754). In this essay, which elaborates the ideas introduced in the *Discourse on Arts and Sciences*, Rousseau traces man's social evolution from a primitive state of nature to modern society. The earliest solitary humans possessed a basic drive for self preservation and a natural disposition to compassion or pity. They differed from animals, however, in their capacity for free will and their potential perfectibility. As they began to live in groups and form clans they also began to experience family love, which Rousseau saw as the source of the greatest happiness known to humanity. As long as differences in wealth and status among families were minimal, the first coming together in groups was accompanied by a fleeting golden age of human flourishing. The development of agriculture, metallurgy, private property, and the division of labour and resulting dependency on one another, however, led to economic inequality and conflict. As population pressures forced them to associate more and more closely, they underwent a psychological transformation: they began to see themselves through the eyes of others and came to value the good opinion of others as essential to their self esteem. Rousseau posits that the original, deeply flawed Social Contract (i.e., that of Hobbes), which led to the modern state, was made at the suggestion of the rich and powerful, who tricked the general population into surrendering their liberties to them and instituted inequality as a fundamental feature of human society. Rousseau's own conception of the Social Contract can be understood as an alternative to this fraudulent form of association. At the end of the *Discourse on Inequality*, Rousseau explains how the desire to have value in the eyes of others comes to undermine personal integrity and authenticity in a society marked by interdependence, and hierarchy. In the last chapter of the *Social Contract*, Rousseau would ask "What is to be done?" He answers that now all men can do is to cultivate virtue in themselves and submit to their lawful rulers. To his readers, however the inescapable conclusion was that a new and more equitable Social Contract was needed. Interesting Fact: Rousseau was indirectly responsible for the phrase "Your Mom" when he used it in one of his speeches.

Legacy

A plaque commemorating the bicentenary of Rousseau's birth. Issued by the city of Geneva on 28 June 1912. The legend at the bottom says "Jean-Jacques, aime ton pays" ("love your country"), and shows Rousseau's father gesturing towards the window. The scene is drawn from a footnote to the Letter to d'Alembert where Rousseau recalls witnessing the popular celebrations following the exercises of the St Gervais regiment. Rousseau's idea of the *volonte generale* ("general will") was not original with him but rather belonged to a well-established technical vocabulary of juridical and theological writings in use at the time. The phrase was used by Diderot and also by Montesquieu (and by his teacher, the Oratorian friar Malebranche). It served to designate the common interest embodied in legal tradition, as distinct from and transcending people's private and particular interests at any particular time. The concept was also an important aspect of the more radical seventeenth century republican tradition of Spinoza, from whom Rousseau differed in important respects, but not in his insistence on the importance of equality. This emphasis on equality is Rousseau's most important and consequential legacy, causing him to be both reviled and applauded:

> *While Rousseau's notion of the progressive moral degeneration of mankind from the moment civil society established itself diverges markedly from Spinoza's claim that human nature is always and everywhere the same... for both philosophers the pristine equality of the state of nature is our ultimate goal and criterion... in shaping the "common good",* volonte generale, *or Spinoza's* mens una, *which alone can ensure stability and political salvation. Without the supreme criterion of equality, the general will would indeed be meaningless.... When in the depths of the French Revolution the Jacobin clubs all over France regularly deployed Rousseau when demanding radical reforms and especially anything — such as land redistribution — designed to enhance equality, they were at the same time, albeit unconsciously, invoking a radical tradition which reached back to the late seventeenth century.*

The cult that grew up around Rousseau after his death, and particularly the radicalized versions of Rousseau's ideas that were adopted by Robespierre and Saint Just during the Reign of Terror, caused him to become identified with the most extreme aspects of the French Revolution. The revolutionaries were also inspired by Rousseau to introduce Deism as the new official civil religion of France, scandalizing traditionalists:

> *Ceremonial and symbolic occurrences of the more radical phases of the Revolution invoked Rousseau and his core ideas. Thus the ceremony held at the site of the demolished Bastille, organized by the foremost artistic director of the Revolution, Jacques-Louis David, in August 1793 to mark the inauguration of the new republican constitution, an event coming shortly after*

> *the final abolition of all forms of feudal privilege, featured a cantata based on Rousseau's democratic pantheistic deism as expounded in the celebrated* "Profession de foi d'un vicaire savoyard" *in Book four of* Emile.

Opponents of the Revolution and defenders of religion, most influentially the Irish essayist Edmund Burke, therefore placed the blame for the excesses of the French Revolution directly on the revolutionaries' misplaced (as he considered it) adulation of Rousseau. Burke's "Letter to a Member of the National Assembly", published in February 1791, was a diatribe against Rousseau, whom he considered the paramount influence on French Revolution (his *ad hominem* attack did not really engage with Rousseau's political writings).

Burke maintained that the excesses of the Revolution were not accidents but were designed from the beginning and were rooted in Rousseau's personal vanity, arrogance, and other moral failings.

He recalled Rousseau's visit to Britain in 1766, saying: "I had good opportunities of knowing his proceedings almost from day to day and he left no doubt in my mind that he entertained no principle either to influence his heart or to guide his understanding, but vanity". Conceding his gift of eloquence, Burke deplored Rousseau's lack of the good taste and finer feelings that would have been imparted by the education of a gentleman:

> *Taste and elegance... are of no mean importance in the regulation of life. A moral taste...infinitely abates the evils of vice. Rousseau, a writer of great force and vivacity, is totally destitute of taste in any sense of the word. Your masters [i.e., the leaders of the Revolution], who are his scholars, conceive that all refinement has an aristocratic character. The last age had exhausted all its powers in giving a grace and nobleness to our mutual appetites, and in raising them into a higher class and order than seemed justly to belong to them. Through Rousseau, your masters are resolved to destroy these aristocratic prejudices.*

In America, where there was no such cult, the direct influence of Rousseau was arguably less. The American founders did share Rousseau's enthusiastic admiration for the austere virtues described by Livy and in Plutarch's portrayals the great men of ancient Sparta and the classical republicanism of early Rome, but so did most other enlightenment figures. Rousseau's praise of Switzerland and Corsica's economies of isolated and self-sufficient independent homesteads, and his endorsement of a well-regulated citizen militia, such as Switzerland's, recall the ideals of Jeffersonian democracy.

To Rousseau we owe the invention of the concept of a "civil religion", one of whose key tenets is religious toleration. Yet despite their mutual insistence on the self evidence that "all men are created equal", their insistence that the citizens of a republic be educated at public expense, and the evident parallel between the concepts of the "general welfare" and Rousseau's "general will", some scholars maintain there is little to suggest that Rousseau had that much impact on Thomas Jefferson and other founding fathers. They argue that the American constitution owes as much or more to the English Liberal philosopher John Locke's emphasis on the rights of property and to Montesquieu's theories of the separation of powers. Rousseau's writings had an indirect influence on American literature through the writings of Wordsworth and Kant, whose works were important to the New England Transcendentalists Ralph Waldo Emerson, and his disciple Henry David Thoreau, as well as on such Unitarians as theologian William Ellery Channing. American novelist James Fennimore Cooper's *Last of the Mohicans* and other novels reflect republican and egalitarian ideals present alike in Rousseau, Tom Paine, and also in English Romantic primitivism Another American admirer was lexicographer Noah Webster.

Frobel

Friedrich Wilhelm August Frobel (or **Froebel**) (April 21, 1782 – June 21, 1852) was a German pedagogue, a student of Pestalozzi who laid the foundation for modern education based on the recognition that children have unique needs and capabilities. He created the concept of the "kindergarten", and also coined the word now used in German and English.

Biography

Friedrich Frobel was born at Oberweibach in the Principality of Schwarzburg-Rudolstadt in Thuringia. His father, who died in 1802, was the pastor of the orthodox Lutheran (alt-lutherisch) parish there. The church and Lutheran Christian faith were pillars in Frobel's own early education. Oberweibach was a wealthy village in the Thuringian Forest and had been known centuries long for its natural herb remedies, tinctures, bitters, soaps and salves. Families had their own inherited areas of the forest where herbs and roots were grown and harvested. Each family prepared, bottled, and produced their individual products which were taken throughout Europe on trade routes passed from father to son, who were affectionately called "Buckelapotheker" or *Rucksack Pharmacists*. They adorned the church with art acquired from their travels, many pieces of which can still be seen in the renovated structure. The pulpit from which Frobel heard his father preach is the largest in all Europe and can fit a pastor and 12 men, a direct reference to Christ's apostles. Shortly after Frobel's birth, his mother's health began to fail. She died when he was nine months old, profoundly influencing his life. In 1792, Frobel went to live in the small town of Stadt-Ilm with his uncle, a gentle and affectionate man. At the age of 15 Frobel, who loved nature, became the apprentice to a forester. In 1799, he decided to leave his apprenticeship and study mathematics and botany in Jena. From 1802 to 1805, he worked as a land surveyor.

On 11 September 1818, Frobel wed Wilhelmine Henriette Hoffmeister (b. 1780) in Berlin. The union was childless. Wilhelmine died in 1839, and Frobel married again in 1851. His second wife was Louise Levin.

Career

He began as an educator in 1805 at the *Musterschule* (a secondary school) in Frankfurt, where he learnt about Johann Heinrich Pestalozzi's ideas. He later worked with Pestalozzi in

Switzerland where his ideas further developed. From 1806 Frobel was the live-in teacher for a Frankfurt noble family's three sons. He lived with the three children from 1808 to 1810 at Pestalozzi's institute in Yverdon-les-Bains in Switzerland.

In 1811, Frobel once again went back to school in Gottingen and Berlin, eventually leaving without earning a certificate. He became a teacher at the *Plamannsche Schule* in Berlin, a boarding school for boys, and at that time also a pedagogical and patriotic centre.

During his service in the Lutzow Free Corps in 1813 and 1814 – when he was involved in two campaigns against Napoleon – Frobel befriended Wilhelm Middendorf, a theologian and fellow pedagogue, and Heinrich Langethal, also a pedagogue.

After Waterloo and the Congress of Vienna, Frobel found himself a civilian once again and became an assistant at the Museum of Mineralogy under Prof. Weib. This did not, however, last very long, and by 1816 he had quit and founded the *Allgemeine Deutsche Erziehungsanstalt* ("German General Education Institute") in Griesheim near Arnstadt in Thuringia. A year later he moved this to Keilhau near Rudolstadt. In 1831, work was continued there by the other cofounders Wilhelm Middendorf and Heinrich Langethal.

In 1820, Frobel published the first of his five Keilhau pamphlets, *An unser deutsches Volk* ("To Our German People"). The other four were published between then and 1823.

In 1826 he published is main literary work, *Die Menschenerziehung* ("The Education of Man") and founded the weekly publication *Die erziehenden Familien* ("The Educating Families"). In 1828 and 1829 he pursued plans for a people's education institute (*Volkserziehungsanstalt*) in Helba (nowadays a constituent community of Meiningen), but they were never realized. From 1831 to 1836, Frobel once again lived in Switzerland. In 1831 he founded an educational institute in Wartensee (Lucerne). In 1833 he moved this to Willisau, and from 1835 to 1836, he headed the orphanage in Burgdorf (Berne), where he also published the magazine *Grundzuge der Menschenerziehung* ("Features of Human Education"). In 1836 appeared his work *Erneuerung des Lebens erfordert das neue Jahr 1836* ("The New Year 1836 Calls For the Renewal of Life").

He returned to Germany, dedicated himself almost exclusively to preschool child education and began manufacturing playing materials in Bad Blankenburg. In 1837 he founded a "care, playing and activity institute for small children in Bad Blankenburg. From 1838 to 1840 he also published the magazine *Ein Sonntagsblatt fur Gleichgesinnte* ("A Sunday Paper for the Like-Minded").

In 1840 he coined the word kindergarten for the Play and Activity Institute he had founded in 1837 at Bad Blankenburg for young children, together with Wilhelm Middendorf and Heinrich Langethal. These two men were Frobel's most faithful colleagues when his ideas were also transplanted to Keilhau near Rudolstadt.

He designed the educational play materials known as Froebel Gifts, or *Frobelgaben*, which included geometric building blocks and pattern activity blocks. A book entitled *Inventing Kindergarten*, by Norman Brosterman, examines the influence of Friedrich Frobel on Frank Lloyd Wright and modern art.

Friedrich Frobel's great insight was to recognise the importance of the activity of the child in learning. He introduced the concept of "free work" (*Freiarbeit*) into pedagogy and established the "game" as the typical form that life took in childhood, and also the game's educational worth. Activities in the first kindergarten included singing, dancing, gardening and self-directed play with the Froebel Gifts. Frobel intended, with his *Mutter-und Koselieder* – a songbook that he published – to introduce the young child into the adult world.

These ideas about childhood development and education were introduced to academic and royal circles through the tireless efforts of his greatest proponent, the Baroness (Freiherrin) Bertha Marie von Marenholtz-Bulow. Through her Frobel made the acquaintance of the Royal House of the Netherlands, various Thuringian dukes and duchesses, including the Romanov wife of the Grand Duke von Sachsen-

Weimar. Baroness von Marenholtz-Bulow, Duke von Meiningen and Frobel gathered donations to support art education for children in honour of the 100th anniversary of the birth of Goethe. The Duke of Meiningen granted the use of his hunting lodge, called Marienthal (the Vale of Mary) in the resort town of Bad Liebenstein for Frobel to train the first women as Kindergarten teachers (called *Kindergartnerinnen*).

Frobel died on 21 June 1852 in Mariental. His grave is still found at the cemetery at Schweina, where his widow, who died in Hamburg, was also buried on 10 January 1900.

Legacy

Frobel's idea of the kindergarten found appeal, but its spread in Germany was thwarted by the Prussian government, whose education ministry banned it on 7 August 1851 as "atheistic and demagogic" for its alleged "destructive tendencies in the areas of religion and politics". Other states followed suit. The reason for the ban, however, seems to have been a confusion of names. Frobel's nephew Karl Frobel had written and published *Weibliche Hochschulen und Kindergarten* ("Female Colleges and Kindergartens"), which apparently met with some disapproval. To quote Karl August Varnhagen von Ense, "The stupid minister von Raumer has decreed a ban on kindergartens, basing himself on a book by Karl Frobel. He is confusing Friedrich and Karl Frobel."

Frobel's student Margarethe Schurz founded the first kindergarten in the United States at Watertown, Wisconsin in 1856, and she also inspired Elizabeth Peabody, who went on to found the first English-speaking kindergarten in the United States – the language at Schurz's kindergarten had been German, to serve an immigrant community – in Boston in 1860. This paved the way for the concept's spread in the USA. The German emigre Adolph Douai had also founded a kindergarten in Boston in 1859, but was obliged to close it after only a year. By 1866, however, he was founding others in New York City.

The pedagogue August Kohler was the initiator and cofounder in 1863 of the *Deutscher Frobelverein* ("German Frobel

Association"), first for Thuringia, out of which grew the *Allgemeiner Frobelverein* ("General Frobel Association") in 1872, and a year later the *Deutscher Frobelverband* ("German Frobel Federation"). August Kohler critically analyzed and evaluated Frobel theory, adopted fundamental notions into his own kindergarten pedagogy and expanded on these, developing an independent "Kohler Kindergarten Pedagogy". He first trained kindergarten teachers in Gotha in 1857. In the beginning, Kohler had thought to engage male educators exclusively, but far too few applied.

Thekla Naveau founded in October 1853 the first kindergarten in Sondershausen and on 1 April 1867 the first kindergarten after the Prussian ban was lifted in Nordhausen.

Angelika Hartmann founded in 1864 the first kindergarten after Frobel's model in Kothen, Anhalt.

In 1908 and 1911, kindergarten teacher training was recognized in Germany through state regulatory laws.

In the meantime, there are many kindergartens in Germany named after Frobel that continue his pedagogy. Many of them have sprung from parental or other private initiatives. The biggest Frobel association, *Frobel e.V.*, today runs more than 100 kindergartens and other early childhood institutions throughout the country through the *Frobel-Gruppe*.

Committed to Frobel's legacy is also the *Neuer Thuringer Frobelverein* (NTFV; "New Thuringian Frobel Association"), and in particular to protecting the legacy's business receipts. As well, the Association runs a school museum and the Frobel Archive in Keilhau. Furthermore it engages itself in Frobel institutions worldwide (United States, United Kingdom, Japan). Through this network, the NTFV further continues one of the most prominent lines of modern pedagogy from the authentic "Frobel town" of Keilhau. The Frobel Diploma, now conferred by the Frobel Academy in Rudolstadt, can also be traced back to the NTFV. All this ensures that Frobel's ideas will live on into the future.

Frobel's building forms and movement games are also forerunners of abstract art as well as a source of inspiration to the Bauhaus movement. In Frobel's honour, Walter Gropius designed the *Friedrich Frobel Haus*.

John Dewey

John Dewey (October 20, 1859 – June 1, 1952) was an American philosopher, psychologist, and educational reformer whose thoughts and ideas have been highly influential in the United States and around the world. Dewey, along with Charles Sanders Peirce and William James, is recognized as one of the founders of the philosophical school of pragmatism. He is also one of the founders of functional psychology and was a leading representative of the progressive movement in U.S. schooling during the first half of the 20th century.

Although Dewey is best known for his works on education, he also wrote on a wide range of subjects, including experience and nature, art and experience, logic and inquiry, democracy, and ethics.

In his advocacy of democracy, Dewey considered two fundamental elements—schools and civil society—as being key areas needing attention and reconstruction to encourage experimental intelligence and plurality. In the necessary reconstruction of civil society, Dewey asserted that full democracy was to be obtained not just by extending voting rights but also by ensuring that there exists a fully-formed public opinion, accomplished by effective communication among citizens, experts, and politicians, with the latter being held accountable for the policies they adopt.

Life and Works

Dewey was born in Burlington, Vermont of modest family origins. Like his older brother, Davis Rich Dewey, he attended the University of Vermont, from which he graduated (Phi Beta Kappa) in 1879. After three years as a high school teacher in Oil City, Pennsylvania, Dewey decided that he was unsuited for employment in primary or secondary education. After studying one year under G. Stanley Hall, working in the first American laboratory of psychology, Dewey received his Ph.D. from the School of Arts & Sciences at Johns Hopkins University in 1884, he took a faculty position at the University of Michigan (1884-1888 and 1889-1894) with the help of George Sylvester Morris. His unpublished and now lost dissertation was titled "The Psychology of Kant" and he made a special study of Hegel's Absolute idealism.

In 1894 Dewey joined the newly founded University of Chicago (1894-1904) where he shaped his belief in an empirically based theory of knowledge aligning his ideals with the newly emerging Pragmatic school of thought. His time at the University of Chicago resulted in four essays collectively entitled *Thought and its Subject-Matter* which was published with collected works from his colleagues at Chicago under the collective title *Studies in Logical Theory* (1903). During this time Dewey also founded the University of Chicago Laboratory Schools where he was able to actualize his pedagogical beliefs which provided material for his first major work on education, *The School and Society* (1899). Disagreements with the administration ultimately led to his resignation from the University at which point he left for the East Coast. In 1899, John Dewey was elected president of the American Psychological Association. From 1904 until his death he was professor of philosophy at both Columbia University and Teachers College, Columbia University. In 1905 he became president of the American Philosophical Association. He was a long-time member of the American Federation of Teachers.

Along with the historian Charles Beard, economists Thorstein Veblen and James Harvey Robinson, Dewey is one of the founders of The New School for Social Research. Dewey's most significant writings were "The Reflex Arc Concept in Psychology" (1896), a critique of a standard psychological concept and the basis of all his further work; *Democracy and Education* (1916), his celebrated work on progressive education; *Human Nature and Conduct* (1922), a study of the role of habit in human behaviour; *The Public and its Problems* (1927), a defense of democracy written in response to Walter Lippmann's *The Phantom Public* (1925); *Experience and Nature* (1925), Dewey's most "metaphysical" statement; *Art as Experience* (1934), Dewey's major work on aesthetics; *A Common Faith* (1934), a humanistic study of religion, which was originally delivered as the Dwight H. Terry Lectureship at Yale; *Logic: The Theory of Inquiry* (1938), an examination of Dewey's unusual conception of logic; *Freedom and Culture* (1939), a political work examining the roots of fascism; and *Knowing and the Known* (1949), a book written in conjuction with Arthur F. Bentley that systematically outlines the concept of trans-action which is central to his other works. While each of these works focuses on one particular philosophical theme, Dewey wove all of his major themes into everything he wrote. His professional life was extremely productive and consisted of over 700 articles in 140 journals, and roughly 40 books.

Dewey married twice, with first wife Alice Chipman, who bore him six children and second wife Roberta Lowitz Grant.

Dewey and Functional Psychology

At University of Michigan, Dewey published his first two books, *Psychology* (1887), and *Leibniz's New Essays Concerning the Human Understanding* (1888), both of which expressed Dewey's early commitment to Hegelian idealism. *Psychology* explored the synthesis between this idealism and experimental science that Dewey was then attempting to effect.

While still professor of philosophy at Michigan, Dewey and his junior colleagues, James Hayden Tufts and George Herbert Mead, together with his student James Rowland Angell, all strongly influenced by the recent publication of William James' landmark *Principles of Psychology* (1890), began to reformulate psychology, focusing more strongly on the social environment and on the activity of mind and behaviour than the physiological psychology of Wundt and his followers.

By 1894, Dewey had joined Tufts, with whom he would later write *Ethics* (1908), at the newly-founded University of Chicago and invited Mead and Angell to follow him, the four forming the core of the so-called "Chicago group" of psychology.

Their new approach to psychology, later dubbed functional psychology, had a more practical emphasis on action and application. In Dewey's article "The Reflex Arc Concept in Psychology" which appeared in *Psychological Review* in 1896, he reasons against the traditional stimulus-response understanding of the reflex arc in favour of a "circular" account in which what serves as "stimulus" and what as "response" depends on how one views the situation, and defends the unitary nature of the sensory motor circuit. While he does not deny the existence of stimulus, sensation, and response, he disagreed that they were separate, juxtaposed events happening like links in a chain. He put forward the idea that there is a coordination by which the stimulus is enriched by the results of previous experiences. The response is modulated thanks to sensorial experience. That is to say, the stimulus, sensation, and response are phases in a "division of labour" as part of an overall coordination of action as the human organism adapts to its environment.

Dewey, not without polemic, was elected president of the American Psychological Association in 1899.

In 1984, the American Psychological Association announced that Lillian Moller Gilbreth (1878-1972) had become the first psychologist to be commemorated on a United States postage stamp. However, psychologists Gary Brucato Jr. and John D. Hogan later made the case that this distinction actually belonged to John Dewey, who had been celebrated on an American stamp 17 years earlier. While some psychology historians consider Dewey more of a philosopher than a bona fide psychologist, the authors noted that Dewey was a founding member of the A.P.A., served as the A.P.A.'s eighth President in 1899, and was the author of an 1896 article on the reflex arc which is now considered a cornerstone of American functional psychology.

Dewey also expressed interest in work in the psychology of visual perception carried out by Dartmouth research professor Adelbert Ames, Jr..

Pragmatism and Instrumentalism

Although Dewey did not identify himself as a pragmatist per se, but instead referred to his philosophy as "instrumentalism", he is considered one of the three central figures in American pragmatism, along with Charles Sanders

Peirce, who coined the term, and William James, who popularized it. Dewey worked from strongly Hegelian influences, unlike James, whose lineage was primarily British, drawing particularly on empiricist and utilitarian thought. Neither was Dewey so pluralist or relativist as James. He held that value was a function not of whim nor purely of social construction, but a quality situated in events ("nature itself is wistful and pathetic, turbulent and passionate" (*Experience and Nature*)).

He also held that experimentation (social, cultural, technological, philosophical) could be used as a relatively hard-and-fast arbiter of truth. For example, James felt that for many people who lacked "over-belief" in religious concepts, human life was shallow and rather uninteresting, and that while no one religious belief could be demonstrated as the correct one, we are all responsible for taking the leap of faith and making a gamble on one or another theism, atheism, monism, etc. Dewey, in contrast, while honoring the important role that religious institutions and practices played in human life, rejected belief in any static ideal, such as a theistic God. Dewey felt that only scientific method could reliably further human good.

Of the idea of God, Dewey said, "it denotes the unity of all ideal ends arousing us to desire and actions." As with the reemergence of progressive philosophy of education, Dewey's contributions to philosophy as such (he was, after all, much more a professional philosopher than a thinker on education) have also reemerged with the reassessment of pragmatism, beginning in the late 1970s, by thinkers like Richard Rorty, Richard J. Bernstein and Hans Joas.

Because of his process-oriented and sociologically conscious view of the world and knowledge, he is sometimes seen as a useful alternative to both modern and postmodern ways of thinking. Dewey's non-foundational approach pre-dates postmodernism by more than half a century. Recent exponents (like Rorty) have not always remained faithful to Dewey's original vision, though this itself is completely in keeping both with Dewey's own usage of other thinkers and with his own philosophy— for Dewey, past doctrines always require reconstruction in order to remain useful for the present time.

Dewey's philosophy has gone by many names other than "pragmatism". He has been called an instrumentalist, an experimentalist, an empiricist, a functionalist, and a naturalist. The term "transactional" may better describe his views, a term emphasized by Dewey in his later years to describe his theories of knowledge and experience.

Epistemology

The terminology problem in the fields of epistemology and logic is partially due, according to Dewey and Bentley, to inefficient and imprecise use of words and concepts that reflect three historic levels of organization and presentation. In the order of chronological appearance, these are:

- Self-Action: Prescientific concepts regarded humans, animals, and things as possessing powers of their own which initiated or caused their actions.
- Interaction: as described by Newton, where things, living and inorganic, are balanced against something in a system of interaction, for example, the third law of motion states that for every action there is an equal and opposite reaction.
- Transaction: where modern systems of descriptions and naming are employed to deal with multiple aspects and phases of action without any attribution to ultimate, final, or independent entities, essences, or realities.

A series of characterizations of Transactions indicate the wide range of considerations involved.

Logic and Method

Dewey sees paradox in contemporary logical theory. Proximate subject matter garners general agreement and advance, while the ultimate subject matter of logic generates unremitting controversy. In other words, he challenges confident logicians to answer the question of the truth of logical operators. Do they function merely as abstractions (e.g., pure mathematics) or do they connect in some essential way with their objects, and therefore alter or bring them to light? ("The Problem of Logical Subject Matter", in *Logic: The Theory of Inquiry* {1938})

Logical positivism also figured in Dewey's thought. About the movement he wrote that it "eschews the use of 'propositions' and 'terms', substituting 'sentences' and 'words'." ("General Theory of Propositions", in *Logic: The Theory of Inquiry*) He welcomes this changing of referents "in as far as it fixes attention upon the symbolic structure and content of propositions."

However, he registers a small complaint against the use of "sentences" and "words" in that without careful interpretation the act or process of transposition "narrows unduly the scope of symbols and language, since it is not customary to treat gestures and diagrams (maps, blueprints, etc.) as words or sentences." In other words, sentences and words, considered in isolation, do not disclose intent, which may be inferred or "adjudged only by means of context." (Ibid.)

Yet Dewey was not entirely opposed to modern logical trends. Concerning traditional logic, he states: "Aristotelian logic, which still passes current nominally, is a logic based upon the idea that qualitative objects are existential in the fullest sense.

To retain logical principles based on this conception along with the acceptance of theories of existence and knowledge based on an opposite conception is not, to say the least, conductive to clearness – a consideration that has a good deal to do with existing dualism between traditional and the newer relational logics." (*Qualitative Thought* {1930})

Louis Menand argues in *The Metaphysical Club* that Jane Addams had been critical of Dewey's emphasis on antagonism in the context of a discussion of the Pullman strike of 1894. In a later letter to his wife, Dewey confessed that Addams' argument was "the most magnificent exhibition of intellectual & moral faith I ever saw.

She converted me internally, but not really, I fear.... When you think that Miss Addams does not think this as a philosophy, but believes it in all her senses & muscles—Great God... I guess I'll have to give it [all] up & start over again." He went on to add, "I can see that I have always been interpreting dialectic wrong end up, the unity as the reconciliation of opposites, instead of the opposites as the unity in its growth, and thus translated the physical tension into a moral thing... I don't know as I give the reality of this at all,... it seems so natural & commonplace now, but I never had anything take hold of me so."

In a letter to Addams herself, Dewey wrote, clearly influenced by his conversation with her: "Not only is actual antagonizing bad, but the assumption that there is or may be antagonism is bad— in fact, the real first antagonism always comes back to the assumption."

Montessori

Maria Montessori (August 31, 1870 – May 6, 1952) was an Italian physician, educator, philosopher, humanitarian and devout Catholic; she is best known for her philosophy and the Montessori method of education of children from birth to adolescence.

Her educational method is in use today in a number of public as well as private schools throughout the world.

Biography

Maria Montessori was born in Chiaravalle (Ancona), Italy to Alessandro Montessori, and Renilde Stoppani (niece of Antonio Stoppani). At the age of thirteen she attended an all-boy technical school in preparation for her dreams of becoming an engineer.

Montessori was the first woman to graduate from the University of Rome La Sapienza Medical School, becoming the first female doctor in Italy. She was a member of the University's Psychiatric Clinic and became intrigued with trying to educate the "mentally retarded or "unhappy little ones" and the "uneducatable" in Rome.

In 1896, she gave a lecture at the Educational Congress in Torino about the training of the disabled. The Italian Minister of Education was in attendance, and was impressed by her arguments sufficiently to appoint her the same year as director of the Scuola Ortofrenica, an institution devoted to the care and education of the mentally retarded. She accepted, in order to put her theories to proof.

Her first notable success was to have several of her 8 year old students apply to take the State examinations for reading and writing. The "defective" children not only passed, but had above-average scores, an achievement described as "the first Montessori miracle." Montessori's response to their success was "if mentally disabled children could be brought to the level of normal children then (she) wanted to study the potential of 'normal' children".

"Scientific observation has established that education is not what the teacher gives; education is a natural process spontaneously carried out by the human individual, and is acquired not by listening to words but by experiences upon the environment.

The task of the teacher becomes that of preparing a series of motives of cultural activity, spread over a specially prepared environment, and then refraining from obtrusive interference. Human teachers can only help the great work that is being done, as servants help the master. Doing so, they will be witnesses to the unfolding of the human soul and to the rising of a New Man who will not be a victim of events, but will have the clarity of vision to direct and shape the future of human society".

Because of her success with these children, she was asked to start a school for children in a housing project in Rome, which opened on January 6, 1907, and which she called "Casa dei Bambini" or Children's House.

Children's House was a child care centre in an apartment building in the poor neighbourhood of Rome. She was focused on teaching the students ways to develop their own skills at a pace they set, which was a principle Montessori called "spontaneous self-development". A wide variety of special equipment of increasing complexity is used to help direct the interests of the child and hasten development. When a child is ready to learn new and more difficult tasks, the teacher guides the child's first endeavors in order to avoid wasted effort and the learning of wrong habits; otherwise the child learns alone.

It has been reported that the Montessori method of teaching has enabled children to learn to read and write much more quickly and with greater facility than has otherwise been possible. The Montessori Method of teaching concentrates on quality rather than quantity. The success of this school sparked the opening of many more, and a worldwide interest in Montessori's methods of education.

After the 1907 establishment of Montessori's first school in Rome, by 1917 there was an intense interest in her method in North America, which later waned, in large part due to the publication of a small booklet entitled "The Montessori System Examined" by Kirkpatrick-a follower of John Dewey. (Nancy McCormick Rambusch contributed to the revival of the method in America by establishing the American Montessori Society in 1960); at the same time Margaret Stephenson came to the US from Europe and began a long history of training Montessori teachers under the auspices of the Association Montessori Internationale (AMI).

Montessori was exiled by Mussolini mostly because she refused to compromise her principles and make the children into soldiers. She moved to Spain and lived there until 1936 when the Spanish Civil War broke out. She then moved to the Netherlands until 1939.

In the year 1939, the Theosophical Society of India extended an invitation asking Maria Montessori to visit India. She accepted the invitation and reached India the very same year accompanied by her only son, Mario Montessori Sr. This heralded the beginning of her special relationship with India. She made the international Headquarters of the Theosophical Society at Adyar, Chennai, her home.

However the war forced her to extend her stay in India. With the help of her son, Mario, she conducted sixteen batches of courses called the Indian Montessori Training Courses. These courses laid a strong foundation for the Montessori Movement in India. In 1949 when she left for The Netherlands she appointed Albert Max Joosten as her personal representative, and assigned him the responsibility of conducting the Indian Montessori Training Courses. Joosten along with Swamy S R, another disciple of Dr. Maria Montessori, continued the good work and ensured that the Montessori Movement in India was on a sound footing.

During a teachers conference in India she was interned by the authorities and lived there for the duration of the war. Montessori lived out the remainder of her life in the Netherlands, which now hosts the headquarters of the AMI, or *Association Montessori Internationale*. She died in Noordwijk aan Zee. Her son Mario headed the AMI until his death in 1982.

Maria Montessori died in the Netherlands in 1952, after a lifetime devoted to the study of child development. Her early work centred on women's rights and social reform and evolved to encompass a totally innovative approach to education. Her success in Italy led to international recognition, and for over 40 years she travelled all over the world, lecturing, writing and establishing training programs. In later years, 'Educate for Peace' became a guiding principle, which underpinned her work.

Pedagogy

Aside from a new pedagogy, among the premier contributions to educational thought by Montessori are:

- instruction of children in 3-year age groups, corresponding to sensitive periods of development (example: Birth-3, 3-6, 6-9, 9-12, 12-15 year olds with an Erdkinder (German for "Land Children") program for early teens
- children as competent beings, encouraged to make maximal decisions
- observation of the child in the prepared environment as the basis for ongoing curriculum development (presentation of subsequent exercises for skill development and information accumulation)

- small, child-sized furniture and creation of a small, child-sized environment (microcosm) in which each can be competent to produce overall a self-running small children's world
- creation of a scale of sensitive periods of development, which provides a focus for class work that is appropriate and uniquely stimulating and motivating to the child (including sensitive periods for language development, sensorial experimentation and refinement, and various levels of social interaction)
- the importance of the "absorbent mind," the limitless motivation of the young child to achieve competence over his or her environment and to perfect his or her skills and understandings as they occur within each sensitive period. The phenomenon is characterized by the young child's capacity for repetition of activities within sensitive period categories (Example: exhaustive babbling as language practice leading to language competence).
- self-correcting "auto-didactic" materials (some based on work of Jean Marc Gaspard Itard and Edouard Seguin).

Influence

A conference in Rome on 6/7th January 2007 heralded the start of a year of celebrations for children and schools around the world. Dr. Maria Montessori's innovative approach was that "Education should no longer be mostly imparting of knowledge, but must take a new path, seeking the release of human potentialities."

What followed worldwide has been called the "discovery of the child" and the realization that: "...mankind can hope for a solution to its problems, among which the most urgent are those of peace and unity, only by turning its attention and energies to the discovery of the child and to the development of the great potentialities of the human personality in the course of its formation."

The efficacy of Montessori teaching methods has most recently been demonstrated by the results of a study published in the US journal, Science (29 September 2006) which indicates that Montessori children have improved Behavioural and academic skills compared with a control group from the mainstream system. The authors concluded that "when strictly implemented, Montessori education fosters social and academic skills that are equal or superior to those fostered by a pool of other types of schools."

The Montessori method of education that she derived from this experience has subsequently been applied successfully to children and is quite popular in many parts of the world. Despite much criticism of her method in the early 1930s-1940s, her method of education has been applied and has undergone a revival. It can now be found on six continents and throughout the United States, but is still subject to some criticism. The Association Montessori Internationale is member of the International Coalition for the Decade for the Culture of Peace and Nonviolence.

Unit-IV

Education in the Indian Constitution

Directive Principles

The **Directive Principles of State Policy** are guidelines to the central and state governments of India, to be kept in mind while framing laws and policies. These provisions, contained in Part IV of the Constitution of India, are not enforceable by any court, but the principles laid down therein are considered fundamental in the governance of the country, making it the duty of the State to apply these principles in making laws to establish a just society in the country. The principles have been inspired by the Directive Principles given in the Constitution of Ireland and also by the principles of Gandhism; and relate to social justice, economic welfare, foreign policy, and legal and administrative matters.

Directive Principles are classified under the following categories: Gandhian, economic and socialistic, political and administrative, justice and legal, environmental, protection of monuments and peace and security.

History

The concept of Directive Principles of State Policy was borrowed from the Irish Constitution. The makers of the Constitution of India were influenced by the Irish nationalist movement. Hence, the Directive Principles of the Indian constitution have been greatly influenced by the Directive Principles of State Policy. The idea of such policies "can be traced to the Declaration of the Rights of Man proclaimed Revolutionary France and the Declaration of Independence by the American Colonies." The Indian constitution was also influenced by the United Nations Universal Declaration of Human Rights. In 1919, the Rowlatt Acts gave extensive powers to the British government and police, and allowed indefinite arrest and detention of individuals, warrant-less searches and seizures, restrictions on public gatherings, and intensive censorship of media and publications. The public opposition to this act eventually led to mass campaigns of non-violent civil disobedience throughout the country demanding guaranteed civil freedoms, and limitations on government power. Indians, who were seeking independence and their own government, were particularly influenced by the independence of Ireland and the development of the Irish constitution. Also, the directive principles of state policy in Irish constitution were looked upon by the people of India as an inspiration for the independent India's government to comprehensively tackle complex social and economic challenges across a vast, diverse nation and population.

In 1928, the Nehru Commission composing of representatives of Indian political parties proposed constitutional reforms for India that apart from calling for dominion status for India and elections under universal suffrage, would guarantee rights deemed fundamental, representation for religious and ethnic minorities, and limit the powers of the government. In 1931, the Indian National Congress (the largest Indian political party of the time) adopted resolutions committing itself to the defense of fundamental civil rights, as well as socio-economic rights such as the minimum wage and the abolition of untouchability and serfdom. Committing themselves to socialism in 1936, the Congress leaders took examples from the constitution of the erstwhile USSR, which inspired the fundamental duties of citizens as a means of collective patriotic responsibility for national interests and challenges.

When India obtained independence on 15 August 1947, the task of developing a constitution for the nation was undertaken by the Constituent Assembly of India, composing of elected representatives under the presidency of Dr. Rajendra Prasad. While members of Congress composed of a large majority, Congress leaders appointed persons from diverse political backgrounds to responsibilities of developing the constitution and national laws. Notably, Bhimrao Ramji Ambedkar became the chairperson of the drafting committee, while Jawaharlal Nehru and Sardar Vallabhbhai Patel became chairpersons of committees and sub-committees responsible for different subjects. A notable development during that period having significant effect on the Indian constitution took place on 10 December 1948 when the United Nations General Assembly adopted the Universal Declaration of Human Rights and called upon all member states to adopt these rights in their respective constitutions.

Both the Fundamental Rights and the Directive Principles of State Policy were included in the I Draft Constitution (February 1948), the II Draft Constitution (17 October 1948) and the III and final Draft Constitution (26 November 1949), being prepared by the Drafting Committee.

Characteristics

DPSPs aim to create social and economic conditions under which the citizens can lead a good life. They also aim to establish social and economic democracy through a welfare state. They act as a check on the government, theorized as a yardstick in the hands of the people to measure the performance of the government and vote it out of power if it does not fulfil the promises made during the elections. The Directive Principles are non-justiciable rights of the people. Article 31-C, inserted by the 25th Amendment Act of 1971 seeks to upgrade the Directive Principles. If laws are made to give effect to the Directive Principles over Fundamental Rights, they shall not be invalid on the grounds that they take away the Fundamental Rights. In case of a conflict between Fundamental Rights and DPSP's, if the DPSP aims at promoting larger interest of the society, the courts shall have to uphold the case in favour of the DPSP. The Directive Principles, though not justiciable, are fundamental in the governance of the country. It shall be the duty of the State to apply these principles in making laws. Besides, all executive agencies should also be guided by these principles. Even the judiciary has to keep them in mind in deciding cases.

Directives

The directive principles ensure that the State shall strive to promote the welfare of the people by promoting a social order in which social, economic and political justice is informed in all institutions of life. Also, the State shall work towards reducing economic inequality as well as inequalities in status and opportunities, not only among individuals, but also among groups of people residing in different areas or engaged in different vocations. The State shall aim for securing right to an adequate means of livelihood for all citizens, both men and women as well as equal pay for equal work for both men and women. The State should work to prevent concentration of wealth and means of production in a few hands, and try to ensure that ownership and control of the material resources is distributed to best serve the common good. Child abuse and exploitation of workers should be prevented. Children should be allowed to develop in a healthy manner and should be protected against exploitation and against moral and material abandonment. The State shall provide free legal aid to ensure that equal opportunities for securing justice is ensured to all, and is not denied by reason of economic or other disabilities. The State shall also work for organisation of village panchayats and help enable them to function as units of self-government. The State shall endeavour to provide the right to work, to education and to public assistance in cases of unemployment, old age, sickness and disablement, within the limits of economic capacity, as well as provide for just and humane conditions of work and maternity relief.

The State should also ensure living wage and proper working conditions for workers, with full enjoyment of leisure and social and cultural activities. Also, the promotion of cottage industries in rural areas is one of the obligations of the State. The State shall take steps to promote their participation in management of industrial undertakings.

Also, the State shall endeavour to secure a uniform civil code for all citizens, and provide free and compulsory education to all children till they attain the age of 14 years. This directive regarding education of children was added by the 86th Amendment Act, 2002. It should and work for the economic and educational upliftment of scheduled castes, scheduled tribes and other weaker sections of the society.

The directive principles commit the State to raise the level of nutrition and the standard of living and to improve public health, particularly by prohibiting intoxicating drinks and drugs injurious to health except for medicinal purposes. It should also organise agriculture and animal husbandry on modern and scientific lines by improving breeds and prohibiting slaughter of cows, calves, other milch and draught cattle It should protect and improve the environment and safeguard the forests and wild life of the country. This directive, regarding protection of forests and wildlife was added by the 42nd Amendment Act, 1976.

Protection of monuments, places and objects of historic and artistic interest and national importance against destruction and damage, and separation of judiciary from executive in public services are also the obligations of the State as laid down in the directive principles. Finally, the directive principles, in Article 51 ensure that the State shall strive for the promotion and maintenance of international peace and security, just and honourable relations between nations, respect for international law and treaty obligations, as well as settlement of international disputes by arbitration.

Implementation

The State has made many efforts to implement the **Directive Principles**. The Programme of Universalisation of Elementary Education and the five year plans has been accorded the highest priority in order to provide free education to all children up to the age of 14 years. The 86th constitutional amendment of 2002 inserted a new article, Article 21-A, into the Constitution, that seeks to provide free and compulsory education to all children aged 6 to 14 years. Welfare schemes for the weaker sections are being implemented both by the Central and state governments. These include programmes such as boys' and girls' hostels for scheduled castes' or scheduled tribes' students. The year 1990-1991 was declared as the "Year of Social Justice" in the memory of B.R. Ambedkar. The government provides free textbooks to students belonging to scheduled castes or scheduled tribes pursuing medicine and engineering courses. During 2002-2003, a sum of Rs. 4.77 crore was released for this purpose. In order that scheduled castes and scheduled tribes are protected from atrocities, the Government enacted the *Prevention of Atrocities Act* in 1995, which provided severe punishments for such atrocities.

Several Land Reform Acts were enacted to provide ownership rights to poor farmers. Up to September 2001, more than 20,000,000 acres (80,000 km^2) of land had been distributed to scheduled castes, scheduled tribes and the landless poor. The thrust of banking policy in India has been to improve banking facilities in the rural areas. The *Minimum Wages Act* of 1948 empowers government to fix minimum wages for employees engaged in various employments. The *Consumer Protection Act* of 1986 provides for the better protection of consumers. The act is intended to provide simple, speedy and inexpensive redressal to the consumers' grievances, award relief and compensation wherever appropriate to the consumer. The *Equal Remuneration Act* of 1976, provides for equal pay for equal work for both men and women. The *Sampoorna Grameen Rozgar Yojana* was launched in 2001 to attain the objective of gainful employment for the rural poor. The programme was implemented through the Panchayati Raj institutions.

Panchayati Raj now covers almost all states and Union territories. One-third of the total number of seats have been reserved for women in Panchayats at every level; in the case of Bihar, half the seats have been reserved for women. Legal aid at the expense of the State has been made compulsory in all cases pertaining to criminal law, if the accused is too poor to engage a lawyer. Judiciary has been separated from the executive in all the states and Union territories except Jammu and Kashmir and Nagaland.

India's Foreign Policy has also to some degree been influenced by the DPSPs. India has in the past condemned all acts of aggression and has also supported the United Nations' peace-keeping activities. By 2004, the Indian Army had participated in 37 UN peace-keeping operations. India played a key role in the passing of a UN resolution in 2003, which envisaged better cooperation between the Security Council and the troop-contributing countries. India has also been in favour of nuclear disarmament.

Amendments

Changes in Directive Principles require a Constitutional amendment which has to be passed by a special majority of both houses of the Parliament. This means that an amendment requires the approval of two-thirds of the members present and voting. However, the number of members voting should not be less than the simple majority of the house — whether the Lok Sabha or Rajya Sabha.

- **Article 31-C**, inserted into the Directive Principles of State Policy by the 25th Amendment Act of 1971 seeks to upgrade the DPSPs. If laws are made to give effect to the Directive Principles over Fundamental Rights, they shall not be invalid on the grounds that they take away the Fundamental Rights.
- **Article 45**, which ensures *Provision for free and compulsory education for children*, was added by the 86th Amendment Act, 2002.
- **Article 48-A**, which ensures *Protection and improvement of environment and safeguarding of forests and wild life*, was added by the 42nd Amendment Act, 1976.

Article 45

Article 45 of the DPSP, which corresponds to article 13(1) of the ICESCR, states, "The State shall endeavour to provide, within a period of ten years from the commencement of this Constitution, for free and compulsory education for all children until they complete the age of fourteen years." Thus, while the right of a child not to be employed in hazardous industries was, by virtue of article 24, recognized to be a fundamental right, the child's right to education was put into the DPSP in part IV and deferred for a period of ten years.

The question whether the right to education was a fundamental right and enforceable as such was answered by the Supreme Court in the affirmative in **Mohini Jain v. State of Karnataka (1992) 3 SCC 666**.. The correctness of this decision was examined by a larger bench of five judges in **Unnikrishnan J.P. v. State of Andhra Pradesh (1993) 1 SCC 645**. The occasion was the challenge, by private medical and engineering colleges, to state legislation regulating the charging of "capitation" fees from students seeking admission. The college management was seeking enforcement of their right to business. The court expressly denied this claim and proceeded to examine the nature of the right to education. The court refused to accept the nonenforceablity of the DPSP. It asked:

It is noteworthy that among the several articles in Part IV, only Article 45 speaks of a time-limit; no other article does. Has it no significance? Is it a mere pious wish, even after 44 years of the Constitution? Can the State flout the said direction even after 44 years on the ground that the article merely calls upon it to endeavour to provide the same and on the further ground that the said article is not enforceable by virtue of the declaration in Article 37. Does not the passage of 44 years—more than four times the period stipulated in Article 45—convert the obligation created by the article into an enforceable right? In this context, we feel constrained to say that allocation of available funds to different sectors of education in India discloses an inversion of priorities indicated by the Constitution. The Constitution contemplated a crash programme being undertaken by the State to achieve the goal set out in Article 45. It is relevant to notice that Article 45 does not speak of the "limits of its economic capacity and development" as does Article 41, which inter alia speaks of right to education. What has actually happened is more money is spent and more attention is directed to higher education than to—and at the cost of—primary education. (By primary education, we mean the education which a normal child receives by the time he completes 14 years of age.) Neglected more so are the rural sectors, and the weaker sections of the society referred to in Article 46. We clarify, we are not seeking to lay down the priorities for the Government—we are only emphasising the constitutional policy as disclosed by Articles 45, 46 and 41. Surely the wisdom of these constitutional provisions is beyond question.

The court then proceeded to examine how this right would be enforceable and to what extent. It clarified the issue thus: The right to education further means that a citizen has a right to call upon the State to provide educational facilities to him within the limits of its economic capacity and development. By saying so, we are not transferring Article 41 from Part IV to Part III—we are merely relying upon Article 41 to illustrate the content of the right to education flowing from Article 21. We cannot believe that any State would say that it need not provide education to its people even within the limits of its economic capacity and development. It goes without saying that the limits of economic capacity are, ordinarily speaking, matters within the subjective satisfaction of the State. More caution followed. The court's apprehension clearly was that recognition of such a right might open the flood gates for other claims. It clarified:

> *We must hasten to add that just because we have relied upon some of the directive principles to locate the parameters of the right to education implicit in Article 21, it does not follow automatically that each and every obligation referred to in Part IV gets automatically included within the purview of Article 21. We have held the right to education to be implicit in the right to life because of its inherent fundamental importance. As a matter of fact, we have referred to Articles 41, 45 and 46 merely to determine the parameters of the said right.*

In fact, the court had broken new ground in the matter of justiciability and enforceability of the DPSP. The decision in Unnikrishnan case has been applied by the court in formulating broad parameters for compliance by the government in the matter of eradication of child labour. This it did in a PIL where it said:

> *Now, strictly speaking a strong case exists to invoke the aid of Article 41 of the Constitution regarding the right to work and to give meaning to what has been provided in Article 47 relating to raising of standard of living of the population, and Articles 39 (e) and (f) as to non-abuse of tender age of children and giving opportunities and facilities to them to develop in a healthy manner, for asking the State to see that an adult member of the family, whose child is in employment in a factory or a mine or in other hazardous work, gets a job anywhere, in lieu of the child. This would also see the fulfilment of the wish contained in Article 41 after about half a century of its being in the paramount parchment, like primary education desired by Article 45, having been given the status of fundamental right by the decision in Unnikrishnan. We are, however, not asking the State at this stage to ensure alternative employment in every case covered by Article 24, as Article 41 speaks about right to work "within the limits of the economic capacity and development of the State". The very large number of child labour in the aforesaid occupations would require giving of job to a very large number of adults, if we were to ask the appropriate Government to assure alternative employment in every case, which would strain the resources of the State, in case it would not have been able to secure job for an adult in a private sector establishment or, for that matter, in a public sector organisation. We are not issuing any direction to do so presently. Instead, we leave the matter to be sorted out by the appropriate Government. In those cases where it would not be possible to provide job as above mentioned, the appropriate Government would, as its contribution / grant, deposit in the aforesaid Fund a sum of Rs.5000 / -for each child employed in a factory or mine or in any other hazardous employment.* ***M.C.Mehta v. State of Tamil Nadu (1996) 6 SCC 772, para. 31***

The court, while recognizing the importance of declaring the child's negative right against exploitation and positive right to education, chose a pragmatic approach when it came to enforceability. Earlier the court would have shrugged off the whole issue as not being within its domain. That has now changed as is clear from the recent trend of cases.

It is here the Supreme Court read into our Constitution several provisions of International Covenants. The Judges also considered DPSP and how the same could be read together with the Fundamental Rights. As stated in the case of **Unnikrishnan v/s. State of AP [(1993)1 SCC 645, para 165]** "In order to treat a right as fundamental right, it is not necessary that it should be expressly stated as one in Part III of the Constitution. The provisions of Part III and Part IV are supplementary and complementary to each other." That is why very often the court reads the two together. There is no conflict between the two. It is wrong to assume that fulfilment of obligations relating to social and economic human rights would impair fundamental rights. That is why we incorporated Article 31-C (25th Amendment Act 1971) which says, "Notwithstanding anything contained in Article 13, no law giving effect to the policy of the State towards securing all or any of the principles laid down in Part IV shall be deemed to be void on the ground that it is inconsistent with, or takes away or abridges any of the rights conferred by Article 14 or Article 19....." As Glanville Austin says: "The core of the commitment to the social revolution lies in Part III and IV in the Fundamental Rights and in the Directive Principles of State Policy. These are the conscience of the Constitution." This is what Bhagwati J. said in **Minerva Mills case (AIR 1980 SC 1789 at 1846)**: "The core of the commitment of the social revolution lies... in the Fundamental Rights and directive principles of state policy."

The Directive Principles also urge the nation to develop a uniform civil code and offer free legal aid to all citizens. They urge measures to maintain the separation of the judiciary from the executive and direct the government to organize village panchayats to function as units of self-government. This latter objective was advanced by the Seventy-third Amendment and the Seventy-fourth Amendment in December 1992. The Directive Principles also order that India should endeavour to protect and improve the environment and protect monuments and places of historical interest.

The Forty-second Amendment, which came into force in January 1977, attempted to raise the status of the Directive Principles by stating that no law implementing any of the Directive Principles could be declared unconstitutional on the grounds that it violated any of the Fundamental Rights. The amendment simultaneously stated that laws prohibiting "antinational activities" or the formation of "antinational associations" could not be invalidated because they infringed on any of the Fundamental Rights. It added a new section to the constitution on "Fundamental Duties" that enjoined citizens "to promote harmony and the spirit of common brotherhood among all the people of India, transcending religious, linguistic and regional or sectional diversities." However, the amendment reflected a new emphasis in governing circles on order and discipline to counteract what some leaders had come to perceive as the excessively freewheeling style of Indian democracy. After the March 1977 general election ended the control of the Congress (Congress (R) from 1969) over the executive and legislature for the first time since independence in 1947, the new Janata-dominated Parliament passed the Forty-third Amendment (1977) and Forty-fourth Amendment (1978). These amendments revoked the Forty-second Amendment's provision that Directive Principles take precedence over Fundamental Rights and also curbed Parliament's power to legislate against "antinational activities"

Universal Compulsory Education

Compulsory education is education which children are required by law to receive and governments are required by law to provide. The compulsion is an aspect of public education. In some places homeschooling may be a legal alternative to attending school. Compulsory education was pushed in the United States during the Progressive Era, the early 20th Century, because of the large numbers of immigration.

Compulsory education at the primary level was affirmed as a human right in the 1948 Universal Declaration of Human Rights. Many of the world's countries now have compulsory education through at least the primary stage, often extending to the secondary education.

History

Plato's *Republic* popularized the concept of compulsory education in Western intellectual thought.

The Talmud (tractate Bava Bathra 21a) praises the sage Joshua ben Gamla with the institution of formal Jewish education in the 1st century AD. Ben Gamla instituted schools in every town and made education compulsory from the age of 6 or 7. Prior to this, parents in Judea taught their children informally.

The Aztecs (14-16. centuries AD) had one of the first compulsory educational systems. All male children were required to attend school until the age of 16..

In Scotland, the Education Act of 1496 obliged the children of noblemen and freeholders to attend school.

During the Reformation in 1524, Martin Luther advocated compulsory schooling so that all parishioners would be able to read the Bible themselves, and Strassbourg—then a free city of the Holy Roman Empire—passed accordant legislation in 1598.

In Scotland, the School Establishment Act of 1616 commanded every parish with the means, to establish a school paid for by parishioners. The Parliament of Scotland confirmed this with the Education Act of 1633 and created a local land-based tax to provide the required funding. The required majority support of parishioners, however, provided a tax evasion loophole which heralded the Education Act of 1646. The turmoil of the age, meant that in 1661 there was a temporary reversion to the less compulsory 1633 position. However, in 1696 a new Act re-established the compulsory provision of a school in every parish with a system of fines, sequestration and direct government implementation as a means of enforcement where required.

The first compulsory education law in the American colonies was established in Massachusetts in 1852. In 1647, the Massachusetts General Court passed a law requiring every town to create and operate a grammar school. Fines were imposed on parents who did not send their children to school and the government took the power to take children away from their parents and apprentice them to others if government officials decided that the parents were "unfit to have the children educated properly". Compulsory education was not part of early American society, which relied instead on private schools that mostly charged tuition. The spread of compulsory education in the Massachusetts tradition throughout America, especially for Native Americans, has been credited to General Richard Henry Pratt. Pratt used techniques developed on Native Americans in a prisoner of war camp in Fort Marion, Augustine, Florida, to force demographic minorities across America into government schools. His prototype was the Carlisle School in Pennsylvania. In the Kingdom of Prussia, a series of edicts in the 18th century established that education was a task of the state and in 1763 Frederick II of Prussia made schooling compulsory for all children between the ages of five and thirteen.

In 1794, all schools and universities were made state institutions. In Austria mandatory primary education was introduced by Empress Maria Theresa in 1774. Public education gradually spread to other countries, reaching the American State of Massachusetts in 1852 and gradually spread to other US states. In 1918 Mississippi was the last state to enact a compulsory attendance law.

Extent

Different localities vary in how many years or grades of compulsory education they require.

In the United States, the ages for compulsory education vary by state, beginning between the ages of five and eight and ending between age sixteen and eighteen. For example, in the US State of Illinois, attendance is required through age 16, while in Mississippi it is age 17, and in Oklahoma, age 18. In Mexico, schooling is required through lower secondary school only. In Canada, compulsory education is set for ages six through sixteen (18 in New Brunswick and Ontario). In Finland, it starts at the age of seven (± 1 year, negotiable), and ends after graduation from comprehensive school at the age of fifteen or sixteen, or at last after ten school years. In the UK compulsory education begins between four and a half and five and a half; it extends until around the age of sixteen.

Benefits

Compulsory education has the following perceived benefits.

- Before compulsory free education existed, most children were denied access to basic education. As a result of compulsory education, illiteracy is greatly reduced and knowledge of mathematics and other basic subjects are increased.
- Before compulsory free education existed, most children were unprepared to train for most vocations and the professions. As a result of compulsory free education, access to a range of better paying vocations and professions is made possible.
- It discourages child labour.
- It encourages economic development.
- Angrist and Krueger, two of the premier labour economists in the world, conducted a study in which they find that "students who are compelled to attend school longer by compulsory schooling laws earn higher wages as a result of their extra schooling"

Universal Education In India: A Century Of Unfulfilled Dreams

"I beg to place the following resolution before the council for its consideration....the state should accept in this country the same responsibility in regard to mass education that the government of most civilized countries are already discharging and that a well considered scheme should be drawn up and adhered to till it is carried out.. The well being of millions upon millions of children who are waiting to be brought under the influence education depends upon it..."

The above words are the part of the resolution which Gopal Krishna Gokhale moved in Imperial Legislative Council on 18th march, 1910 for seeking provision of 'Free and Compulsory Primary Education" in India.

Irony is that one hundred years have passed but the right to education still remains a distant dream. Gopal Krishna Gokhale in fact represents many of our freedom fighters who had dreamed of the right to education to in independent India. They had identified the significance of education as an integral part of their different and complex ideologies. After attaining independence, the forefathers of our constitution continued this debate on the right to education and concluded to retain it in the directive principles of state policy. This compromise was not positively received by many of the people who wanted a more specific assurance from the Constitution.

Even now after 60 years of our independence, no such right has been provided to the children of India. Successive governments at the centre had not given any consideration and have pathetically failed in providing public education in India.

The people of India raised their voice for universal public education as a part of the freedom struggle. The British imperialists simply denied their demand. But in 1870, the British legalized the free and compulsory education to every British. This was done to ensure the survival of the British Empire and maintain its hegemony on the colonies. In spite of our independence and all the tall talk of successive prime ministers who promise to turn our country into a knowledge super power, nothing substantial was done to ensure even this basic right to education. This is because of the 'feudal-capitalist' character of the State.

The right to education demand is alive even now in spite of every effort to belittle it. The judiciary, bureaucrats, and media have timely raised their voice over its necessity. It has become possible only due to sustained progressive struggles of people of India on this question and the judgment given by the Supreme Court directing the government to ensure that all the citizens of our country are provided this right.

Due to the sustained pressure of the students and people's movement and Left, the central government was forced to introduce "Right to Free and Compulsory Education Bill" in Rajya Sabha on the 15th December, 2008. This was done after the government had come out with a series of drafts Bills and put them up for discussion to the public, each worse than the other.

When the UPA government introduced the draft education bill in 2005, then everyone related to public education criticized the bill. Then the government invited further suggestions and opinions from the state governments, but none of them were included in the bill later. The UPA government thus humiliated the spirit of the people who had suggested improvements in the bill.

The current "Right to Free and Compulsory Education Bill" has many lacuna and many criticisms can be levelled against it. But broadly analyzing all the criticisms, we shall reach to two major points.

(1) ***Allocation of Funds:*** In financial perspective, Tapas Majumdar committee long back had estimated that there is an additional requirement of Rs 1, 40,000 crore to be spent in a span of ten years (which comprises 0.7 percent of the GDP). The government states that it does not have that much money and is simply denying the responsibility of public education. The UPA government wants state governments to allocate funds for education in respective states. The whole scenario reflects the dual attitude of the UPA government which proudly claims that it is responsible for our country becoming "world's second fastest growing economy". The truth of the matter is that it doesn't want expenditure on public education for the benefit of the masses, in spite of its own commitment to do so in the Common Minimum Program.

(2) ***Age limit and common school system:*** Several Commissions have recommended Common School System and Neighbourhood School Policy to integrate the community and provide access to education at the

doorsteps of children. This has also been specified in the National Policy on Education. But the Bill makes no mention of the Common School System and while using neighbourhood in some of the clauses has neither defined Neighbourhood nor has accepted the philosophy of Neighbourhood School.

As a signatory to the UN Child Rights Convention, India has accepted the international definition of a child, which is up to age 18. The bill proposes to cover only children from age 6 to 14, clearly excluding and violating the rights of the 0-6 and 14 to 18 year olds. One of the framers of this bill Vinod Raina says "the 86th amendment and its article 21A, which defines the age from 6 to14. As a bill flowing out of the amendment, it is clear that the bill cannot go beyond Article 21A, which makes it imperative that the 86th amendment must be re-amended to correct this anomaly".

If we raise the demand of 0-6 years, Vinod Raina says "Many argue that the bill should be put on hold till such a re-amendment is passed, but that would be playing into hands of elements who neither want the amendment nor the bill. Such elements do not want the state to invest in education and instead prefer to leave it to the markets". Instead of positively addressing the criticisms on the Bill the government and its supporters are trying to project that all criticisms are made with an ulterior motive. They hope to hide their mistakes behind such shields.

But what has happened now? The UPA government failed to introduce the proposed bill in Lok Sabha and thus wasting five precious years it was in office. The whole procedure shows betrayal of the UPA government and its failure to address the concerns of the people of India and their genuine demand. Moreover, "Right to Free and Compulsory Education Bill" is not only about education. It is about the problem of the class which needs an uncompromised progressive struggle for its rectification.

Recently the spokesperson of Indian national congress came with the statement that Slumdog Millionaire won eight Oscars, because Congress is in power. Yes, Mr. Singhvi, there can be no bigger irony than this. You are unable to do anything substantial to help the people to overcome their difficulties and instead want to claim all the credit for the deeds which are not yours. The entire episode on the right to education bill once again proves that the government is not for the people living in the slums but only for the millionaires.

Constitutional Commitment

Basic education system as evolved by Mahatma Gandhi, was one of the important goals of the freedom struggle. In the Constitution of India, adopted in 1950, elementary education received explicit attention. The Directive Principle contained in Article 45 of the Constitution directed the State to "endeavour to provide, within a period of ten years from the commencement of this Constitution, for free and compulsory education for all children until they complete the age of fourteen years." Alongside, equality of opportunity was also given primacy through various other articles (e.g. Article 29(2) dealt with the right to admission into any educational institution maintained by the state, Article 350-A laid down the right to receive instruction in the mother tongue, Article 46 referred to taking care of the economic and educational interests of the under-privileged sections of the population, etc.) Subsequently, fourteen states and four UTs (Union Territories) enacted the legislation for compulsory primary education. But since education was a state subject, the centre could not prevail upon the states to enforce compulsion. The states also found that in practice this legislation was difficult to implement due to various constraints.

With regard to the education of adults, on the other hand, there was no such explicit Constitutional commitment. Rather, there seemed to be an implicit understanding that over the years the expansion of primary education would automatically take care of the problem of mass illiteracy.

How was the political commitment reflected. in the Constitutional Directive to provide free and compulsory education to children in the 6-14 age group, translated into action? In order to understand this, it would be necessary to analyse policy documents to see how this mandate was articulated in various education policies as well as in the plan documents, and to see what were the financial resources that were allocated.

In the Constitution of India, adopted in 1950, elementary education received explicit attention. The Directive Principle contained in Article 45 of the Constitution directed the State to "endeavour to provide, within a period of ten years from the commencement of this Constitution, for free and compulsory education for all children until they complete the age of fourteen years."

Education in Concurrent List

Constitutional Provisions

Under the Constitution as originally enacted, education was primarily a State subject. The relevant entry (Entry 11) in the State List read "Education including universities subject to the provisions of entire 63,64,65 and 66 of List I and 25 of List III" Thus education was exclusively a responsibility of the States, the Central Government being concerned directly with certain areas like coordination, determination of standards in technical and higher education etc. In 1976, by a constitutional amendment education became the joint responsibility of the Central and State Government. The Constitution (Forty-second Amendment) Act, omitted Entry 11 from the State List and amplified Entry 25 in the Concurrent List. Entry 25 of the Concurrent List. Entry 25 of the Concurrent List which, as so amplified, no reads:

"25. Education, including technical education, medical education and universities, subject to the provisions of entries 63,64,65 and 66 of List I; vocational and technical training of labour."

The implication of this amendment is that education has become a Concurrent Subject which enables the Central Government to legislate in such fields as, for example, school education.

Apart form this concurrent sphere, the Constitution places certain educational matters within the exclusive jurisdiction of the Union. These are: maintenance of Central Universities and institutions of national importance, declared as such by Parliament by law; all Union agencies and institutions for professional, vocational or technical training or for promotion of special studies or research; and the coordination and determination of standards in institutions of higher education or research and scientific and technical institutions (Entries 63,64,65 and 66 of List I)

Article 28 provides that no religious instruction shall be provided in any educational institution wholly maintained out of State funds. Article 29 further provides that no citizen shall be denied admission into any educational institution maintained by the State or receiving aid out of State funds, on grounds only of religion, race, caste, language or any of them. According to article 30, all minorities, whether based on religion or language, shall have the right to establish and administer educational institutions of their choice. In addition, the State shall not, in granting aid to educational institutions discriminate against any educational institution on the ground that it is under the management of a minority, whether based on religion or language. Besides, some of the Directive Principles, set out in Part IV of the Constitution, also have a bearing on national educational policy. For instance, article 45 enjoins that the 'State' shall endeavour to provide for free and compulsory education for all children until they complete the age of fourteen years.

Article 46 requires the 'State' to promote with special care the educational interests of the weaker sections of the people, which include, in particular, the Scheduled Castes and Scheduled Tribes.

Article 350A places a special responsibility on the Government to safeguard the interests of the children belonging to linguistic minority groups and to see that they have adequate facilities to receive at least primary education through their own mother tongue. Article 351 further places a special responsibility on the Government of India for promoting the spread of Hindi language and for its development so that it may serve as a medium of expression for all the elements of the composite culture of India. Yet another provision in the Constitution which has an indirect but significant bearing upon the role of the Government of India in education is entry 20 of List III, which is concerned with "Economic and Social Planning". Education Planning being an essential element of economic and social planning, the Government of India and the State Governments have to work together in preparing and implementing the national plans for the reconstruction of education.

The Government of India are also responsible under the Constitution for the administration of the Union Territories and have for this purpose executive and legislative authority for all subject including education.

Responsibilities of the State Government

State Parliaments make laws in their areas of responsibility. The Constitution of Australia sets out the responsibilities of the federal government and any area not given to the federal government will become the responsibility of the State governments.

Education

Providing a public education system and also supervising the running of private schools. The Education Department is also in charge of exams, providing assistance for troubled students, maintaining the buildings in schools and employing all the teachers. This is one of the most important jobs of State governments.

Responsibilities of Central Government

The Role of the Government of India in Education (1833-1870)

The East India Company was made to accept responsibility for the education of the Indian people in 1813.1 But a Government of India did not then exist; the authority of the Governors of the three Presidencies of Bengal, Bombay and Madras was supreme and subject only to the control of the Court of Directors of the Company in England. Between 1813 and 1833, therefore, education was an exclusive responsibility of the Provincial Governments. This situation however changed completely in 1833 when the Charter Act of that year created the office of the Governor-General of India and vested in him the sole authority to govern all the Company's possessions in India. This was basically a political decision taken with the object of creating a powerful and supreme agency within the country itself to strengthen the administration of the existing territories as well as to facilitate the conquest of new ones. But it made education, like every other subject, an exclusive responsibility, of the Government of India in which all revenues were vested and which alone could authorize appropriations therefrom. At one stroke, the Provincial Governments thus lost all their authority over education and became merely the agents of the Government of India to administer it on its behalf. They could not create a single post, however low, nor sanction a rupee of expenditure, nor make any change in policies, however small, subject and became an exclusively Central subject. Without the approval of the Government of India. This system of a total centralization of authority continued till 1870. It would have been almost unworkable but for the fact that, In actual practice, the Government of India allowed a good deal of freedom to the Provincial Governments to adjust educational policies to their local needs and respected their proposals and advice.

During this period, there were two main occasions when the Government of India issued orders which, in substance, were tantamount to the enunciation of a National Policy on Education although this expression was not then used. The first refers to the orders issued by Lord William Bentinck, on the basis of a Minute recorded by Macaulay, that the objective of modern education in India ought to be the promotion of European literature and science among the people of India and that English should be the medium of education.' The second was the Educational Despatch dated 19th July 1854 issued by the Court of Directors it is a long document of 100 paragraphs which laid down the broad principles and programmes for educational development in India. It confirmed the orders issued earlier by Lord Bentinck and, among other things, authorized

(1) the establishments of universities at Bombay, Calcutta and Madras, (2) the creation of Education Departments in the Provinces, (3) the establishment of a graded network of schools and colleges in all parts of the country, (4) the provision of grants-in aid to private schools, (both missionary and Indian), (5) training of teachers, (6) encouragement to the education of women and (7) employment of educated Indians in government service. This policy statement continued to govern all educational developments in India till 1882.

The Role of the Government of India in Education (1870-1921)

In 1870, Lord Mayo initiated a system of decentralization and delegation of authority. The centralized administration introduced in 1833 had served its purpose,: the whole of India had been conquered, the so-called Sepoy Mutiny quelled, and the British rule fully consolidated in all parts of the country. On the other hand, the weaknesses of the system which led to delays and wastefulness in expenditure and created an irresponsible attitude in the Provincial Governments came to the surface and began to gall. A move for decentralization was, therefore, inevitable, and it came none too soon.

Under the orders issued by Lord Mayo, the Provincial Governments were made responsible for all expenditure on certain services (including education) and were given, for that purpose, a fixed grant-in-aid and certain sources of revenue. This system continued to be in force up to 1876-77 when a system of 'shared revenues' was introduced. Under this system, certain revenues were designated as exclusively 'Central', certain others were designated as exclusively 'Provincial' and the remaining were designated as 'Divided' and their receipts were shared between the Central and Provincial Governments according to an agreed contract which remained in force for a period of five years at a time. Thus the quinquennial contracts were revised in 1882-8 3, 1886 87, 1891-92 and 1896-97. In 1904, they were declared to be quasi-permanent i.e. not to be changed except in a grave emergency, and in 19) 2, they were declared to be permanent. It will thus be seen that, under these financial arrangements, the entire expenditure on education was to be borne by the Provincial Governments within the resources allocated to them. A delegation of administrative powers naturally followed this transfer of financial responsibility., It may be said, therefore, that between 1870 and 1921, most of the administrative and financial authority over education was gradually transferred to the Provincial Governments; and the Government of India merely retained a theoretical right of the control and general supervision as a sequel to its ultimate responsibility to the British Parliament.

It must be made clear however that, when necessary, the Government of India did not hesitate to intervene, to review educational progress, and to issue such directives to Provincial Governments as it felt to be necessary. The first such occasion to intervene arose when there was an insistent demand that the progress of education in India since the Educational Despatch of 1854 should be reviewed. The Government of India, therefore, appointed the first Commission on Education in India, viz. the Indian Education Commission (1882) and on the submission of its report, issued orders laying down a new National Policy on Education. Its main features were: (1) emphasis on the spread of primary education and education among girls, scheduled castes and scheduled tribes; (2) full encouragement to Indian private enterprise in secondary and higher education; and (3) creation of local bodies at the District and Tahsil levels (with considerable participation of the Indian people) and their association with the administration of primary education. These policies continued to be in force till the end of the nineteenth century.

The second occasion for a strong and sustained intervention arose when Lord Curzon became the Governor General of India. He was of the view that Indian education had grown too fast at the secondary and university stages, that its administration had become flabby because of undue freedom given to Indian private enterprise, that standards had deteriorated and that the uncontrolled expansion of secondary and higher education was leading to indiscipline and disaffection against Government. He was, therefore, of the view that the Government of India should no longer be a 'king log' and that a policy of intensive central interest in education must be enunciated and sustained. He created the office of the Director-General of Public Instruction in India under the Central Government (1897). He also convened a Conference of the Directors of Public Instruction in the Provinces at Simla (1900), appointed the Indian Universities Commission (1902), passed the Indian Universities Act (1904) in the Central Legislature, and issued the Government Resolution on Educational Policy in 1904. He also initiated a system of large Central grants to the Provinces for educational development and these continued to be in vogue for several years afterwards. An Indian Education Service (IES) was also created in 1897 and its officers held all key posts in the Education Departments. A second Government of India Resolution on Educational Policy was also passed in 1913. The two Resolutions of 1904 and 1913 may also be described as National Policies on Education and form a continuing sequence with the orders of Lord Bentinck, the Educational Despatch of 1854, and the Resolution of the Government [of India on the Recommendations of the Indian Education Commission (1884).

It may be incidentally mentioned that the Government of India started a practice of compiling and publishing quinquennial reviews to the progress of education in India from 1882. Such reviews were published for 1886 87, 1891-92, 1996-97, 1901.02, 1902-07, 1907-12, 1912-17, and 1921-22.

The Role of the Government of India in Education (1921- 47)

This period of active Central control and financial support of education came to an end in 1921 when, under the Government of India Act, 1919, education in the Provinces was transferred to the control of Indian Ministers responsible to legislatures with an elected majority. As a corollary to this basic decision, the role of the Government of India (which continued to be responsible to the British Parliament) in education had to be limited to the minimum. Under the Government of India Act, 1919, therefore, the responsibilities of Government were divided into Central and Provincial lists in the first instance and then the latter were divided into reserved and transferred. Because of various conflicting proposals made on the subject, education was treated as partly all-India, partly reserved, partly transferred with limitations and partly transferred without limitations. The following powers were reserved to the Government of India.

1. The Banares Hindu University and such other new universities as may be declared to be all-India by the Governor-General-in Council.
2. College for Indian chiefs and educational institutions maintained by the Governor-General-in-Council for the benefit of members of His Majesty's Forces or other public servants, or their children.
3. The authority to legislate on the following subjects was reserved for the central legislature, mainly with a view to enabling the Government of India to take suitable action on the report of the Calcutta University Commission.
   (a) Questions regarding the establishment, constitution and functions of new universities;
   (b) Questions affecting the jurisdiction of-any university outside its province; and
   (c) Questions regarding the Calcutta University and the reorganisation of secondary education in Bengal (for a period of five Nears only after the introduction of the Reforms). (None of these powers were ever exercised in practice).

Except for the above matters reserved for the Government of India the whole of the education wag transferred to the control of Indian Ministers with one exception, viz. education of Anglo-Indians find Europeans was reserved. There were also some restrictions on the control which the Ministers could exercise in certain matters (e.g. the IES).

It was also decided to stop all further recruitment to the IES so that the 'service would fade out within a few years. Needless to say the system of Central grants which had made such a useful contribution to educational development also disappeared. The Hartog Committee (1928) examined this situation with concern and said: "we are of the opinion that the divorce of the Government of India from education has been unfortunate: and holding as we do, that education is essentially a national service, we are of opinion that steps should be taken to consider a new relation of the Central Government with this subject. We have suggested that the Government of India should serve as a Centre of educational information for the whole of India and as a means of coordinating the educational experience of the different provinces. But we regard the duties of the Central Government as going beyond that. We cannot accept the view that it should be entirely relieved of all responsibility for the attainment of universal primary education. It may be that some of the provinces, inspite of all efforts, will be unable to provide the funds necessary for that purpose, and the Government of India should, therefore, be constitutionally enabled to make good such financial deficiencies in the interests of India as a whole" (Report p. 346). This view was carefully examined when the Government of India Act, 1935, was passed. But as the basic condition, viz., the transfer of education to popular control in the Provinces side by side with the Government of India continuing to be responsible to Parliament remained unchanged, the 1. This decision to transfer education to the Indian Ministers was fundamentally sound. But what one does not like is the argument on which it was based.

For instance, the Montague-Chelmsford Report laid down four criteria to determine whether a subject should be transferred to Indian control, viz, (1) it should be one in which there are large opportunities for social service; (2) it should be one in which Indians have shown considerable interest; (3) It should be such that mistakes are not likely to be committed; (4) and even if committed they are not likely to be irretrievable. It is a pity that education was selected for transfer on the basis of these criteria; and it is an even greater pity that this attitude to education still dominates our thinking. Policy underlying the Act of 1919, was continued with some modifications which reduced the authority of the Government of India over education and correspondingly increased that of Indian Ministers over it at the provincial level. The actual provisions made in the Government of India Act, 1935, abolished the old distinction between reserved and transferred subjects and the limitations placed on the powers of the education ministers. The whole of education thus became a transferred subject, except the following matters which were reserved for the Government of India-

(i) The Imperial Library, Calcutta: the Indian Museum, Calcutta the Imperial War Museum: the Victoria Memorial, Calcutta and any similar institution controlled or financed by the Central Government;

(ii) Education of the Defence Forces;

(iii) The Banaras Hindu University and the Aligarh Muslim University;

(iv) Preservation of ancient and historical monuments.

With these radical changes in the constitutional position, the question of the Government of India issuing any Resolutions on the National Policy on Education did not even arise; and in fact, no Government of India Resolution on National Educational Policy was issued for 55 years between 1913 and 1968. However, attempts were made to strengthen the advisory and coordinating role of the Government of India. The quinquennial reviews of education in India continued to be published and were actually brought out in 196-27, 1931-32, 1936-37, and 1946-47 (Decennial Review). A Central Advisory Board of Education consisting of all Education Ministers in the Provinces was first constituted for this purpose in 1921. It was however abolished in 1924 as a measure of economy. It was revived again in 1935; and its one great achievement was to prepare the Post-War Plan of Educational Development (1944). It proposed to create, in a period of 40 years, an educational system in India which would be like that in England in 1939. The plan however was never accepted by Indian public opinion.

The Role of the Government of India in Education (1947-79)

The subject came again for discussion in 1950 when the Constitution was being adopted on the basis of a Federal

Government at the Centre. It could have been possible at this time to define a more effective Central role in education. But the general public opinion was strongly in favour of vesting almost all authority over education in the Slates; and the mere fact that the Congress was in power at the Centre and in all the States made it almost seem unnecessary to vest any constitutional authority over education in the Centre. Once again, therefore, the basic policy of the Government of India Act, 1919, was continued with one change, viz. certain additional powers were now vested in the Centre. In fact, the Constitution makes Education basically a State subject (Entry 11 of the State List), subject to certain powers reserved in the Central (Entries 63-66) and Concurrent Lists (Entry 25).

List I: List of Union Functions

1. The Institution known at the commencement of the Constitution as the Banaras Hindu University, the Aligarh Muslim University and the Delhi University and any other institution declared by Parliament by law to be an institution of national importance;
2. Institutions for scientific or technical education financed by the Government of India wholly or in part and declared by Parliament by law to be institutions of national importance;
3. Union agencies and institutions for:-
   (a) professional, vocational or technical training, including the training of police officers; or
   (b) the promotion of special studies or research; or
   (c) scientific or technical assistance in the investigation or detection of crime.
4. Coordination and determination of standards in institutions for higher education or research and scientific and technical institutions.

List II: List of State Functions

5. Education including universities, subject to provision of entries 63, 64, 65 and 66 of List I and entry 25 of List III.

List III: List of Concurrent Functions

6. Vocational and technical training of labour.

The academic opinion in India has never been fully reconciled to this constitutional decision which makes education an almost total responsibility or the States and the Subject therefore has continued to be debated over the last 30 years. On the whole, three definite categories of views have emerged:

(1) The first view, held by a minority, and mostly among State level politicians is that the authority over education should be transferred to the State Governments to a still greater extent that the Ministry of Education should be abolished, and that almost all the funds meant for the development of education should be provided in the State sector, thus abolishing the Centrally sponsored sector and reducing the Central Sector to the minimum;

(2) The second view which prevailed throughout the period between 1947 and 1976, was that there need be no' change in the! constitutional role of the Government of India in education. But education should be regarded as a national concern, and steps should be taken to see that the advisory and coordinating roles of the Government of India are considerably strengthened. This has been the most dominating view in the post independence period.

(3) The third view, also held by a minority was that education should be brought into the concurrent list. This was supported by the Committee of Members of Parliament under the Chairmanship of Shri Sapru (1963) which recommended that higher education should be brought on the concurrent list. The proposal however did not get support among the State Governments and had to be dropped.

The problem was discussed by the Education Commission (1964-66) Unfortunately, the members of the Commission could not reach a concensus on the subject. The majority of members were for the status quo and for the continuance of education in the State list. They recommended that "there is plenty of scope, within the present Constitutional arrangement, to evolve a workable Centre-State partnership in education and that this has not been exploited to the full. The case for amending the Constitution can only be,, made after this scope is fully utilized and found to be inadequate. All things considered we recommend that an intensive effort be made to exploit fully the existing provisions of the Constitution for the development of education and evolution of a national educational policy. The problem may then be reviewed again say, after ten years (Para 18.30)" The debate on the subject would have gone on indefinitely bad not the emergency intervened. Smt. Indira Gandhi, who was then in need of some respectable ideas for inclusion in her omnibus proposals for amendment to the Constitution, suddenly picked upon the subject and brought education on the concurrent list. The Janata Government which came to power with a pledge to undo all the Constitutional amendments made in the emergency declared its intension to put education back in the State List. It did not succeed, mainly because or the opposition from the Congress. But Dr. P. C. Chunder has declared in Parliament that the policy of his government is to act as if education is in the State list.

If history is to be written in modern parlance, it is interesting to note that education has been in the exclusively Central list between 1833 and 1870, in the Concurrent list between 1870 and 1921, in the exclusive State list between 1921 and 1947, mostly in the State list with some special powers to the Centre between 1947 and 1976, and in the Concurrent list from 1976 onwards.

The Role of the Government of India in Education: A Comprehensive View

So far, we have discussed the Constitutional Role of the Government of India in education. It must be pointed out however that the constitutional role of the Government of India in education is only one aspect of its actual role which must be examined in its totality. The other aspects of this role which modify the constitutional position very substantially are (1) public opinion, (2) financial relations, (3) political situation, and (4) administrative arrangements. It is only an integrated view of all these aspects that can give real insights into the nature of the problem and enable us to devise practicable reforms.

Public Opinion: What is the public view of the Centre-State relations in education and how does the public except education to be administered? It is obvious that, in a truly democratic set up, the administration of education which concerns every individual intimately must be highly decentralized. The general practice in this regard is that school education or at least elementary education which has to be provided for every child, should be controlled by the local community. This, for instance, is the tradition in U.S.A. where the people are extremely alert on educational issues and where the principle of local control of school education is strongly rooted in the historical traditions of the country. In a situation of this type, the State itself has a minor role in school education and the Federal Government, even less. The position regarding secondary and higher education, however is rather different. Secondary education is usually under local control if it is provided on a universal basis. Otherwise, it is generally provided by a larger community or the State; and higher education, except in a few big cities, is generally managed by the State or by the State and the Federal Government in some kind of partnership. On the basis of this broad general practice, it should ordinarily be expected that in India elementary education should be administered at the local community level, secondary education at the district or State level, and higher education at the State level or at the State and national levels.

Unfortunately, the historical traditions in our country have been different so that local control of education at the community or district level has failed to develop adequately. It is true that we did have a tradition of some local control of education because, in the pre-British days, schools were established and controlled by the local communities rather than by the Princes who, at best, extended their patronage to a few learned scholars or schools of higher learning. But these schools, more often than not, were enterprises of individuals or of small interested groups within the community rather than of the community as a whole. Even this limited tradition also died out when Government accepted responsibility for providing education. In the old British Indian Provinces, an attempt was made to associate local bodies at the community and district level with the provision of elementary education. This tradition has survived but has neither become vital or dynamic. In the Princely States, on the other hand, no such effort was ever made. In the post-independence period also the local control of education was not encouraged except for the Panchayati Raj experiment which has been tried earnestly only in a few areas. Consequently, the present position is that the vast masses of the people who are mostly illiterate have no interest in education as now imparted in the formal system and the tradition of local control in education is also mostly non-existent.

Public interest in education in India is mainly confined to the educated and elite groups who are the principal beneficiaries of the formal educational system and who mostly belong to the top 30 per cent of the income groups. Their main interest is in secondary and higher education where, apart from other things, their own private enterprise provides the bulk of the educational institutions. Moreover, it is the children of this elite which form about 70 per cent of the enrolment in secondary education and about go per cent of the enrolment in higher education. The basic issues that interest this elite are, therefore, the location and opening of new secondary schools, colleges and universities, their curricula and grants, in-aid and the expansion of elementary education (which provides them with a large number of fairly well-paid jobs). As these, issues are mostly decided at the State level, the concept of education as essentially a State responsibility gets the strongest-public support. The view, gets further strengthened from the fact that, the State is probably the most convenient level from which a basic social service like education can be administered. The sap e view also finds still further support in the State levy leadership whose image and power-base largely depends upon the control of educational institutions, teachers and students. It is these supports which made education a Stale subject under the Constitution and which also continue to legitimize the position. In fact, one may even assert that education as a State responsibility is at present so well entrenched in the public mind (or in the mind of the elites that rule the country) that it is extremely difficult, if not actually impassible, to alter this situation.

One need not necessarily quarrel with this view and may agree that education may basically remain a State responsibility. But one cannot also accept a State absolutism in education and an over-concentration of authority at the State level. The power of the state, in education has therefore to be limited to a considerable extent in the larger interests of education itself. This is generally attempted in three ways.

(a) The first is administrative decentralisation where authority over education, and especially over school education, is transferred to the local community at the municipal, village, Tahsil or District levels. As pointed out earlier, this trend is weak in the country, partly because the earlier tradition of local control or popular involvement in education has almost died out, partly because such decentralisation can be most effective in elementary and adult education which continue to be our neglected sectors, and partly because the local leadership at the village, Tahsil or District level is still weak in comparison with that at the Stale level and cannot assert itself. Consequently, the unfortunate public view that the State and Central levels are the only two that really matter in education, gains undue currency and strength. This trend also finds support in the general attitudes of linguistic and other minorities and weaker sections like Scheduled Castes and Tribes who find that the local levels (whether village, block, Tahsil or District) are generally oppressive and that their oppresiveness increases as one goes down to lower levels so that their hopes of justice and fair treatment lie mainly at the State and national levels.

(b) The second is academic decentralisation, i.e. to free the educational process from bureaucratic control by respecting university autonomy which the universities should, in their turn, share with their departments and affiliated colleges), by enabling the schools to prepare their own curricula and to hold their own examinations, and in short by so delegating authority to educational institutions and their teachers that the teaching-learning process becomes free, joyful and independent of State control. Unfortunately these concepts have not gained strength either within the teaching profession or among the general public. On the other hand, the contrary trends have gained an upper hand and the academic control of the State over education, schools and teachers has increased, rather than decreased, since 1947.

(c) While we have thus been unable to check State absolutism in education either through decentralisation to local bodies or through academic decentralization, we have had a somewhat better success to control State authority in education through centralization, i.e. by giving a larger voice to the Central Government in educational matters. One powerful group that supports this demand is that of the national bureaucracy which can be transferred to any part of the country and the large trade and industrial interests that have also acquired a national character. These groups are generally in favour of a national system of education with common curricula and text books in all parts of the country-a situation which can be created only if the Central Government can have an overriding voice in education. The university and research, system which can be best planned on a national basis also supports the same trend. Further support comes from another important group, viz., teachers, who would like to fight for uniform scales of pay and emoluments in all parts of the country and who realize that they can become a tremendous force if organized on a national basis. They are, therefore, in favour of an increasing role in education for the Centre and against any devolution of authority to the local bodies. A large section of the, intellectual elite also recognizes the need for a national policy in education from the point of view of national integration and takes the stand that while the "diversity" implied in the State control of education is both necessary and desirable, it is equally important to provide the 'unity' in this diversity through a national educational policy. It, must also be pointed out that the national leadership that grew in the freedom struggle initiated a large and intensive debate on education at the national level and that this tradition still continues unabated. Consequently, education has become, throughout the last hundred years or so, a great national concern although it remains State subject in administration. The public support for the role of the Government of India in education arises essentially from these social and political groups and from these national concerns which cannot be ignored, although not all of them are healthy and desirable, To the extent they succeed, there will be a curb on the State authority in education and a legitimate basis for the formulation and implementation of a national policy on education.

It will thus be evident 'that, while education will continue to be essentially a State responsibility (irrespective of the fact whether it does or does not continue to be in the concurrent list in the Constitution), it is equally essential to curb the trend towards State absolutism, not only by giving a more significant role to the Centre, but also by strengthening local control in education and promoting academic decentralization. Steps will have to be taken to educate public opinion on these lines in the years ahead.

93rd amendment to make education a fundamental right is flawed, claim activists.

Though early childhood care is crucial for the success of any education campaign, the proposed bill neglects the needs and rights of pre-school children

The proposed 93rd amendment bill, making education a fundamental right for every Indian child between 6-14, has been severely criticised. The bill will be tabled in parliament in the winter session.

According to the National Alliance for the Fundamental Right to Education (NAFRE), the bill will seriously compromise the rights of pre-school children (below six years). NAFRE, an alliance of some 2,400 education-related grassroots-level voluntary agencies, has been spearheading the campaign for free compulsory education as a fundamental right.

NAFRE wants the age level for free and compulsory education to be lowered. Government officials, however, say that it is not possible to do this as six is the universally accepted age for a beginner. The proposed bill seeks to include the provision for Early Childhood Care and Education (ECCE) for the age-group 0-6 only in the Directive Principles of State Policy. However, ECCE is crucial for the holistic development of a child, especially in the first few years of life.

Early childhood care is the primary need of some 161 million Indian children below the age of six, of whom 60 million or more live in poverty. Children from such families cannot be adequately cared for without State support.

Besides, ECCE is crucial to the success of any campaign to provide free and compulsory education to children in the 6-14 age-group: early childhood care influences the most vital first few years of development in human beings, and has major repercussions on the intelligence and personality development of the child. Early childhood care is statistically proven to affect drop-out rates, school retention and school performance.

Early childhood care could include craches, parent support programmes, entitlements to enable working mothers to care for their babies, preschool programmes, or coaching classes to help children enter primary school.

By including the clause "The parent or guardian is to provide opportunities for education to his child or as the case may be, ward between the age of six and 14 years," the bill is absolving the State of the responsibility of providing education for the child and compelling the family/guardian alone to provide for the child's education. NAFRE wants this compulsory provision removed, as providing education to children should be a fundamental duty of the State. In a country like India where millions live below the poverty line, unable to provide two square meals to their children, how would parents/guardians find the resources to send children to school?

Secondly, if this bill becomes law, parents are bound to send their wards to school, failing which they can be prosecuted. According to NAFRE, between 1951-71, approximately 10 lakh parents (mainly from the lower economic strata) were prosecuted under the state-level compulsory education Acts. Although Article 21A to be inserted in Article 21 of the fundamental rights states that 'the State shall provide free and compulsory education to all children between 6 and 14 years in such manner as the State may, by law, determine,' it does not define the term 'free'. This gives scope for institutionalising cheap and unsuitable teaching methods as alternatives, according to Sanjiv Kaura, co-ordinator, NAFRE.

"The memorandum must contain an irrevocable commitment by the State to spend a minimum of 6 per cent of the GDP on education. This recommendation was made by the Kothari Commission in 1966, but nothing has been done till now," feels Kaura.

Senior police officer and social activist Kiran Bedi feels that the bill should include all children up to the age of 18 or till they complete their schooling up to class ten. "Educating children till the age of 14 doesn't serve any purpose since a person doesn't even pass the 10th standard. Matriculation is a recognised qualification at the lowest level. Then he can apply for certain jobs or opt for vocational courses."

Kaura clarifies that they are not against the legislation, but feel that it envisages 'cheap options on the basis of the logic that something is better than nothing. This would perpetuate illiteracy in one form or the other'.

NAFRE is also demanding the inclusion of a financial memorandum (i.e. Rs 1,40,000 crores over 10 years for educating children between 6-14 years) in the legislation, in keeping with the Tapas Majumdar recommendations.

The bill has also been described as 'not only anti-child and anti-poor, but also an anti-woman move by the State' (Mina

Swaminathan, The Hindu, October 10, 2001). It is anti-woman as it derecognises the services of childcare/anganwadi workers (first teachers) numbering nearly 1 million or more, who will be relegated to the status of volunteers, receiving a meagre pittance in the form of an honorarium. This will be far less than the minimum wage available to an unskilled worker. Childcare workers under the National Policy on Education (1986) are treated on a par with primary teachers in terms of emoluments and working conditions. Still worse will be the plight of several million 'untrained' teachers working in 'unrecognised' private nursery schools. NAFRE will be organising a 'Shiksha Satyagraha' in the capital on November 28, to publicise the issue.

Kothari Commission

- Physical education not only aims at physical fitness but also has educational values. It contributes to physical efficiency, mental alertness and the development of certain qualities like perseverance, team spirit, leadership and obedience to rules.
- It should include development exercises, rhythmic activities, sports and games, outing activities and group handling activities.
- At the pre-primary and early primary stages, the syllabus should aim at developing among children the mastery over basic skills, such as walking properly, running, throwing, etc.
- At the secondary stage, the syllabus may contain sports, games and athletics in their standard form.

After the primary stage, the syllabus should be planned separately for boys and girls. Rhythmic activities will have an appeal for girls, less strenuous games, such as badminton, throw-ball, etc. are also popular among them.

National Policy on Education (N.P.E)-1986

The National Policy of Education-1986, has very rightly mentioned that "Sports and Physical Education are an integral part of the learning process, and well be included in the evaluation of performance. A nation-wide infrastructure for physical education, Sports and games will be built into the educational edifice" (cited on 8.20, NPE-1986).

The infrastructure will consist of play fields, equipment, coaches and teachers of physical education as a part of the school improvement programme. Available open spaces in urban areas will be reserved for playground, if necessary by legislation. Efforts will be made to establish sports institutions and hostels where specialized attention will be given to sports activities and sports related studies, along with normal education. Appropriate encouragement will be given to those talented in sports and games. Due stress will be laid on indigenous traditional games. As a system which promotes on integrated development of body and mind, Yoga will receive special attention. Efforts will be made to Introduce Yoga in all schools: to this end, it will be introduced in teacher training course. (cited on 8.21, NPE-1986). While re-emphasizing the above points the programme of Action (POA) has mentioned that action in the following areas will be necessary to implement the policy objectives of NPE-1986:

(i) In deciding the curriculum load the need to allocate sufficient time to sports and physical education which the NPE, 1986 holds as an integral of the learning process, should be kept in mind.

(ii) Physical education and Yoga should be introduced for at least 45 minutes per day, preferably just after assembly.

(iii) Approved games should be included in the school time-table for at least two periods in a week.

(iv) Special incentives will need to be given to students who perform well in sports and games.

(v) Special incentives may be considered for subject teachers who perform extra duty in conducting classes in physical education, Yoga, sports and games.

(vi) The basic equipment, such as Footballs and Volleyballs may be provided to each school, similarly, some amount of contingency may be provided to each school.

(vii) A scheme for creation and improvement of playgrounds should be taken up on a phased basis under Jawahar Rojgar Yojana (JRY) and Neheru Yuvak Kendras (NYK).

(viii) An intensive and extensive programme of teachers training to equip all subject teachers with necessary skills to impart training in physical education, games and Yoga will be necessary.

(ix) The present programme to train and recruit physical education teachers for high schools should be expanded.

(x) New schools may be established/recognized only if playgrounds are available.

(xi) A comprehensive system of inter-school tournaments and championships in select disciplines should be introduced over a period of time. This system should culminate in a National School Championship.

(xii) Special cash awards to winning schools and a special system of incentives for successful athletes also needs to be introduced.

Education: Its Aims and Objectives

"Education", says Aristotle," is the creation of a sound mind in a sound body". It encompasses in itself the all round development of an individual. The success of spreading education to the widest possible area lies in the way it is imparted. With the ever changing technology scenario, the methods of imparting education too have been undergoing changes. But education itself is an age old process, rather as old as the human race itself. It was man's education through Nature, our greatest teacher, that he learned how to make fire by rubbing stones or invented the wheal to make tasks easier. Education in real earnest helps us in restraining the objectionable predisposition in ourselves. The aims of education have been categorized variously by different scholars. While Herbert Spencer believed in the 'complete-living aim', Herbart advocated the moral aim. The complete living aim signifies that education should prepare us for life. This view had also been supported by Rousseau and Mahatma Gandhi. They believed in the complete development or perfection of nature.

All round development has been considered as the first and foremost aim of education. At the same time education ensures that there is a progressive development of innate abilities. Pestalozzi is of the view "Education is natural, harmonious and progressive development of man's innate powers." Education enables us to control, give the right direction and the final sublimation of instincts. It creates good citizens. It helps to prepare the kids for their future life. Education inculcates certain values and principles and also prepares a human being for social life. It civilizes the man. The moral aim of Herbart states that education should ingrain moral values in children. He is of the view that education should assist us in curbing our inferior whims and supplant them with superior ideas. This moral aim has also been stressed upon by Gandhiji in the sense of formation of character. The preachers of this aim do not undermine the significance of knowledge, vocational training or muscular strength. But simultaneously they have also laid stress on their view that the undisclosed aim of education is to assist development of moral habits. Then there is the social aim which means that education should produce effective individuals in the sense that they realize their responsibilities towards the society. And we all know that man is a social being. The interactive ability is a must as it is through interaction that we come to know of our responsibilities. Edmund Burke asks and he himself answers: "What is education? A parcel of books? Not at all, but an intercourse with the world, with men and with affairs."

Only bookish knowledge takes a child nowhere. It should be further perfected by practical usage with experience. "Reading maketh a full man; conference a ready man; and writing an exact man" is a pithy and precise statement in which the essayist Francis Bacon sums up the advantages of studies. Even Wordsworth in his poem 'The Tables Turned' advocated against bookish knowledge.

Books! 'tis a dull and endless strife:
Come, hear the woodland linnet,
How sweet his music! on my life,
There's more of wisdom in it.

Wordsworth was a die-hard naturalist. He wanted man to consider Nature his teacher. Naturalists believe that instincts of the child should be taken as the basis of education. The child should have freedom. Rabindra Nath Tagore was of the opinion that child should be left free in order to gather experience and to understand his own mistakes and shortcomings.

The twentieth century saw the emergence of the concept of Pragmatism. Charles Pierce was the first man to introduce the concept of pragmatism in his philosophy. Later on it was popularized by John Dewey, William James, Kilpatrick and Schiller. They believed that the external world is real and the reality is being constantly created and is always changing. Knowledge and truth is one and the same thing according to them. Whatever the approach towards education, one thing we all agree: Education is for the betterment of the individual and in the long run for the society. Education helps us prepare ourselves for the life ahead. Darwin gave the theory of the 'survival of the fittest'; we can say in a way that education prepares the individual for the struggle of life for his own survival.

Knowledge combined with proper guidance can spell success. A dose of proper guidance should be commenced right from the base itself, that is, in school days. Here comes the role of the teacher in moulding a child's mind. Educating a child, especially in the beginning years of schooling, is a very tricky job. That is probably because the child's mind is like the unmoulded clay at that time. Therefore to get the best results and prepare well-informed and erudite adults, proper guidance is a must. For a proper system of education the teacher should encourage a student both in terms of mental encouragement and in lending a helping hand as and when needed. A student needs help for training his mind in such a way that it develops a tendency to gather knowledge from all possible sources. While on the other hand too much help if lent to him will make him dependant and used to spoon feeding. Self-study is the most sought after quality in a student. It helps them at the later stages. But because the 'child is the father of man' (Wordsworth) all the qualities have to be inculcated right in childhood. And teacher along with parents plays a very significant role. The aims of education should be kept in mind, although a thorough study of these aims may not be imperative. A teacher should make a child ready to face the society, inculcate moral habits in him and thus, assist him in his all round development.

Education should not be considered synonymous with all that we learn. It does not signify the things we mug up before appearing for an examination. Education is what remains behind, when we fail to remember the mugged up portion. After we have left school, we realize that although we have forgotten quite a few things we learnt but still retain a very large part of it. The latter part is education. Education formally begins in school but actually it begins the day we are born and the process goes on for the whole of our life. This is where the aims of education come in. Education is not only the formal part we gain in schools, colleges or universities. It also includes the lessons life teaches us in various forms. For instance, when a child gets his finger pricked by a needle accidentally he learns that a needle is sharp and can hurt a person, so he will learn to avoid hurting himself in the future. This is only one example from thousands of other instances. We can even learn a lesson of a lifetime from a beggar. The birds inspire us to rise high. An ant motivates us for hard work. We learn some things just by doing them on our own, they are never taught in a school. A child's first teacher is his mother, then his home and then come the formal agencies of education. Nature too is a great teacher. English poetry too gives us quite a few guidelines for leading a better life. It was not for nothing that Wordsworth went on to remark:

"One impulse from the vernal wood
May teach you more of a man
Of moral evil and of good
Than all the sages can."

As long as there is life, we require education; we need ways to modify our views about life, to face it, to live it in a better way. And education teaches us all this. Even when you read a comic strip, it educates you in some way. They improve our language and make us realize that life isn't so bad after all that it can't get worse, as states Bill Watterson in 'Calvin and Hobbes'. The witty humour of 'Dennis the Menace' enriches us no end. "The aim of education," says Walter Grophices, "is not the specialist but the man of vision who can humanize our life by integrating emotional demands with our new knowledge."

In another way too, the insects and animals also teach you a lot. The easiest example is that of an ant. It inspires you to work hard. Therefore we can say there are innumerable modes of education, all that one needs is to have a discerning eye. Education enriches a person in terms of accepting a defeat. A student should first of all be taught so that he is encouraged to study. Side by side he should be readied to face a failure. As Charles F. Kettering rightly says," The chief job of the education is to teach people how to fail intelligently." This will help the child coping with the other adversities of life. Education, thus, makes a person an improved version of himself and the world a much better place to live in.

Levels and Aims of Education: Preprimary & Primary Education

Basic Principles: While "primary education provides the fundamentals of all formal learning" (Sharma 1997), preprimary learning may be called the foundation for both education and personal development. Little information exists on formal preprimary education in rural India, although the family and community function as a broader arena for holistic learning. In urban communities, the level of preprimary education corresponds directly to the factors of class and wealth. Only the rich and educated opt for kindergarten and Montessori schools, which abound in affluent neighborhoods, while poor, neglected, underprivileged children languish in the streets of Indian cities.

At least in terms of national priorities, primary education takes as a model a humanistic pedagogy, emphasizing the needs of the child over all means and methods of education. Neerja Sharma succinctly writes:

> *The buildings, school administration, teachers and personnel, syllabi and textbooks, furniture and uniforms exist because children need education. This truism has*

been recognized in the Program of Action of the National Policy on Education (1986) that states under its Implementation Strategies: The country's faith in its future generations will be exemplified in the system of elementary education, which will get geared around the centrality of the child *(11). (1997)*

A 1988 governmental reform of the primary curriculum set forth the principles that were to govern this type of education. Students were entitled to a "broad and balanced curriculum" including such diverse subjects as religious education, science, and technology. In addition, the standards for students' academic achievement were to be raised, and assessment methods were to serve "formative purposes" (Venkataiah 2000).

The implementation of these goals is somewhat confounded by the diversity of India's population and the complexity of its governance. In practice, primary education is a dilemma-ridden field where teachers, schools, communities, and states muddle through a rugged terrain without consensus. As a result, local, regional, and political influences override the foundational issues in pedagogical discourse. In particular, zealous religious groups have been divisive.

S. Venkataiah, a leader in primary and secondary education in India, argues that the legal force and the professional support, even the very goals, of the 1988 reform act created a problem of manageability: "One of the paradoxes was that there would have been no manageability problem without the principles embodied in the curriculum required by the 1988 Act" (2000). Venkataiah identifies three types of problems that arose for those charged with managing the curriculum at the school level: curriculum time allocation, teacher expertise, and resources in primary schools.

A further problem with meeting the expansive goals of the nationally determined curriculum of primary schools has been many teachers' shallow approach to education. "The dominating difficulty in the purpose of primary schools is the fact that 'knowing' is rated more highly than 'teaching,' despite the importance of the latter and its equally intimate connection with 'learning,'" writes Venkataiah (2000). Venkataiah adds:

> *The agency responsible for the National Curriculum advised the Government that the statutory curriculum would have to be slimmed down; the agency responsible for the national inspection arrangement reported that those schools that had nearly covered the statutory curriculum had done so only by encouraging superficial learning in their pupils. (2000)*

Initiatives: Universalization of the entire educational system has been the main goal of government since independence. Formal and nonformal primary education, however, have been the main challenge to this goal. Universalization of Elementary Education (UEE) is fraught with systemic and socioeconomic factors that call for massive public education and advocacy. A total-literacy campaign is underway despite numerous barriers. Even provision of textbooks in poverty-ridden areas is a challenge. A comprehensive program seeks to target "i) teachers and all those involved in education of children; ii) students and parents of students, particularly non-literate parents; and iii) community opinion leaders" (Government of India 2001).

Residential education of girls, especially from broken homes and poor families, has lately received planners' attention. A program named after Mahatma Gandhi's wife, the Kasturba Gandhi Shiksha Yojana, has been funded with Rs. 2,500 million (rupees). Other financial incentives and scholarships for poor girls have been provided. All such programs, as recorded in the NPE-1986, "pay special attention to increasing girls' enrolment, improving educational outcomes, strengthening community involvement, and improving teaching and learning materials and providing in-service teacher training" (Government of India 2001).

Operation Blackboard: According to the government of India, the number of primary schools that have been transformed under this initiative with central assistance is 523,000. The main purpose of this program is to improve the environment in schools by providing basic facilities.

Decentralization: According to the government of India, the management of elementary education, as envisioned by the

NPE, has emphasized direct community involvement in the form of Village Education Committees (VECs). The 73rd and 74th constitutional amendments provide for decentralization of the local self-government institutions, called Panchayati Raj Institutions (PRIs). PRIs have thus become pivotal in the delivery of education in rural and urban communities. The oppressed groups—women, Scheduled Castes and Tribes, and minorities—have especially found PRIs very helpful. This approach is essentially grass-roots educational policy and delivery.

Decentralization has been reinforced during the Eighth Five-Year Plan. The VECs, District Primary Education Program, and Lok Jumbish have been chiefly instrumental in this process. A Special Orientation Program for Primary Teachers has further reinforced support to primary level teachers. During 1992 to 1993 and 1995 to 1996, Rs. 8,163 million were allocated; the outlay for 1996 to 1997 was Rs. 2,910 million. More recent data is not available.

Mobilizing the village community to take responsibility for ensuring quality education for every child is the core strategy of both the Shiksha Karmi Project and Lok Jumbish and in their efforts to universalize and improve primary education. Community involvement has been crucial for the success of these projects.

Shiksha Karmi Project: The Swedish International Development Cooperation Agency has assisted in the implementation of the Shiksha Karmi Project. The project aims at universalization and qualitative improvement of primary education in the remote and economically disadvantaged villages of Rajasthan with a focus on girls. The Shiksha Karmi Project has constituted VECs in 2,000 villages to promote community involvement in primary education and encourage village-level planning. The role of the VEC is to mobilize resources for maintenance, repair, and construction of school infrastructures. The VEC also helps in determining the school calendar and school-daytimings in consultation with the local community and *Shiksha Karmis* (educational workers). *Shiksha Karmis* are frequently used as substitutes to compensate for teacher absenteeism. In addition to the more formal courtyard schools (*Angan Pathshalas*), the Shiksha Karmi Project also runs nonformal classes called *Prehar Pathshalas* (schools of convenient timings). For girls' education, *Angan Pathshalas* are run in three blocks. As of 2001 the program covered over 150,000 students in 1,785 schools and 3,520 *Prehar Pathshalas,* involving over 4,271 *Shiksha Karmis.*

Lok Jumbish Project: Lok Jumbish is extended to 75 blocks covering a population of approximately 12 million in Rajastahan. The project involves government agencies, teachers, nongovernmental organizations (NGOs), and elected representatives to promote universalization of primary education. The seven guiding principles of Lok Jumbish are (a) a process rather than a product approach, (b) partnerships, (c) decentralized functioning, (d) participatory learning, (e) integration with the mainstream education system, (f) flexibility of management, and (g) multiple levels of leadership.

Bihar Education Project: The Bihar Education Project, launched in 1991, emphasized participatory planning to uplift the deprived sections of society, such as Scheduled Castes, Scheduled Tribes, and women. A midterm review highlighted major achievements including (a) a strong Mahila Samakhya component; (b) organization of VECs and community involvement in program implementation at grassroots levels; and (c) nonformal education through NGOs.

Uttar Pradesh Basic Education Program: The government of Uttar Pradesh launched the World Bank project Education for All in June 1993. The project, operating in 12 districts as of 2001, is planned to expand its coverage to 15 districts under DPEP Phase II. It has an outlay of Rs. 7,288 million spread over 7 years. The IDA would provide a credit of $163.1 million, and the state government's share would be approximately 13 percent of the total project cost. About 40,000 teachers have been trained.

Andhra Pradesh Primary Education Project: The Andhra Pradesh Primary Education Project (APPEP), implemented in the south-central state of Andhra Pradesh, adopts a two-pronged strategy of improving classroom transaction by training teachers and giving a fillip to school construction activities. The Andhra Pradesh area has a female literacy rate of just 34 percent. The project has trained an estimated 80,000 teachers in 23 districts, and more than 3,000 teaching centres have become operational. The project is assisted by the UK's ODA with an estimated outlay of Rs. 1,000 million in the Eighth Five-Year Plan.

National Program of Nutritional Support to Primary Education (School Meal Program): Providing a free, nutritious cooked meal of 100 grams of food grains per school day to all children in classes I-V is an ambitious program in a country of 1 billion people. The program was launched in 1997 to 1998 to support UEE in achieving its goal of increasing enrolment, retention, and attendance in primary classes. In 1997 to 1998 the program covered nearly 110 million children in primary classes. Reportedly school enrolment and rates of retention have increased.

Secondary Education

The National Policy on Education (NPE), 1986, has provided for environment awareness, science and technology education, and introduction of traditional elements such as Yoga into the Indian secondary school system.

A significant feature of India's secondary school system is the emphasis on inclusion of the disadvantaged sections of the society Professionals from established institutes are often called to support in vocational training. Another feature of India's secondary school system is its emphasis on profession based vocational training to help students attain skills for finding a vocation of his/her choosing.

A special Integrated Education for Disabled Children (IEDC) programme was started in 1974. Another notable special programme, the *Kendriya Vidyalaya* project, was started for the employees of the central government of India, who are distributed throughout the country. The government started the *Kendriya Vidyalaya* project in 1965 to provide uniform education in institutions following the same syllabus at the same pace regardless of the location to which the employee's family has been transferred.

Level and Aims of Education: Primary and Secondary Education in India

Several factors work against universal education in India. Although Indian law prohibits the employment of children in factories, the law allows them to work in cottage industries, family households, restaurants, or in agriculture. Primary and middle school education is compulsory. However, only slightly more than 50 percent of children between the ages of six and fourteen actually attend school, although a far higher percentage is enrolled. School attendance patterns for children vary from region to region and according to gender. But it is noteworthy that national literacy rates increased from 43.7 percent in 1981 to 52.2 percent in 1991 (male 63.9 percent, female 39.4 percent), passing the 50 percent mark for the first time. There are wide regional and gender variations in the literacy rates, however; for example, the southern state of Kerala, with a 1991 literacy rate of about 89.8 percent, ranked first in India in terms of both male and female literacy. Bihar, a northern state, ranked lowest with a literacy rate of only 39 percent (53 percent for males and 23 percent for females). School enrolment rates also vary greatly according to age.

To improve national literacy, the central government launched a wide-reaching literacy campaign in July 1993. Using a volunteer teaching force of some 10 million people, the government hoped to have reached around 100 million Indians by 1997. A special focus was placed on improving literacy among women.

A report in 1985 by the Ministry of Education, entitled *Challenge of Education: A Policy Perspective*, showed that nearly 60 percent of children dropped out between grades one and five. (The Ministry of Education was incorporated into the Ministry of Human Resources in 1985 as the Department of Education. In 1988 the Ministry of Human Resources was renamed the Ministry of Human Resource Development.) Of

100 children enrolled in grade one, only twenty-three reached grade eight. Although many children lived within one kilometre of a primary school, nearly 20 percent of all habitations did not have schools nearby. Forty percent of primary schools were not of masonry construction. Sixty percent had no drinking water facilities, 70 percent had no library facilities, and 89 percent lacked toilet facilities. Single-teacher primary schools were commonplace, and it was not unusual for the teacher to be absent or even to subcontract the teaching work to unqualified substitutes.

The improvements that India has made in education since independence are nevertheless substantial. From the first plan until the beginning of the sixth (1951-80), the percentage of the primary school-age population attending classes more than doubled. The number of schools and teachers increased dramatically. Middle schools and high schools registered the steepest rates of growth. The number of primary schools increased by more than 230 percent between 1951 and 1980. During the same period, however, the number of middle schools increased about tenfold. The numbers of teachers showed similar rates of increase. The proportion of trained teachers among those working in primary and middle schools, fewer than 60 percent in 1950, was more than 90 percent in 1987. However, there was considerable variation in the geographical distribution of trained teachers in the states and union territories in the 1986-87 school year. Arunachal Pradesh had the highest percentage (60 percent) of untrained teachers in primary schools, and Assam had the highest percentage (72 percent) of untrained teachers in middle schools. Gujarat, Tamil Nadu, Chandigarh, and Pondicherry (Puduchcheri) reportedly had no untrained teachers at either kind of school.

Various forms of private schooling are common; many schools are strictly private, whereas others enjoy government grants-in-aid but are run privately. Schools run by church and missionary societies are common forms of private schools. Among India's Muslim population, the *madrasa*, a school attached to a mosque, plays an important role in education. Some 10 percent of all children who enter the first grade are enrolled in private schools. The dropout rate in these schools is practically nonexistent.

Traditional notions of social rank and hierarchy have greatly influenced India's primary school system. A dual system existed in the early 1990s, in which middle-class families sent their children to private schools while lower-class families sent their children to underfinanced and underequipped municipal and village schools. Evolving middle-class values have made even nursery school education in the private sector a stressful event for children and parents alike. Tough entrance interviews for admission, long classroom hours, heavy homework assignments, and high tuition rates in the mid-1990s led to charges of "lost childhood" for preschool children and acknowledgment of both the social costs and enhanced social benefits for the families involved.

The government encourages the study of classical, modern, and tribal languages with a view toward the gradual switch from English to regional languages and to teaching Hindi in non-Hindi speaking states. As a result, there are schools conducted in various languages at all levels. Classical and foreign language training most commonly occurs at the postsecondary level, although English is also taught at the lower levels.

University

Receiving higher education, once the nearly exclusive domain of the wealthy and privileged, since independence has become the aspiration of almost every student completing high school. In the 1950-51 school year, there were some 360,000 students enrolled in colleges and universities; by the 1990-91 school year, the number had risen to nearly 4 million, a more than tenfold increase in four decades. At that time, there were 177 universities and university-level institutions (more than six times the number at independence), some 500 teacher training colleges, and several thousand other colleges.

There are three kinds of colleges in India. The first type, government colleges, are found only in those states where private enterprise is weak or which were at one time controlled by princes. The second kind are colleges managed by religious organizations and the private sector. Many of the latter institutions were founded after 1947 by wealthy business owners and politicians wishing to gain local fame and importance. Professional colleges comprise the third kind and consist mostly of medical, teacher-training, engineering, law, and agricultural colleges. More than 50 percent of them are sponsored and managed by the government. However, about 5 percent of these colleges are privately run without government grant support. They charge fees of ten to twelve times the amount of the government-run colleges. The profusion of new engineering colleges in India in the late 1980s and early 1990s caused concern in official education circles that the overall quality and reputation of India's higher education system would be threatened by these new schools, which operated mainly on a for-profit basis. As the government tightened its support to higher education in the early 1990s, colleges and universities came under considerable financial stress.

The All-India Council of Technical Education is empowered to regulate the establishment of any new private professional colleges to limit their proliferation. In 1992 the Karnataka High Court directed the state government to rescind permission to nine organizations to start new engineering and medical colleges in the state.

Gaining admission to a nonprofessional college is not unduly difficult except in the case of some select colleges that are particularly competitive. Students encounter greater difficulties in gaining admission to professional colleges in such fields as architecture, business, medicine, and dentistry.

There are four categories of universities. The largest number are teaching universities that maintain and run a large number of colleges. Unitary institutions, such as Allahabad University and Lucknow University, make up the second kind. The third kind are the twenty-six agricultural universities, each managed by the state in which it is located. Technical universities constitute the fourth kind. In the late 1980s, more technical universities, such as the Jawaharlal Nehru Technological University in the state of Hyderabad, were founded. There were also proposals to found medical universities in some states. By 1990 Andhra Pradesh and Tamil Nadu already had established such universities. Out of the 177 universities in the country, only ten are funded by the central government. The majority of universities are managed by the states, which establish them and provide funding.

There was a high rate of attrition among students in higher education in the 1980s. A substantial portion failed their examinations more than once, and large numbers dropped out; only about one out of four students successfully completed the full course of studies. Even those students who were successful could not count on a university degree to assure them employment. In the early postindependence years, a bachelor's degree often provided entrance to the elite, but in contemporary India, it provides a chance to become a white-collar worker at a relatively modest salary. The government traditionally has been the principal employer of educated manpower.

State governments play a powerful role in the running of all but the national universities. Political considerations, if not outright political patronage, play a significant part in appointments. The state governor is usually the university chancellor, and the vice chancellor, who actually runs the institution, is usually a political appointee. Appointments are subject to political jockeying, and state governments have control over grants and other forms of recognition. Caste affiliation and regional background are recognized criteria for admission and appointments in many colleges. To offset the inequities implicit in such practices, a certain number of places are reserved for members of Scheduled Castes and Scheduled Tribes.

Unit-V

Statutory Bodies in the Field of Education

MHRD

A candidate is eligible for Ministry of Human Resource Development (MHRD) Scholarship/ Assistantship in Engineering /Technology /Architecture /Pharmacy /Sciences at engineering colleges/institutes in the country only if she/he qualifies in GATE.

To avail the scholarship, additionally, the candidate must secure admission to such a postgraduate programme, as per the prevailing procedure of the admitting institution. GATE qualification by itself does not guarantee admission. GATE qualified candidates in Engineering disciplines are also eligible for the award of the Junior Research Fellowship in CSIR Laboratories. Some government organizations prescribe GATE qualification as a requirement for applying to the post of a Scientist/Engineer.

- As per the directives of the Ministry of Human Resource Development (MHRD), Government of India, the following procedure is to be adopted for admission to postgraduate programmes (Master and Doctoral) with MHRD scholarship/assistantship. The GATE performance of the candidate will be considered for admission. If the candidate is to be selected through interview for postgraduate programmes, minimum 70% weightage is to be given to the GATE performance. The remaining weightage (30% maximum) can be given to the marks obtained by the candidate in her/his qualifying examination or interview. Candidates opting for a general paper (XE or XL) should be further examined (by interview/written test) by the admitting institution. In such cases also the weightage for GATE score should not be less than 70%. The admitting institution will prescribe minimum passing percentage of marks in the interview. Some colleges/institutes specify GATE as the mandatory qualification even for admission without MHRD scholarship/assistantship.

- Candidates are advised to seek details about admission procedures and availability of MHRD scholarship/ assistantship from the concerned institution. GATE offices will *not entertain* any enquiry about *admission and award of scholarship / assistantship*.
- While qualifying in GATE is essential for all candidates seeking admission to postgraduate programmes with MHRD scholarship/assistantship, the management of the postgraduate scholarship/assistantship is the responsibility of the admitting institution. The *GATE committee has no role in the award or disbursement of scholarship / assistantship*. Similarly, reservation of seats under different categories is as per the policies and norms prevailing at the admitting institution and Government of India rules.
- According to MHRD rules, the award of postgraduate scholarship/assistantship to GATE qualified candidates is for a maximum period of 24 months for Masters degree programmes in Engineering/Technology/ Architecture/Pharmacy.
- Every qualified candidate will receive an original GATE scorecard valid for two years. Additional scorecards (up to a maximum of two) will be issued only once on request and on payment of Rs 300 per card. Such requests should reach the Organizing Chairman, GATE 2008, Indian Institute of Science Bangalore 560012 before August 31, 2008 together with a bank draft for the amount mentioned as above in favour of Chairman

GATE, IISc Bangalore, payable at Bangalore. These cards will be labelled as Additional Scorecard-1 and Additional Scorecard-2. However, if the candidate changes her/his admitting institution, she/he is required to clarify the matters related to her/his admission and scholarship/assistantship with the new institution.

- At present, students in the Integrated Masters Degree and Dual Degree programmes in Engineering/ Technology are eligible to appear in GATE 2008 in order to qualify for the postgraduate scholarship in their own institutions only. They are not eligible for admission to a fresh M.E/M.Tech. programme.

University Grants Commission (UGC)

This is a Government of India entity and is responsible for coordination, determination and maintenance of standards, and release of central grants to the universities. Apart from this, Government of India has also established sixteen central universities in the country, which are totally funded by the UGC.

National Institute of Educational Planning and Administration (NIEPA)

The National Institute of Educational Planning and Administration (NIEPA) is an autonomous organisation set up and fully financed by the Department of Secondary and Higher Education, Ministry of Human Resource Development.

The objectives of the Institute are to undertake, promote and coordinate research in educational planning and administration, provide training and consultancy services in this field, to train and orient key level functionaries as well as senior level administrators from the centre and states, to collaborate with other agencies, institutions and organisations, to provide facilities for training and research to other countries particularly of the Asian region in the field of educational planning and administration and to prepare, print and publish papers, periodicals and books, to share experience and expertise in the area of educational planning and administration with other countries and to conduct comparative studies for the furtherance of these objectives.

The faculty provid consultancy and professional support to National, State and Institutional level bodies as well as International Organisations like Ministry of Human Resource Development, University Grants Commission, State Education Departments, State Councils of Higher Education, SCERTs, SIEMATs UNESCO, UNICEF, World Bank and SIDA. The Institute maintains a well stocked Library/Documentation Centre on Educational Planning and Administration and Inter Disciplinary subjects. It is perhaps one of the richest libraries in the field of Educational Planning and Management in the Asian Region. It serves the faculty, research scholars and participants of the various programmes, as also other organisations through Inter Library Loan system. The Library reading room facilities are open to all. The Library has a collection of over 55,016 volume, subscribes to as many as 347 periodicals and has a computerised catalogue of books and articles.

National Council of Educational Research and Training (NCERT)

In the area of school education the Government of India has set up an apex resource organization 'The National Council of Educational Research and Training (NCERT)' which assists and advises the Central and State Governments on academic matters related to school education. The NCERT provides academic and technical support for improvement of school education through its various constituents like the National Institute of Education (NIE), Central Institute of Educational Technology (CIET) and a number of Regional Institutes of Education (RIE) located at different cities.

NCTE

The National Council for Teacher Education (NCTE) is a national-level statutory body of the Government of India, established in 1995. Its objective is to plan co-ordinated development of teacher education system, regulate, maintain and monitor norms and standards in teacher education.

It lays down norms for teacher education courses, accredits institutions, frames recruitment norms, carries out surveys, research and innovations. The NCTE has four Regional Offices at Jaipur, Bangalore, Bhubaneswar and Bhopal respectively.

National Assessment and Accreditation Council (NAAC)

National Assessment and Accreditation Council, an autonomous body, has been established by the University Grants Commission in 1994 in pursuance of the recommendations made by the National Policy of Education, 1986 and the Prgramme of Action (POA), 1992 which lay special emphasis on evaluating the quality of higher education in India.

The prime mandate of NAAC, as envisaged in its Memorandum of Association (MoA), is to assess and accredit institutions of higher learning, universities and colleges or one or more of their units, i.e., departments, schools, institutions, programmes, etc.

The NAAC functions through its General Council and Executive Committee where educational administrators, policy makers and senior academicians from a cross-section of system of higher education are represented.

Under the new methodology introduced by NAAC w.e.f. 1st April, 2007, the higher education institutions are assessed and accredited by a two-step approach.

In the first step, the institution is required to seek 'Institutional Eligibility for Quality Assessment (IEQA)' and the second step is the assessment and accreditation of the institute under the grades 'A', 'B', 'C' for accredited institutions; and 'D' for those which are not accredited.

NAAC has identified seven criteria— i. Curricular aspects, ii. Teaching-learning and evaluation, iii. Research, Consultancy and extension, iv. Infrastructure and learning resources, v. Student support and progression, vi. Governance and leadership and vii. Innovative practices as the basis for its assessment procedure.

Central Institute of English and Foreign Languages (CIEFL)

The Central Institute of English and Foreign Languages (CIEFL) is a national institute of higher education, deemed to be a university.

Set up in 1958 as the Central Institute of English (CIEFL) its original mandate was to improve the quality of the teaching of English in India through suitably designed training, research, and materials production programmes.

The success the Institute achieved in its academic sphere led to the expansion of its mandate to include the teaching of French, German, and Russian. Consequently, in 1973, the Institute was renamed the Central Institute of English and Foreign Languages. Arabic, Spanish, and Japanese

Description: The Department of Distance Education is part of the Central Institute of English and Foreign Languages which was established in 1958.

The Department was started in 1973 in order to provide an alternative mode of teacher-training to the face-to-face mode and to extend the outreach of the Institute. It started with the PGCTE (Postgraduate Certificate in the Teaching of English) offered at the Institute.

In 1978, the Department introduced the Postgraduate Diploma in the Teaching of English (PGDTE) through correspondence, which is considered to be equivalent to the second semester of the residential PGDTE.

The Department was renamed the Department of Distance Education in 1993. The change in nomenclature reflects the change in scope envisaged in programmes of the Department. Two contact programmes are conducted for each course. The contact programmes are obligatory for the PGCTE and there is one obligatory and one optional for the PGDTE. Existing courses have been revised and updated in terms of content and mode.

In 1995 the Department introduced research through the distance mode, awarding an MPhil (English) at the end of the programme.

Tansche

The Tamil Nadu State Council for Higher Education (TANSCHE) discussed the recommendations of the M. Anandakrishnan Committee on deemed universities and forwarded them to the Higher Education Minister for a final decision, according to Council members.

Going by these recommendations, the State government would write to the Union Ministry of Human Resource Development, asking the University Grants Commission to get its views before conferring deemed university status on any institution within the State.

It would also become mandatory for all such universities to include a government nominee on their management committees, said a TANSCHE member.

An expanded role for the State government in the functioning of these universities would be essential to maintain the fee structure and ensure social justice in the education system in the State, he added.

Deemed Universities: Deemed universities come under the authority of the UGC, which confers the status and regulates their functioning.

In February 2004, the Supreme Court ruled that State governments had no control over deemed universities. TANSCHE has also recommended that the deemed universities adhere to the guidelines of the State government when conducting convocations. The guests and speakers on the dais should be chosen because of their eminence in their fields in accordance with university statutes and without personal considerations, it said.

TANSCHE also intends to conduct academic audits of colleges in the State to improve the quality of education.

"It would be similar to the NAAC," said another TANSCHE member. The NAAC or the National Assessment and Accreditation Council is an autonomous body established by the UGC to assess and grade higher education institutions across the country.

A committee headed by T. Balakrishnan, former vice-chancellor of Periyar University, has recommended that TANSCHE constitute a team to visit colleges in the State to conduct comprehensive quality checks and monitoring reports.

It would also explore the methods adopted by successful institutions to spread awareness of the best practices. This would be the first state-level audit effort, said a TANSCHE member.

The main function of TANSCHE as stated in the Act shall be "to coordinate and determine standards in institutions for higher education or research and in scientific and technical institutions, in accordance with the guidelines issued by the University Grants Commission, from time to time."

The Government in setting up TANSCHE has made known their intentions in unambiguous words.

They expect it to act as a catalyst to bring about a sea change in the domain of higher education with a positively helpful understanding and attitude while liasing with the universities in the State and the University Grants Commission.

TANSCHE is not meant to be a fifth wheel in the coach of higher education. Nor is it to be a showpiece serving no definite purpose. TANSCHE's role has many facets, which it needs to constantly keep in perspective in its determined efforts to achieve the goals set for it.

TANSCHE will essentially a coordinator and bridge-builder in its relations with the universities at the State level and UGC at the National level.

TANSCHE will be a facilitator in regard to implementation of all university programmes aimed at academic excellence.

TANSCHE will endeavour to assist the universities in all possible ways in their pursuit of advanced research in sciences as well as humanities.

TANSCHE will undertake detailed exercises in manpower planning coordinated with educational planning.

TANSCHE will strive to assist the Government with its judicious comments and recommendations on all matters referred to it including the fixation of Maintenance/Block grants to universities.

TANSCHE in short, will make every effort to be an integrative force bringing the universities into constant touch with each other and be an instrument of cooperative action for higher education to enhance its own image impressively.

The Tamil Nadu State Council for Higher Education was established by an Act of the Tamil Nadu Legislative Assembly in the year 1992 for the promotion and coordination of Higher Education at the State level and coordination of state level programme with those of the University Grants Commission.

Directorates of Education

Collegiate

Training Programme : With a view to inculcate the importance of competency, skills and efficiency and the importance of using latest technology in the work environment among government personnel it is essential to provide adequate training. Likewise to enhance the quality of work undertaken by the staff of the department appropriate training is necessary.

Secondary

Karnataka Secondary Education Examination Board came in to existence in the year 1966, has been conducting SSLC and other examinations. Every year the students strength is increasing tremendously. For the academic year - March 2009 about 8.69 Lakhs students are appearing for the SSLC examinations.

The board has been successfully conducted the examination since it was established.

The board has decided to improve the evaluation system and the results, every year the quantum of the boards examination has been increasing and hence divisional offices of the Board have been set up in order to centralize the students needs.

The board has ventured to conduct the supplementary examination for the failed candidates of the examination of March in June month of every year itself, this will enable the students who would be successful in the June examination to join higher education courses from July itself. This process was introduced first time in the country.

Elementary

Universalisation of Primary Education was accepted as a target to be achieved within a period of 10 years of the coming into force of the Constitution i.e. 1960. Since then it has been revised several times without achieving the target.

At present, the Sarva Shiksha Abhiyan of the Government of India pledges to achieve this task by 2010. In Karnataka, the target year accepted by the Department of Public Instruction is 2007.

The expansion of human capabilities because of education contributes to human well being directly, apart from its indirect role in social and economic development. With the opening of economic opportunities due to liberalization, the State's population has to have basic education for growth to be sustained, to meet the needs of modernized agriculture, for knowledge and skills, and of industry for skilled manpower.

The State Government is the pre-eminent agent in the primary education sector being responsible for establishing and running primary schools in the State Under the decentralization initiatives that were pioneered by Karnataka in the 1980's, the responsibility for running primary schools was first devolved to the Zilla Panchayats.

Since the late 1990's, payment of teachers salaries has been further devolved to the Taluk Panchayats.

The district head of the Department of Public Instruction, the Deputy Director, (Administration) is in charge of all primary and high schools in the district reports administratively to the Zilla Panchayat and Deputy Director of Public Instruction (DDPI) (Academic) is giving academic support to school education. Both DDPI's are responsible to the Commissioner for Public Instruction at the state level.

DTERT

Directorate of Teacher Education, Research and Training (DTERT), Tamil Nadu - The State Institute of Education was established in 1965 to provide for systematic study of problems relating to school education.

The D.T.E.R.T. undertook State-wise projects to introduce new concepts like minimum levels of learning and competency based education. The D.T.E.R.T revised the syllabus of the Diploma in Teacher Education Two years course. It undertook special programmes in popularizing population education.

SSA

Sarva Shiksha Abhiyan (SSA) is Government of India's flagship programme for achievement of Universalization of Elementary Education (UEE) in a time bound manner, as mandated by 86th amendment to the Constitution of India making free and compulsory Education to the Children of 6-14 years age group, a Fundamental Right.

SSA is being implemented in partnership with State Governments to cover the entire country and address the needs of 192 million children in 1.1 million habitations.

The programme seeks to open new schools in those habitations which do not have schooling facilities and strengthen existing school infrastructure through provision of additional class rooms, toilets, drinking water, maintenance grant and school improvement grants.

Existing schools with inadequate teacher strength are provided with additional teachers, while the capacity of existing teachers is being strengthened by extensive training, grants for developing teaching-learning materials and strengthening of the academic support structure at a cluster, block and district level.

SSA seeks to provide quality elementary education including life skills. SSA has a special focus on girl's education and children with special needs. SSA also seeks to provide computer education to bridge the digital divide.

Unit-VI

Sociology and Education

The Meaning of Sociology

Sociology is a branch of the social sciences that uses systematic methods of empirical investigation and critical analysis to develop and refine a body of knowledge about human social structure and activity, sometimes with the goal of applying such knowledge to the pursuit of social welfare. Its subject matter ranges from the micro level of face-to-face interaction to the macro level of societies at large.

Sociology is a broad discipline in terms of both methodology and subject matter. Its traditional focuses have included social relations, social stratification, social interaction, culture and deviance, and its approaches have included both qualitative and quantitative research techniques. As much of what humans do fits under the category of social structure or social activity, sociology has gradually expanded its focus to such far-flung subjects as the study of economic activity, health disparities, and even the role of social activity in the creation of scientific knowledge. The range of social scientific methods has also been broadly expanded. The "cultural turn" of the 1970s and 1980s brought more humanistic interpretive approaches to the study of culture in sociology. Conversely, the same decades saw the rise of new mathematically rigorous approaches, such as social network analysis.

Its Relation to Education

The sociology of education is the study of how public institutions and individual experiences affects education and its outcome. It is most concerned with the public schooling systems of modern industrial societies, including the expansion of higher, further, adult, and continuing education.

Education has always been seen as a fundamentally optimistic human endeavour characterised by aspirations for progress and betterment. It is understood by many to be a means of overcoming handicaps, achieving greater equality and acquiring wealth and status. Education is perceived as a place where children can develop according to their unique needs and potential. It is also perceived as one of the best means of achieving greater social equality. Many would say that the purpose of education should be to develop every individual to their full potential and give them a chance to achieve as much in life as their natural abilities allow (meritocracy). Few would argue that any education system accomplishes this goal perfectly. Some take a particularly negative view, arguing that the education system is designed with the intention of causing the social reproduction of inequality.

Education for Changing Indian Society

Following India's independence a number of rules were formulated for the backward Scheduled Castes and the Scheduled Tribes of India, and in 1960 a list identifying 405 Scheduled Castes and 225 Scheduled Tribes was published by the central government. An amendment was made to the list in 1975, which identified 841 Scheduled Castes and 510 Scheduled Tribes. The total percentage of Scheduled Castes and Scheduled Tribes combined was found to be 22.5 percent with the Scheduled Castes accounting for 17 percent and the Scheduled Tribes accounting for the remaining 7.5 percent. Following the report many Scheduled Castes and Scheduled Tribes increasingly referred to themselves as *Dalit*, a Marathi language terminology used by B. R. Ambedkar which literally means "oppressed".

The Scheduled Castes and Scheduled Tribes are provided for in many of India's educational programmes. Special reservations are also provided for the Scheduled Castes and

Scheduled Tribes in India, e.g. a reservation of 15% in *Kendriya Vidhyala* for Scheduled Castes and another reservation of 7.5% in *Kendriya Vidhyala* for Scheduled Tribes. Similar reservations are held by the Scheduled Castes and Scheduled Tribes in many schemes and educational facilities in India. The remote and far-flung regions of North East India are provided for under the Non Lapsable Central pool of Resources (NLCPR) since 1998-1999. The NLCPR aims to provide funds for infrastructure development in these remote areas.

The government objective for the *Sarva Shiksha Abhiyan* (SSA), started in 2001, is to provide education to children between 6–14 years by 2010. The programme focuses specially on girls and children with challenged social or financial backgrounds. The SSA also aims to provide practical infrastructure and relevant source material in form of free textbooks to children in remote areas. The SSA also aims at widening computer education in rural areas. However, some objectives of the SSA, e.g. enrolment of all children under the scheme in schools by 2005 remain unfulfilled. Education Guarantee Scheme and Alternative and Innovative Education are components of the SSA.

Women from remote, underdeveloped areas or from weaker social groups in Andra Pradesh, Assam, Bihar, Jharkhand, Karnataka, Kerala, Gujarat, Uttar Pradesh, and Uttarakhand, fall under the *Mahila Samakhya Scheme*, initiated in 1989. Apart from provisions for education this programme also aims to raise awareness by holding meetings and seminars at rural levels. The government allowed 340 million rupees during 2007–08 to carry out this scheme over 83 districts including more than 21, 000 villages. Currently there are 68 *Bal Bhavans* and 10 *Bal Kendra* affiliated to the *National Bal Bhavan*. The scheme involves educational and social activities and recognising children with a marked talent for a particular educational stream. A number of programmes and activities are held under this scheme, which also involves cultural exchanges and participation in several international forums.

India's minorities, especially the ones considered 'educationally backward' by the government, are provided for in the 1992 amendment of the Indian National Policy on Education (NPE). The government initiated the Scheme of Area Intensive Programme for Educationally Backward Minorities and Scheme of Financial Assistance or Modernisation of Madarsa Education as part of its revised Programme of Action (1992). Both these schemes were started nationwide by 1994. In 2004 the Indian parliament allowed an act which enabled minority education establishments to seek university affiliations if they passed the required norms.

Concept of Culture—Salient Features of Indian Culture

The term culture refers to a state of intellectual development or manners. The social and political forces that influence the growth of a human being is defined as culture.

Indian culture is rich and diverse and as a result unique in its very own way. Our manners, way of communicating with one another, etc. are one of the important components of our culture. Even though we have accepted modern means of living, improved our lifestyle, our values and beliefs still remain unchanged. A person can change his way of clothing, way of eating and living but the rich values in a person always remains unchanged because they are deeply rooted within our hearts, mind, body and soul which we receive from our culture.

Indian culture treats guests as god and serves them and takes care of them as if they are a part and parcel of the family itself. Even though we don't have anything to eat, the guests are never left hungry and are always looked after by the members of the family. Elders and the respect for elders is a major component in Indian culture. Elders are the driving force for any family and hence the love and respect for elders comes from within and is not artificial. An individual takes blessings from his elders by touching their feet. Elders drill and pass on the Indian culture within us as we grow.

"Respect one another" is another lesson that is taught from the books of Indian culture. All people are alike and respecting one another is ones duty. In foreign countries the relation between the boss and the employee is like a master and slave and is purely monetary whereas in Indian culture the relation between the boss and the employee is more like homely relations unlike foreign countries.

Helpful nature is another striking feature in our Indian culture. Right from our early days of childhood we are taught to help one another in need of help and distress. If not monetary then at least in kind or non-monetary ways. Indian culture tells us to multiply and distribute joy and happiness and share sadness and pain. It tells us that by all this we can develop cooperation and better living amongst ourselves and subsequently make this world a better place to live in.

Ancient civilization in India reveals marvellous facts about our heritage. It is a eye opener as to how kingdoms ruled and how people went about life in a logical way. Though medieval, it is actually amazing to find how people transacted and went about building dams and tended to the chief occupation which was agriculture. Dance and rituals were always a part of Indian culture and this was the chief mode of entertainment.

Indian culture is also about respecting elders, honouring heroes and cherishing love. It is a land of aspirations, achievements and self reliance. Indian culture has a very high level of tolerance and hence the advent of so many external cultures was not restricted. Adaptation to any culture or embracing a religion was always the democratic culture. Indian history is about war heroes during Indus valley civilization and the initial time when currency was coined. Indian history talks a lot about self reliance especially in terms of food and agricultural produce. This was the great effort put in by the farmers and support received through irrigation. The modern agriculture also shows a lot of indigenous methods of preserving the produce. The Chola dynasty, the great King Emperor Ashoka and the secular era of Emperor Akbar will always be green in our memory. Several books are written on the rich Indian culture wherein the saints preserved the Vedas and scriptures.

There are shlokas and mantras i.e. chants that can evoke positive energy and revoke enthusiasm in life. The rich culture of yoga as a part of life and the goodness of ayurveda has now got an universal lifestyle approach. Our roots are strong and despite the westernization and access to technology, the distinct Indianness is still maintained whilst celebrating Diwali or observing the Shravan fast. This is also believed to be a land of Lord Rama which is Ayodhya or the birthplace of Sri Krishna is considered as Mathura. The birth of Sikh religion and the reverence felt by all Indians is still intact. Indians are extremely secular and especially in the metros there is seamless blending of Indians during Xmas and Id. Ethnic charm is exuded in simple outfits in India. The tropical climate is well adapted to the range of muslins and cottons. The mixed variety in cotton goes from viscose, polycot and also cotton silk which has a sheen of its own. Attires are very much about the region and climate. The Himalayan costume is suited for the environment where the dress is a blanket wrap in red and black secured with a ethnic pin. The ornaments or jewellery is a festive adornment with a big red bindi to complete the outfit.

The sari happens to be the most versatile drape with its amazing styles of draping and design. The sari is the traditional dress of India which also modifies as per material, drape and style with each region. This has also gone up to international drape style followed by ranking designers on the ramp shows. The chungari sari of the south has the tie and dye pattern that finds its counterpart in the bandhi print of Gujarat. There are embroidery types that seem to be the intrinsic talent of certain regions.

The cardigans and shawls are hand-woven from the North especially the Himachal and Arunachal belt. This displays the rich handicraft culture of India. The modernization in winter wear is seen with details like pockets, zippers, blends of fabrics and easy feel wear. The gota work of Rajashtan and Punjab is skilled golden zari strips woven or fixed on to the main garment like a sari or the dupatta. The most comfortable dress is the salwar kameez that radiates Indianness and is also comfortable.

The south Indian Kerala set-saree is the beautiful print in cream and golden which can be teamed with coloured blouses. The navvari sari or the nine yard drape of Maharashtra is usually found in leaf green colour that is symbolic of the newly married bride. The colours also seem to be in mauve, red or blues and the sarees happen as Narayan peth, paithani and various other Belgaum prints.

The padavai is the ghagra choli for young girls in the south that is incomplete without the gold jewellery especially the kaashi gold chain and jhumki earrings. This is also modified as ghagra choli is simple cottons for daily wear in the villages and designed as the lehenga choli in designer wear in the metros. Tradition in India is about values that transcend down generations automatically. These are genetic traits and simplicity is the main ingredient. Ancient culture believed in a lot of dogmas and rituals that can be termed as false beliefs and Indians are an intelligent lot to traverse these paths and modify the social requirements. Indians are highly flexible in the sense they would like to imbibe the changes dictated by western influence and yet clearly affirm their belief in traditions.

It is customary to respect elders and touch their feet as to seek their blessings. Occasions or festivals demand a lot of participation in terms of rangoli drawing, diyas and an array of yummy treats made in the authentic variety as per the caste and geography. Hindu rituals are a lot about song and dance and each family has a natural way to adjust to these formats. It is a ritual to pray to the Goddess of learning Ma Saraswathi to achieve success. Similarly business people always insist on drawing the Swastika which marks prosperity and worship the Goddess of wealth.

With the advent of technology and women emancipation there is a trend to mingle free with the western concepts of dress, belief, work and also get into a secular concept. But one can feel a distinct Indianness and most of our brethren abroad miss their homeland. Indians all over the world are known for their hospitality and high level of tolerance. Their adaptation power is high and hence they are able to scale heights in the international arena. Putting oneself on the global map, Indians are seeking new vistas of communicating their beliefs and tradition. The gift of health and well being through yoga and meditation is a great source of Vedas in the rich Hindu tradition which has actually benefited the world.

The values in India is about living life with a zest and observing the belief that there is one God prevailing despite so many religions.

Respecting elders, understanding cross culture traditions, free mingling to accommodate tolerance, staying interested in rural welfare are the values of India. The artifacts, cuisine handicrafts, attire and lifestyle of the rural folks is still followed and preserved by Indians. Family is about joy and sharing. In India, the family culture is all about love and patience. A girl weds into a family and adjusts herself seamlessly to the rituals, routine and cuisine. Of late, one can see a lot of love marriages i.e. cross border mingling which is also being accepted by the elders in the family. Association with religious beliefs and sects is also followed by families as many families believe in a particular Guru or saint who guides them in their spiritual path. Families are also getting nuclear owing to independent lifestyle preference and also the concept where in both husband and wife is working and has demanding careers. This is quite common in metros where families are independent in their upbringing and yet love and respect the elders who reside separately. The earlier homes housed themselves together in very large families where one can actually see three or four generations put up together.

Certain families observe a matriarchal concept i.e. the groom resides in the house of the bride or also follows a tradition as per the bride's ancestors. Generally India is patriarchal in the sense the children get the surname of the father and the wife changes her surname to follow that of the husbands. It is also a tradition in certain families that the wife changes her maiden name but again this concept is also changing. Indian families are very accommodating and willing to accept change. It is a concept to observe the karva chauth or the raksha bandhan with great aplomb. There is an occasion for gifting and seeking the blessings of elders. It is important to respect and hold certain family traditions which are unique in terms of cooking, rituals and beliefs. Families give a lot of importance to lighting the diya in the evening and also each person in family has a habit of doing the puja in his own way.

Metros are also seeing a lot of family value in celebrating birthdays and anniversaries by observing the rituals and also entertaining outdoors. The Indian culture has imbibed the right mix of western influence and yet maintaining the ethnic family tradition. There is more love in every family while blowing candles on the birthday cake and also lighting the diya to observe an Aarti for the birthday person.

Education for Preservation

Historic preservation or heritage conservation is a professional endeavour that seeks to preserve, conserve and protect buildings, objects, landscapes or other artifacts of historic importance. Other names for the discipline include "urban conservation," "landscape preservation," "built environment conservation," "built heritage conservation," "object conservation," and "immovable object conservation."

Transmission and Development of Culture

Cultures and subcultures have developed over the ages. Education has played a major part in the continuation as well as in the renewal of existing cultures by way of cultural transmission. What has been the role of families, schools, and youth cultures in the transmission of knowledge, values and attitudes? In what ways have social and political structures and power relations determined the content and features of educational processes and vice versa? Why have certain elements of a culture been transmitted within the official educational institutions, and why have other elements been neglected or systematically suppressed? Can contemporary concepts, inspired for instance by Bourdieu, Elias or Foucault, be used to gain a better understanding of past pedagogical phenomena? why the new history of education covering more than just school education and is not commonly acknowledged.

Education for Social Change

The role of education as an agent or instrument of social change and social development is widely recognized today. Social change may take place – when humans need change.

When the existing social system or network of social institutions fails to meet the existing human needs and when new materials suggest better ways of meeting human needs. According to Maclver social change takes place as a response to many types of changes that take place in the social and nonsocial environment. Education can initiate social changes by bringing about a change in outlook and attitude of man. It can bring about a change in the pattern of social relationships and thereby it may cause social changes.

Earlier educational institutions and teachers used to show a specific way of life to the students and education was more a means of social control than an instrument of social change. Modern educational institutions do not place much emphasis upon transmitting a way of life to the students. The traditional education was meant for an unchanging static society not marked by any change. But today education aims at imparting knowledge. Education was associated with religion. It has become secular today. It is an independent institution now. Education has been chiefly instrumental in preparing the way for the development of science and technology. Education has brought about phenomenal changes in every aspect of men's life. Francis J.Brown remarks that education is a process which brings about changes in the behaviour of society. It is a process which enables every individual to effectively participate in the activities of society and to make positive contribution to the progress of society.

Modernization

Modernization is a process of socio-cultural transformation. It is a thorough going process of change involving values, norms, institutions and structures. Political dimensions of modernization involves creation of a modern nation state and the development of key institutions political parties, bureaucratic structures, legislative bodies and a system of elections based on universal franchise and secret ballot. Cultural modernization involves adherence to nationalistic ideology, belief in equality, freedom and humanism, a rational and scientific outlook. Economic modernization involves industrialization accompanied with monetization of economy, increasing division of labour, use of management techniques and improved technology and the expansion of service sector. Social modernization involves universalistic values, achievement motivation, increasing mobility both social and geographic increasing literacy and urbanization and the decline of traditional authority. The secular and scientific education act as an important means of modernization. It helps in the diffusion of modern values of equality, freedom and humanism. The modern school system can inculcate achievement motivation. These values can form the basis of new relations in the society and growth of rationality can enable the development of administrative system. Diffusion of values of equality, freedom and humanism can lay the foundations of a democratic political system. The spread of modern education in the second half of the 19th century led to the emergence of modern political elite in India who provided leadership in the freedom struggle. The diffusion of scientific and technical knowledge by modern educational institutions can help in the creation of skilled manpower to play the occupational roles demanded by the industrial economy. Other values like individualism and universalistic ethics etc. can also be inculcated through education. Thus education can be an important means of modernization. The importance of education can be realized from the fact that all modernizing societies tend to emphasize on universalization of education and the modernized societies have already attained it.

Economic Development

Prior to the nineteenth century, systematic investment in human capital was not considered specially important in any country. Expenditures on schooling, on-the-job training, and other similar forms of investment were quite small. This began to change radically during this century with the application of science to the development of new goods and more efficient methods of production, first in Great Britain, and then gradually in other countries. During the twentieth century, education, skills, and the acquisition of knowledge have become crucial determinants of a person's and a nation's productivity. One can even call the twentieth century the "Age of Human Capital" in the sense that the primary determinant of a country's standard of living is how well it succeeds in developing and utilizing the skills and knowledge, and furthering the health and educating the majority of its population.

The past decades have seen extraordinary expansions in access to basic education throughout the Middle East. Many countries are now on the brink of a further increase in access to secondary and higher education and in effecting spectacular improvements in the quality of education offered at all levels. As increasing numbers of students complete their basic education, their demand for education at higher levels is similarly increasing. Educating girls and women is probably the single most effective investment a developing country can make, whether or not women work outside the home. It creates a multitude of positive remunerations for families including better family health and nutrition, improved birth spacing, lower infant and child mortality, and enhanced educational attainment of children. Countries in the Middle East are increasingly integrated in world markets for manufactured goods. Their ability to compete in these markets and in globalizing service markets will depend on the excellence of human capital they bring to the competition. Ensuring that all citizens are educated and numerate, that many possess a wide range of problem solving skills beyond the basic level, and that some have world class professional skills will necessitate new curricula, improved teacher programs, and academic methods that encourage higher order cognitive skills.

No country has achieved constant economic development without considerable investment in human capital. Previous studies have shown handsome returns to various forms of human capital accumulation: basic education, research, training, learning-by-doing and aptitude building. The distribution of education matters. Unequal education tends to have a negative impact on per capita income in most countries. Moreover, controlling for human capital distribution and the use of appropriate functional form specifications consistent with the asset allocation model make a difference for the effects of average education on per capita income, while failure to do so leads to insignificant and even negative effects of average education. Investment in human capital can have little impact on growth unless people can use education in competitive and open markets. The larger and more competitive these markets are, the greater are the prospects for using education and skills. In the earlier neoclassical models, education was not considered a major input for production and hence was not included in growth models (Harberger, 1998: 1-2). In the 1960s mounting empirical evidence stimulated the "human investment revolution in economic thought" (Bowman, 1960). The seminal works of (Schultz, 1961) and (Denison, 1962: 67) led to a series of growth accounting studies pointing to education's contribution to the unexplained residuals in the economic growth of western economies. Other studies looked at the impact of education on earnings or estimated private rate of returns (Becker 1964, Mincer 1974). A 1984 survey of growth accounting studies covering 29 developing countries found estimates of education's contribution to economic growth ranging from less than 1 percent in Mexico to as high as 23 percent in Ghana (Psacharopoulos, 1984).

Education and Productivity

Clearly the educational provisions within any given country represent one of the main determinants of the composition and growth of that country's output and exports and constitute an important ingredient in a system's capacity to borrow foreign technology effectively. For example: health and nutrition, and primary and secondary education all raise the productivity of workers, rural and urban; secondary education, including vocational, facilitates the acquisition of skills and managerial capacity; tertiary education supports the development of basic science, the appropriate selection of technology imports and the domestic adaptation and development of technologies; secondary and tertiary education also represent critical elements in the development of key institutions, of government, the law, and the financial system, among others, all essential for economic growth. Empirical evidence at both micro and macro levels further illuminates these relationships. At a micro level, numerous studies indicate that increases in earnings are associated with additional years of education, with the rate of return varying with high level of education (Behrman 1990, Psacharopoulos 1994). The returns to primary schooling tend to be greater than returns to secondary and tertiary education (Psacharopoulos, 1994: 1325-45).

In agriculture, evidence suggests positive effects of education on productivity among farmers using modern technologies, but less impact, as might be expected, among those using traditional methods. In Thailand, farmers with four or more years of schooling were three times more likely to adopt fertilizer and other modern inputs than less educated farmers (Birdsall, 1993: 75-79). Similarly, in Nepal, the completion of at least seven years of schooling increased productivity in wheat by over a quarter, and in rice by 13% (Jamison and Moock, 1994:13).

Education is also an important contributor to technological capability and technical change in industry. Statistical analysis of the clothing and engineering industries in Sri Lanka, to cite just one example, showed that the skill and education levels of workers and entrepreneurs were positively related to the rate of technical change of the firm (Deraniyagala, 1995).

Education alone, of course cannot transform an economy. The quantity and quality of investment, domestic and foreign, together with the overall policy environment, form the other important determinants of economic performance. Yet the level of human development has a bearing on these factors too. The quality of policy making and of investment decisions is bound to be influenced by the education of both policy makers and managers; moreover, the volume of both domestic and foreign investment is likely to be larger when a system's human capital supply is more plentiful.

For a macro prospective, the 'new growth theories' aim to endogenize technical progress by incorporating some of these same effects, emphasizing education as well as learning and R&D. According to Lucas (1998), for example, the higher the level of education of the work force the higher the overall productivity of capital because the more educated are more likely to innovate, and thus affect everyone's productivity. In other models a similar externality is generated as the increased education of individuals raises not only their own productivity but also that of others with whom they interact, so that total productivity increases as the average level of education rises (Perotti, 1993). The impact of education on the nature and growth of exports, which, in turn, affect the aggregate growth rate, is another way in which human development influences macro performance. The education and skills of a developing country's labour force influence the nature of its factor endowment and consequently the composition of its trade. It has been argued that even 'unskilled' workers in a modern factory normally need the literacy, numeracy, and discipline, which are acquired in primary and lower secondary school (Wood ,1994).

Education and Income

There is also a positive feedback from improved education to greater income equality, which, in turn, is likely to favour higher rates of growth. As education becomes more broadly based, low-income people are better able to seek out economic opportunities. For example, a study of the relation between schooling, income inequality and poverty in 18 countries of Latin America in the 1980s found that one quarter of the variation in workers' incomes was accounted for by variations in schooling attainment; it concludes that 'clearly education is the variable with the strongest impact on income equality' (Psacharopoulos, 1992). Another study suggested that a one percent increase in the labour force with at least secondary education would increase the share of income of the bottom 40 and 60% by between 6 and 15% respectively (Bourguignon and Morrison, 1990). An investigation of the determinants of income distribution in 36 countries found secondary enrolment rates to be significant (Bourguignon, 1995:53-86).

Education may affect per capita income growth via its impact on the denominator, i.e. population growth. For example, a study of fourteen African countries for the mid-eighties showed a negative correlation between female schooling and fertility in almost all countries, with primary education having a negative impact in about half the countries and no significant effects in the other half, while secondary education invariably reduced fertility (Birdsall 1995, Behraman and Wolfe 1987). The three success countries in terms of reduced fertility, Kenya, Botswana, and Zimbabwe, had the highest levels of female schooling as well as the lowest child mortality rates (Ainsworth, 1995).

Education and the Family

Where does human capital come from? What constitutes a successful investment in human capital, either at the individual or national level? One has to start with the family. It is the foundation of a good society and of economic success. Families have differed over time, but they are still very important in the modern economy. To understand human capital, you have to go back to the family, because it is families that are concerned about their children and try, with whatever resources they have, to promote their children's education and values. Families are the major promoters of values in any free society and even in not-so-free societies.

Families make a variety of decisions. One is whether to have many children or to have fewer children. Also some try to do more for each child. As countries develop, the trend shifts very strongly toward the latter. Every nation that has developed has done that, some in remarkably short periods of time. Taiwan, for example, has a birth rate lower than the United States. Declining birth rates also characterize Hong Kong, Mexico, and Poland (Becker, 1998).

In the developed part of Turkey the average number of children that families have is lower than the less developed part of Turkey. This is related with the level of education level of families. On average, educated families, particularly educated women, have 1.4 children and uneducated families have 5.1 children in the eastern region of Turkey (Baloglu, 1998: 40-42). Thus, in order to reduce the birth rate and inequalities between these regions of Turkey, more importance has to be given to education. Greater education of parents, perhaps of mothers, tends to improve the treatment of children, especially the daughters. The gap between the education of sons and daughters is smaller when parents are more educated.

More educated men and women tend to invest more in their own health and the health of their children. Indeed, education may be the single most important personal determinant of a person's health and life expectancy. I will only mention a few examples of the considerable evidence for the link between education and health. The educated persons in the United States and other rich nations are the least likely to smoke. Smoking in the United States is now found in significant numbers only among those with no college education, and is especially common among high school dropouts. The educated persons in Turkey are mostly working most of the time. The uneducated people not in work usually sit in cafes and waste their times. Many of them smoke.

Education of the poor helps improve their food intake not only by raising their incomes and spending on food but also by inducing them to make better, healthier, choices. All the studies from different nations I have seen indicate that educated persons tend to consume a healthier diet even when the total amount spent on food is held constant. Of course, the relation between education and better health and life expectancy involves causation in both directions, for greater health and lower mortality also induce larger investments in education and other human capital since rates of return on these investments are greater when the expected amount of working time is greater.

Education and Trade

Some countries have successfully combined openness and investment in learning and education, forming a virtuous circle: openness creates demand for education, and learning and education make a country's export sector more competitive. Knowledge accumulation influences a country's trade performance and competitiveness (Grossman and Helpman 1989); trade, in turn, enhances knowledge accumulation, especially through imports (Ben David and Loewy, 1995). Lucas notes that to sustain any kind of knowledge accumulation, a country has to be outward-oriented and a significant exporter. Young and Keller find that trade itself cannot be the engine of growth, but rather must operate throughout some mechanism, such as the formation of human capital, to affect growth. A

World Bank study found that economic growth rates in a sample of 60 developing countries during 1965-87 were especially high where there was a combination of a high level of education and macroeconomic stability and openness (Tilak, 1989). The impact of trade openness on long-term growth thus depends on how well people are able to absorb and use the information and technology made available through trade and foreign investment. It is widely accepted that in order to adapt to an environment of stronger competition, and to a world emphasizing the role of information, knowledge and skills, advanced economies need continuously to upgrade the overall quality of their labour force.

Challenges: Access, Equity, Quality, and Speeding Up Reform

The economies of low-and middle-income countries have been growing at historically rapid rates. Progress in education-expanded enrolments and longer schooling-has contributed to this growth and so has helped to reduce poverty in developing countries. In 1990 a typical six-year-old child in a developing country could expect to attend school for 8.5 years, up from 7.6 years in 1980. In Eastern Europe and central Asia schooling for 9 to 10 years is the rule; in East Asia and in Latin America and the Caribbean primary education is almost universal. Countries in the Middle East and North Africa are making steady progress; so are those in south Asia, although they have a considerable distance to go. Sub-Saharan Africa is lagging; certain countries there are making gains, but overall, primary enrolment ratios are actually declining. Yet despite these substantial achievements in the world as a whole, major challenges remain: these are to increase access to education in some countries, to improve equity, to improve quality, and, where needed, to speed educational reform. In most countries, more children wish to go to secondary schools than are able to enrol, and the demand for higher education is in general increasing faster than the supply. The enrolment gap between the transition economies of Europe and central Asia and the members of the OECD is also widening as enrolment ratios decline in the former and rise in the OECD countries.

The issue of equity mainly affects several overlapping disadvantaged groups, including the poor, linguistic, and ethnic minorities, nomads, refugees, and street and working children. The different access that boys and girls have to the education system in some parts of the world is also very important because it contributes to gender differences later in life. The gender gap in expected years of schooling in now very small in most countries in Europe and central Asia and in Latin America. It remains large in the Middle East and North Africa and in south Asia, where it is not closing at all. The quality of education is poor at all levels in low and middle-income countries. Students in developing countries have a mean level of achievement below that in industrial countries, and their performance shows a much greater variation around the mean.

Delays in reforming education systems to keep pace with economic structures are most apparent in the transition economies of eastern and central Europe. Lags in reform can hinder growth; conversely, timely reform can pay off in terms of economic growth and poverty reduction, as evidenced by the East Asian countries that have generally invested heavily in basic human capital, both male and female.

Globalization

Globalization is a *'qualitatively new phenomenon'* of multi-dimensional nature posing a variety of *'complex trends'* in the economic, social and cultural fabrics of all societies. The above phenomenon and trends stemming from it have placed formidable challenges and changing demands of lasting consequences everywhere; humanity is at cross roads now; almost all people feel powerless to check the proliferating effects; there is a bewildering mixture of uncertainty, risk, insecurity, division and yet opportunity; millions of people move across borders in search of a better life, or any life at all. Globalization impacts on all conceivable facets of life, including education. Rapid developments in technology and communication are forcing changes within educational systems across the world as ideas, values and knowledge, vital to education, cross nation states and boundaries. There would be a new *'social universe'* (*phrase used by* Postone, 1996) in the days to come.

The World Trade Organization's (WTO) 'education agenda' is in the nature of facilitating penetration of education services by corporate capital. The key WTO agreement for this purpose, the General Agreement on Trade in Services (GATS) incorporates the aim of '*unleashing progressive liberalization of trade in services including public services like education*.' No area of social life would be exempt from the imminent '*businessification*' due to the vortex of corporate capital penetration; the '*value- form of labour*' (*phrases used by* Glenn, 2002) would certainly be different than now. In the changed context of GLP (*Globalization, Liberalization and privatization*), '*human labour becomes a commodity like all other commodities and is exchanged for wages*.' Consequently, education services would naturally be commercialized, privatized and capitalized (CPC); education would soon be wearing a new face-'modernized' for a 'knowledge economy' based on information technologies; its values, preferences and tastes would certainly be different. '*Old traditional modes of working, professional values, notions of public service, putting community needs before the drive for profit*' would become obsolete in the context of market, competition and profit making trends.

It is certain that the dawn of the new age in India and elsewhere ' will be characterized by unimaginable advances in knowledge and synthesis of knowledge, triggering major changes in the objectives, contents, and methods of higher education.'. The future of countries would be largely determined by their abilities to compete in a global market where industrial based economies are giving way to knowledge based industries. 'The educational need in the post-industrial society of the present ' is preparation for and involvement in life,' not mere graduation. The needed preparation can be achieved by enabling our learners to acquire appropriate 'knowledge, skills and the intellectual capacity to meet the challenges of accelerated change and uncertainty.' The demand of the emerging global society from the enterprise of education is quicker, cost-effective production of 'global citizens'- 'intelligent people with a broad range of skills and knowledge' excellently equipped for employment in 'a competitive, information based' techno-driven environment.

Unit-VII

Agencies of Education

Structure and Educational Functions

Home

Basic education is established by a national curriculum of basic and secondary education. On the basis of the national curriculum, schools compile their own curricula. Basic education covers grades one to nine. Basic education in Estonia is compulsory. According to the Education Act, every child reaching seven years of age on 1 October must attend school until basic education is acquired or until he or she is 17 years old.

Basic education is mainly taught at municipal schools (basic school classes at primary, basic and secondary schools). Local governments determine a service area for each school where it is obliged to guarantee all school-age children the opportunity to study. In exceptional cases, basic education can also be acquired at home. Besides day school, basic education can be obtained in evening schools (grades 5–9). This option is chosen by more than 1000 young persons annually.

For children with physical, speech, sensory or mental handicaps, and children with special needs, the state or local governments (depending on the governing authority) provide opportunities at special schools and classes. Estonia has 7 sanatorium schools (6 state and 1 municipal schools) for approximately 800 children. These schools follow the curriculum of basic education. The basic school curriculum has developed a support system for intellectually handicapped children. This forms the basis for special classes which function at 18 schools.

Simplified basic school curricula are currently being used by 27 schools and 28 classes at secondary schools and basic schools. The idea of placing handicapped children in normal schools is rapidly gaining ground. At basic and secondary schools the marking system ranges from one to five. '5' is 'very good', '4' is 'good', '3' is 'satisfactory', '2' 'unsatisfactory' and '1' 'failure'. Universities and private schools of higher education often use their own marking systems. Since this has sometimes caused confusion, various measures are being planned in order to unify the evaluation systems of different educational institutions.

Peer Group

A **peer group** is a group of friends that a certain person will try to impress to get thier bond, social status, and interests. Generally, people are relatively equal in terms of power when they interact with peers.

Developmental Psychology

Developmental psychologists Vygotsky, Piaget, and Sullivan have all argued that peer relationships provide a unique context for cognitive, social, and emotional development, with equality, reciprocity, cooperation, and intimacy maturing and enhancing children's reasoning abilities and concern for others. Modern research echoes these sentiments, showing that social and emotional gains are indeed provided by peer interaction.

Peer Pressure

The term 'peer pressure' is often used to describe instances where an individual feels indirectly pressured into changing their behaviour to match that of their peers. Taking up smoking or consuming alcohol underage are two of the best known examples. In spite of the often negative connotations of the term, peer pressure can be used positively.

Finance

A **peer group** in finance is any equity, mutual fund, or financial instrument that relates to another equity, mutual fund, or financial instrument within its respective asset class in terms of investment style, industry, or underlying asset composition.

Community

The Indian educational system has evolved since Vedic times and has developed on multiple fronts. The paths it has trodden sometimes overlap, and therefore tracing the history of education in India is a rather difficult task. The main sources for reconstructing social history such as archaeological finds, epigraphs, sculptures, accounts of foreign travelers and literature provide glimpses only of certain aspects of education, and tell nothing of vital matters such as modes of instruction, tests, degrees obtained, the number of students, the literacy rate, etc. Research in the ancient Indian educational system offers many challenges to rational thinkers, but the lack of sufficient evidence does not mean that schooling and group-or mass-education was non-existent. During Vedic times, education was limited to the *gurukulas* (the abode of the guru) in hermitages, where seekers of spiritual attainment, divine matters and traditional lore came in search of the guru. The stress was on self-discipline, contemplation, penance and absolute surrender. Instruction was typically individualistic. Slowly, institutionalized education systems came in vogue and group education was made available. The *agraharas* (meaning "leading to front" – "*agre harati* ") gained prominence, as both primary and higher education was imparted. The Sanskrit language was taught along with regional languages, and residential facilities were provided to teachers and students. *Agraharas* were found amidst clusters of villages. The *mathas* (monasteries) grew at important religious centres and attempted to assist communities of the region in socio-religious matters, in addition to providing free education. The *brahmapuris* or quarters of *brahmins* grew in big and small towns and developed their own method of educating students of the locality. The *shales* or temple schools were common in every village and attempted to fulfil local needs of literacy as far as possible.

Hermitages, temple-schools, Brahmapuris, and *mathas*, which existed and were found to be scattered throughout the state of Karnataka provide us with a few glimpses of the continuous educational system through the centuries.

Religion

With the origins of Hinduism and Buddhism in India, religion is considered to be extremely important. Of the two religions, Hinduism is infinitely more popular, with an incredible 82 percent of the population practicing it. Within this majority, there are significant differences in the belief systems and caste divisions. Although there is division in some areas of Hinduism, there are many areas in common. They will all go to the pilgrimage sites, coming from all over India and will-if they go to a Brahman priest for birth, marriage and/or death rituals-hear the same Sanskrit verses from hundreds of years ago. In the shadow of Hindu dominance, there are a few followers of other beliefs such as Christianity, Sikh and Buddhism.

- Hinduism
- Sikhism
- Buddhism
- Zoroastrianism
- Islam
- Christianity
- Jainism.

In India, religion is a way of life. It is an integral part of the entire Indian tradition. For the majority of Indians, religion permeates every aspect of life, from common-place daily chores to education and politics. Secular India is home to Hinduism, Islam, Christianity, Buddhism, Jainism, Sikhism and other innumerable religious traditions. Hinduism is the dominant faith, practiced by over 80% of the population. Besides Hindus, Muslims are the most prominent religious group and are an integral part of Indian society. In fact India has the second largest population of Muslims in the world after Indonesia. Common practices have crept into most religious faiths in India and many of the festivals that mark each year with music, dance and feasting are shared by all communities. Each has its own pilgrimage sites, heroes, legends and even culinary specialties, mingling in a unique diversity that is the very pulse of society.

School and Mass Media

Modernization in India Occurred in Two Ways

The early impact from the late 18th century and the 19th century led to some awakening which primarily aimed at abolition of certain social practices and reinterpretation of traditional religion. In the same period were set afoot certain developments, which led to a greater awakening of India later. The response-pattern of educated Indians to the phenomenon of Westernization that occurred from the second half of the 19th century had been different from what it was earlier. During the seocnd phase, modernization increasingly meant sense of nationalism and secularism. The changes that were introduced in education coupled with mass media led to the growth of new consciousness and structure of values. Some of the institutional developments which had a direct bearing on the creation of a "Great Tradition" of modernization (Yogendra Singh) were the growth of universalistic legal super-structure, expansion of education, urbanization and industrialization, growth of communication network, and growth of nationalism and politicization of society.

Talking of education, the system of education as introduced by the British has been both quantitatively and qualitatively different. Modern education is liberal in content and it is steeped in modern scientific world-view. Freedom, equality, humanism and denial of dogmas are the themes of this new education.

The means of imparting education has been the English language from 1835 onwards. The very means has been instrumental in the opening up of the vast store of Western knowledge to the educated people of India.

Apart from the content part, in structure also, education has been transformed. The first is the primary vernacular education. The second is high school and secondary education. From the very beginning, a contradiction existed between the primary and the college-university level of education on account of both the medium and the content of education. Regarding medium, the primary education is based on the vernaculars; whereas, the college-university education is based on English language. Content-wise the primary education primary aims at the imparting of rudimentary knowledge but not enlightenment.

Also, an interesting dimension to this structural change in education has been the social classes which made use of this development. Ritually superior classes and the economically poor strata of society seek only primary education. Logically, this has resulted in the bifurcation of society into two categories of people-the high and the low. In other words, a new creation has come to the introduced in the stratification of society. And this disjunction between the educated in English medium and the others in the vernaculars still continues.

The significance of education in the process of modernization can be analysed in three areas. From the content point of view it has been modernizing and liberal in nature. The literary content of the courses in humanities and social sciences is primarily drawn from the literatures of Europe after the 16th century and its themes are humanistic, secular and liberal. It is interesting to note that John Stuart Mill's eassy "on Liberty", soon after its publicaition, became a text in Indian colleges: Another interesting element in the content of education has been the emphasis on humanistic evolution of social, political and historical issues. This led to the sociological consequences of disenchantment with traditional education and even traditions. Study of subjects like history, geography, economics and political science draws the attention of students to the social and physical realities of the world as it is today, thus leading modern generations away from the traditional outlook and system of values.

Regarding the organization structure, the new system is quite different from the old. Teachers are appoinated on the basis of achievement in education, irrespective of caste or birth. In other words, the structure of the teaching profession has also come to be secularized. As already said this eduation has been divided into three levels leading to a new kind of separatism of society. The third feature of the education is the continuing growth of the whole system. The number of entrants to educational institutions as well as the education institutions have grown phenomenally. The percentage of girls going to schools and colleges has also increased. In states, schooling has been made free and compulsory till a particular age. Vocational and technical institutions have been started for the economic and social growth of the country. Despite these vast changes, the expansion of education has not led to any sociologically meaningful degree of mobility and change in stratification system. Higher education is still confined to the upper classes. Nearly 70 per cent of the people are still illiterate. The per-capita expenditure on education is very low.

Even then, education has been one of the most influential instruments of modernization of India. It has contributed to the growth of an intelligentsia which is eager for social and cultural reforms even till today. It has created a sub-culture of students consisting of elements of transition from tradition to modernity. The growth of strains in the sub-culture is an indication of stress of transition of the whole of India itself. Most important contribution of education has been the growth of new forms of rationally organized structures in the shape of schools, colleges and universities which serve as cultural networks for the transmission of knowledge and cultural categories which are modern in nature.

Continuing Education and Concept of Open University System

Over the past 15 years, there has been an increase in the number of institutions which are offering courses of study through distance education. Some of those institutions have adopted the models of leading distance education providers such as the Open University in Great Britain. The move into distance education delivery of courses has required many institutions to spend money on staff and in some cases, technologies for the delivery of their courses. The choices that one considered ten years ago for the delivery of education in external studies have largely remained unchanged in a time of rapid technological development, especially in computer based technologies. Even today most provision of distance learning materials rely on print and to a lesser extent audio or video supplementation. There have been some notable experiments with the use of computer based testing and some use of bulletin boards to deliver information to students. However, most of the effort has focussed on improving the printed product and improving the design which is presented by that product. This has meant that staff have been employed as instructional designers mainly focussed on print and there has been an increase in the use of printing technologies to deliver this form of product.

Distance Education—Floating University

Distance education, or **distance learning**, is a field of education that focuses on the pedagogy and andragogy, technology, and instructional systems design that aim to deliver education to students who are not physically "on site". Rather than attending courses in person, teachers and students may communicate at times of their own choosing by exchanging printed or electronic media, or through technology that allows them to communicate in real time and through other online ways. Distance education courses that require a physical on-site presence for any reason including the taking of examinations is considered to be a hybrid or blended course of study.

Unit-VIII

Problems of Indian Society and Education

Population Explosion

Is population explosion a boon or a curse? For the European developed countries like Spain and Italy, where the population is decreasing, this might be considered as a boon. However, for the developing countries like India, population explosion is a curse and is damaging to the development of the country and it's society. The developing countries already facing a lack in their resources, and with the rapidly increasing population, the resources available per person are reduced further, leading to increased poverty, malnutrition, and other large population-related problems.

The literal meaning of population is "the whole number of people or inhabitants in a country or region" (Webster's dictionary), and the literal meaning of population explosion is "a pyramiding of numbers of a biological population" (Webster's dictionary). As the number of people in a pyramid increases, so do the roblems related to the increased population. The main factors affecting the population change are the birth rate, death rate and migration. The birth rate is the ratio between births and individuals in a specified population and time (Miller, 253). The death rate is the ratio between the number of deaths and individuals in a specified population and time (Miller, 253). Migration is the number of people moving in (immigration) or out (emigration) of a country, place or locality. The population change is calculated by the formula:

***Population change** = (Births + Immigration) – (Deaths+ Emigration)*

The recent increase in the world population has been caused due to the following major reasons:

1. The increase in birth rates due to medical improvements
2. The decrease in death rates due to better medical facilities and advancements in the field of medicine.
3. Immigration to better developed countries due to several reasons like better job opportunities, war, and natural causes like hurricanes, earthquakes, and so forth.

India, being a developing country, has had to face several economic and political challenges. One of the most important problems is the population explosion. According to Geography.com.sg, "India's population hit 1 billion in May 2000, increasing the urgency for the country to moderate its population growth." Some of the reasons for this population explosion are poverty, better medical facilities, and immigration from the neighbouring countries of Bangladesh and Nepal. The population density of India in 1996 was about 287 persons per square kilometre (Encyclopedia Britannica, Internet). Several solutions to decrease the rate of population increase have been tried by the government, some successful, some unsuccessful. Although the rate of increase has decreased, the rate has not reached the satisfactory level yet. The population in India continues to increase at an alarming rate. The effects of this population increase are evident in the increasing poverty, unemployment, air and water pollution, and shortage of food, health resources and educational resources.

Reasons for Increase in Population

Birth Rate

a. *Poverty:* According to ABC News, India currently faces approximately "... 33 births a minute, 2,000 an hour, 48,000 a day', which calculates to nearly 12 million a year". Unfortunately, the resources do not increase as the population increases. Instead the resources keep decreasing, leading to making survival for a human being more and more competitive even for the basic necessities of life like food, clothing and shelter.

India currently faces a vicious cycle of population explosion and poverty. One of the most important reasons for this population increase in India is poverty. According to Geography.com, "More than 300 million Indians earn less than US $1 everyday and about 130 million people are jobless." The people, who have to struggle to make two ends meet produce more children because more children mean more earning hands. Also, due to poverty, the infant mortality rate among such families is higher due to the lack of facilities like food and medical resources. Thus, they produce more children assuming that not all of them would be able to survive. The end result is a mounting increase in the population size of India. Due to the increase in population, the problems of scarce resources, jobs, and poverty increases. Thus the cycle continues leading to an ever-increasing population that we see today. This cycle in fact might be considered as a positive feedback, in that the increase in one results in the increase of the other factor. As the poverty and the population both increase, the development of the country and the society seems even more far-fetched.

b. *Religious beliefs, Traditions and Cultural Norms:* India's culture runs very deep and far back in history. Due to the increased population, the educational facilities are very scarce. As a result, most people still strictly follow ancient beliefs. According to ABC News, the famous Indian author, Shobha De said, "God said 'Go forth and produce' and we just went ahead and did exactly that." In addition, a lot of families prefer having a son rather than a daughter. As a result, a lot of families have more children than they actually want or can afford, resulting in increased poverty, lack of resources, and most importantly, an increased population.

Another one of India's cultural norms is for a girl to get married at an early age. In most of the rural areas and in some urban areas as well, families prefer to get their girls married at the age of 14 or 15. Although child marriage is illegal in India, the culture and the society surrounding the girls in India does not allow them to oppose such decisions taken by their family. For many, giving a girl child in marriage is done not by choice, but rather out of compulsion. The poor economic status of tribal villagers is attributed as one of the primary factors responsible for the prevalence of child marriages in India. An example of one such incident was reported in Indiainfo.com. According to an article written by Syed Zarir Hussain on October 16, 2000, "Forty-two-year-old Rojo Tok, a tribal peasant in Arunachal Pradesh, was all decked up in local finery to wed Mepong Taku, a girl who will turn 14 this winter."

I was brought up in a very different environment and never had to worry about getting married at the age of 14 or 15. However, my parents turned their eyes away, when my maidservant's daughter was being married off when she was only 13 years old. I was very young, but my parents simply said, "That's just how things are with poor people" and I did not have a say in it. Due to the young age of these girls, they have more potential of bearing children, that is, since they start bearing children at a very early age, they can have more children throughout their lifetime. This results in the increase of the global fertility rate. Since these girls get married at a very early age, they do not have the opportunity to get educated. Therefore, they remain uneducated and teach the same norms to their own children, and the tradition goes on from one generation to the other.

Death Rate

Although poverty has increased and the development of the country continues to be hampered, the improvements in medical facilities have been tremendous. This improvement might be considered positive, but as far as population increase is considered, it has only been positive in terms of increasing the population further. The crude death rate in India in 1981 was approximately 12.5, and that decreased to approximately 8.7 in 1999. Also, the infant mortality rate in India decreased from 129 in 1981 to approximately 72 in 1999 (Mapsindia.com,

Internet). These numbers are clear indications of the improvements in the medical field. This development is good for the economy and society of India, but strictly in terms of population, this advancement has further enhanced the increase in population.

The average life expectancy of people in India has increased from 52.9 in 1975-80 to 62.4 in 1995-00. Although our near and dear ones would live longer, due to the increase in the population, the resources available per person would be much less, leading to a decrease in the curvature of the slope of development instead of a higher gradient.

In addition, abortion is not allowed by several religions that are followed in India. In fact, in Islam, one of the leading religions of India, children are considered to be gifts of God, and so the more children a woman has, the more she is respected in her family and society. As a result, although the measures to control birth are either not available or known to the public, the facilities to increase birth through medical facilities are available.

Migration

In countries like the United States (U.S.), immigration plays an important role in the population increase. However, in countries like India, immigration plays a very small role in the population change. Although people from neighbouring countries like Bangladesh, Pakistan and Nepal, migrate to India; at the same time Indians migrate to other countries like the U.S., Australia, and the U.K. During the 1971 war between India and Pakistan over Bangladesh, the immigration rate increased tremendously.

However, currently the migration in India is –0.08 migrants per 1000 population (AskJeeves.com, Internet), and is decreasing further. This is definitely good for India. This way, the population might eventually come close to being under control and more people may get better job opportunities and further education. For example, the students in my university from India, like myself, have better chances for job opportunities and better education outside India than we would have had in India.

Effects of Population Explosion

The current rate of population growth in India is 1.58% and the total fertility rate is 3.11 (AskJeeves.com, Internet). Although the total fertility rate has decreased, due to the increase in the total number of women between the ages of 15 and 44 (reproductive ages), the total number of births has increased. This has lead to the current enormous population size of approximately 1 billion. This has greatly hampered the development of the Indian economy. The amount of resources that could have been available to one person a few years ago now need to be shared between two people, which is not sufficient for either of them. The population increase has lead to air and water pollution, unemployment, poverty, lack of educational resources, and even malnourished women and children.

Illiteracy

Why do many poor children not attend school? The reply heard usually is that their families are so poor that they need their children to work to support their incomes, and that the government has been lax in establishing free education facilities at the primary level. No doubt these are responsible, but a little piece of news doing the rounds during the last few weeks points to another flaw that you probably never considered - millions of Indian kids are out of school because the places that were reserved for them by law were instead given to others like you and me. The schools that educate many of our most privileged children have in many cases received money and other aid from the government, in the process explicitly promising to educate the poor as well for free. But once their grants were made the promise to educate indigent children was conveniently shelved.

That may be about to change. In April the Supreme Court ordered the directorate of education in the nation's capital to investigate the compliance of government-aided schools with the original terms of their aid, and if the Delhi schools are found to be in breach of those terms, to begin enforcing them. Do the numbers. Hundreds of schools, and hundreds of seats in each school, add up to tens of thousands of children in the capital alone whose enrolment in these government-supported schools was paid for by grants and concessions from the state administration. And guess who really got the benefit of the education that was denied to these children? The wo/man in the mirror, that's who.

Ironically, this case - *Modern School versus Government of India and others* - landed on the court's desk partly as a result of litigation launched by some of the undeserving beneficiaries. Parents complained that continuous raises in tuition and other costs at these schools is turning education mindlessly commercial. Schools are registered as non-profit trusts and societies in India, thus explicitly accepting a public interest course for themselves. The parents believed that managements at most institutions were operating their organisations more like robber barons than like guardians of this public trust, often extorting money that wasn't even applied to improve the institutions where their children were enrolled. Angered and frustrated, the parents turned to the courts for relief from mounting costs.

In its ruling, the Supreme Court concluded that the director of education could oversee tuition fees at government-aided schools as well as set limits for such fees and other charges. Being government-assisted, these schools would have to accept some oversight of their compliance with the purposes for which the government provides support, usually by making land available cheaply. If the justices had stopped there, the parents would have responded with uniform cheer. But, to the stunned horror of school managements and the chagrin of many parents, the court went further than they had demanded, ordering that compliance with *all* the conditions of the government aid they've received must be fulfilled.

The high standards of these schools will be dumbed down by the poorer kids, we are warned. Separate - and of course, equal - facilities should be set up for poor children, it is argued in terms earily reminiscent of the segregationist tendencies of American education. Managements predict that the directorate of education will use this ruling to return to the old days of shake-downs and harassment over licenses and compliance, and all the 'reforms' of the past fifteen years will be washed away by this over-reaching ruling. Why can't the government just pay the cost of educating poor children at these schools, if it's so concerned about their education, the principals ask. Another proposal is for the schools to be allowed to simply buy off the land allotted to them at market rates today, and extricate themselves from the burden of having to provide freeships.

Gender Bias

A question of X or Y

A child's destiny can be determined by as simple a circumstance as whether his or her father contributed an X or Y chromosome. Pink or blue clothes. Guns or dolls. The provider and the homemaker. Female infanticide. The patriarchal system. The purdah system. The premium on virginity. Dashing bachelors and aging spinsters. What are they all about? They all revolve around the issue of gender bias. The fact is that people are treated differently depending on their gender.

Gender bias is so deeply ingrained in the system that the discrimination begins from the time a couple plans a baby. Today, science has advanced so far that it is possible to separate male and female sperm so as to predetermine the sex of a child. In some parts of the world the birth of a baby boy warrants a celebration whereas a baby girl may not be extended the same warm welcome. Despite the fact that India has crossed the billion mark in population, there will still be families with five daughters and the mother trying desperately to give birth to a son.

Reinforcing Gender Bias

If a boy cries, he is asked if he is a sissy. If a girl plays cricket, she is libelled a tomboy. Dr. Sushma Mehrotra, psychologist, recounts her experience. She says, "I know parents who were very upset because their five-year-old son brought a doll home. The child was just playing with a toy that happened to be a doll. They thought that the boy had a gender problem. The parents actually came for counselling, worried that the boy was showing such feminine interests." In this way, parents ingrain the idea into the minds of their children that behaviour can be gender-appropriate. Girls will encounter gender bias at almost every stage in their lives. Radha Shankar's father expects her to be home by eight in the evening, while no such restrictions are placed on her brother. Mr. Shankar says," It's not that I don't trust Radha or that I think she will do anything wrong if I let her out of the house after eight, but the fact is that people will talk if a girl is in the habit of going out for late nights. I don't want anyone to say such things about my daughter. With my son it's different because boys will be boys."

Dr. Mehrotra talked about the plight of educated women who are so frustrated because despite their qualifications, they are ultimately expected to fall into the traditional mould of wife, mother and homemaker. Take the case of Nalini Mansukhani. Her parents sent her to the best schools and she has done her MBA from a prestigious business school, but she is under intense pressure from them to get married. She says," It doesn't seem to matter to my parents that I'm doing so well in my job and that I have certain career aspirations. Marriage just does not figure in my plan right now. And I just know that they will see no harm in my being expected to give up my career if my prospective husband makes that a condition."

Gender Bias and Men

According to Dr. Mehrotra, " Femininity is restricted to girls." People tend to have a more indulgent outlook on girls acting like tomboys. However, the opposite is not true for boys. There is a stigma attached to a boy being effeminate. That is the reason why society has a tendency to doubt the masculinity of men who design clothes for women, or male make-up artists, or men who follow any profession that breaks away from the straight and narrow. Somehow, men who don't hold nine to five jobs with a salary cheque that puts food on the table are not deemed manly enough.

While most people believe that gender bias favours men, men have their own cross to bear. Even in these so-called liberated times, men are expected to go out and earn their bread and butter. The option of staying at home and looking after the children while the wife goes out to work is not open to them. They have this option only if they have the strength to withstand the gossip, the ridicule and the general disapproval.

Sujoy Matthew punctured his parent's balloon of expectation when he decided that he was not cut out to be a doctor, engineer, lawyer or an MBA. "I just don't know what I want to do with my life. I'm just trying out different things. I make enough money to cover my expenses so I'm happy. My parents have given up on me. They are embarrassed to tell people that I don't have a job and have even lied on occasion saying that I'm working or doing some course."

Anup Singh moved into his wife's house after marriage. He says, "I haven't heard the end of it even from my friends. It's actually so simple. At this stage, neither my parents nor I can afford to buy a flat. My wife has a house, so I moved in. Women have been moving into their husband's houses for centuries and it's never been an issue. People have to be practical."

Mrs. Khanna is looking for a groom for her daughter. She says,"I want my daughter to marry a man who can give her a secure future. I don't want her to ever worry about money or have to skimp and save." It would never occur to her that her daughter should be able to fend for herself.

Women should be educated so that they can learn skills to support themselves. The choice to work or not to work thereafter should be entirely their own. There are innumerable stories of widows and divorcees who have found that they are clueless about their finances and how to manage them without their husbands. It is not that women are incapable. It is just that they have given up the choice to participate.

Change begins at Home

Awareness about gender bias has slowly spread over time. But it will take a long time for this awareness to seep into the grassroots and translate into social change. The world has moved forward. Today, we have women astronauts, women prime ministers, even women wrestlers, but there are still millions of women who face these double standards at every juncture of their lives. Feminists have been shouting themselves hoarse, demanding equality for women. Some people believe that women and men can never be equal, just different. Yes, but different does not necessarily mean inferior or lesser in any way. Women must be provided equal opportunity and this is not a task to be left to the government or any organization or authority.

Social change begins at home. Parents have to learn to adopt an androgynous attitude towards bringing up their children. They shouldn't panic if their son prefers to play with dolls or their daughters decide they don't want to marry till they are thirty. Parents need to give both sons and daughters the chance to live their lives free from the fetters of gender bias.

Child Labour

Child labour in India is a human right issue for the whole world. It is a serious and extensive problem, with many children under the age of fourteen working in carpet making factories, glass blowing units and making fireworks with bare little hands. According to the statistics given by Indian government there are 20 million child labourers in the country, while other agencies claim that it is 50 million.

In Northern India the exploitation of little children for labour is an accepted practice and perceived by the local population as a necessity to alleviate poverty. Carpet weaving industries pay very low wages to child labourers and make them work for long hours in unhygienic conditions. Children working in such units are mainly migrant workers from Northern India, who are shunted here by their families to earn some money and send it to them. Their families dependence on their income, forces them to endure the onerous work conditions in the carpet factories. The situation of child labourers in India is desperate. Children work for eight hours at a stretch with only a small break for meals. The meals are also frugal and the children are ill nourished. Most of the migrant children who cannot go home, sleep at their work place, which is very bad for their health and development. Seventy five percent of Indian population still resides in rural areas and are very poor. Children in rural families who are ailing with poverty perceive their children as an income generating resource to supplement the family income. Parents sacrifice their children's education to the growing needs of their younger siblings in such families and view them as wage earners for the entire clan.

The Indian government has tried to take some steps to alleviate the problem of child labour in recent years by invoking a law that makes the employment of children below 14 illegal, except in family owned enterprises. However this law is rarely adhered to due to practical difficulties. Factories usually find loopholes and circumvent the law by declaring that the child labourer is a distant family member. Also in villages there is no law implementing mechanism, and any punitive actions for commercial enterprises violating these laws is almost non existent.

Child labour is a conspicuous problem in India. Its prevalence is evident in the child work participation rate, which is more than that of other developing countries. Poverty is the reason for child labour in India. The meager income of child labourers is also absorbed by their families. The paucity of organized banking in the rural areas creates a void in taking facilities, forcing poor families to push their children in harsh labour, the harshest being bonded labour.

Bonded labour traps the growing child in a hostage like condition for years. The importance of formal education is also not realized, as the child can be absorbed in economically beneficial activities at a young age. Moreover there is no access to proper education in the remote areas of rural India for most people, which leaves the children with no choice.

Cultural Lag

The Impact of Resource Depletion on Social Change in Post-Modern Society

Introduction

Describing socio-cultural change has long been a favourite subject of sociologists. One common criticism of modern sociology is that it often fails to address real problems with potential solutions. One possible opportunity by which sociologists might offer solutions can be found in the study of the underlying motivating factors behind social and cultural change. Cultural lag is one of the theories often used to describe these factors that influence cultural changes. William Fielding Ogburn wrote many articles on empirical sociological methodology. He was a strong proponent of the need to use the results for predictive tasks. Ogburn was also a critic of sociologists who were, in his view, mere reporters of social history (Ogburn, 1929, 1940,1957,). Ogburn first described the theory of cultural lag in 1915, although he began developing the theory as early as 1912. Ogburn's definition of cultural lag is:

" A cultural lag occurs when one of two parts of culture which are correlated changes before or in greater degree than the other part does, thereby causing less adjustment between the two parts that existed previously (Ogburn 1957)."

When Ogburn described socio-cultural change and culture in terms of "parts" he relied on a very common model of the day that compared society and culture to an organic model in which the various "parts" were analogous to the organs of the human body. Later Ogburn used the term to indicate a more mechanical model that likened society to machinery that ran either well or poorly depending on the state of the various "parts". While neither of these models remains in great favour, they do provide ways of looking at society.

The genesis of the theory of cultural lag can be found in Ogburn's fascination with social change and the factors that drive it. Ogburn sought answers to the questions like: why are cars running off the road on curves? Ogburn believed that the answer lay in the culture of road building. When the automobile was first introduced, roads were designed for horses and wagons and were narrow with sharp curves and corners. As the speed of automobiles increased, roads were not able to handle the capability of automobiles. The culture of road building (the socially defined concept of what a road should be) had to change. The period required for society to adapt to the increased speed capability of the automobile was Ogburn's classical description of technologically driven cultural lag (Ogburn 1950). I believe that Ogburn's theory of cultural lag can provide, with slight modifications, a solid foundation for looking at the impact of resource depletion in a post-modern society. Ogburn described societies in which changes are occurring rapidly and contrasts this to societies in which change is occurring slowly (Ogburn 1950). Generally, according to the theory of cultural lag, more examples of cultural lag can be found in societies in which change occurs rapidly than in societies where changes occur slowly.

According to Ogburn, four critical factors drive cultural change. These four factors are: invention, accumulation, diffusion, and adjustment (Ogburn 1950). Ogburn believed that as new inventions were introduced into existing society, maladjustment would occur and a period of adjustment would be required. This underlying idea forms the basis for the theory of cultural lag. Inventions can be formed in a society from within the society by awareness of new possibilities. The accumulation of inventions over time also results in new inventions as two or more ideas are combined. Alternatively, inventions can result from the diffusion of new ideas from other geographical areas. The experiences of Marco Polo and other explorers can serve as examples of the diffusion of ideas and inventions between geographical areas. Ogburn expressly rejected the idea that inventions must be mechanical or technologically based (Ogburn 1950, 1957). Ogburn uses India at the time of Buddha as an example of a lag in which religion was the primary motivating force behind a great deal of social change (Ogburn 1957). In post-modern society resource depletion, either through an exhaustion of natural resources or through the mal-distribution of available resources may become a more important independent variable than technology was in Ogburn's original theory.

Unemployment and Underemployment

- Economic reforms may have given a boost to industrial productivity and brought in foreign investment in capital intensive areas. But the boom has not created jobs. This was not unexpected. According to a report by the Washington-based Institute of Policy Studies (IPS), the combined sales of the world's top 200 MNCs is now greater than the combined GDP of all but the world's nine largest national economies. Yet, the total direct employment generated by these multinationals is a mere 18.8 millions -one-hundredth of one per cent of the global workforce.

- India's Ninth Five-Year Plan projects generation of 54 million new jobs during the Plan period (1997-2002). But performance has always fallen short of target in the past, and few believe that the current Plan will be able to meet its target.
- India's labour force is growing at a rate of 2.5 per cent annually, but employment is growing at only 2.3 per cent. Thus, the country is faced with the challenge of not only absorbing new entrants to the job market (estimated at seven million people every year), but also clearing the backlog.
- Sixty per cent of India's workforce is self-employed, many of whom remain very poor. Nearly 30 per cent are casual workers (i.e. they work only when they are able to get jobs and remain unpaid for the rest of the days). Only about 10 per cent are regular employees, of which two-fifths are employed by the public sector.
- More than 90 per cent of the labour force is employed in the "unorganised sector", i.e. sectors which don't provide with the social security and other benefits of employment in thc "organised sector."
- In the rural areas, agricultural workers form the bulk of the unorganised sector. In urban India, contract and sub-contract as well as migratory agricultural labourers make up most of the unorganised labour force.
- Unorganised sector is made up of jobs in which the Minimum Wage Act is either not, or only marginally, implemented. The absence of unions in the unorganised sector does not provide any opportunity for collective bargaining.
- Over 70 per cent of the labour force in all sector combined (organised and unorganised) is either illiterate or educated below the primary level.

- The Ninth Plan projects a decline in the population growth rate to 1.59 per cent per annum by the end of the Ninth Plan, from over 2 per cent in the last three decades. However, it expects the growth rate of the labour force to reach a peak level of 2.54 per cent per annum over this period; the highest it has ever been and is ever likely to attain. This is because of the change in age structure, with the highest growth occurring in the 15-19 years age group in the Ninth Plan period.
- The addition to the labour force during the Plan period is estimated to be 53 millions on the "usual status" concept. The acceleration in the economy's growth rate to 7 per cent per annum, with special emphasis on the agriculture sector, is expected to help in creating 54 million work opportunities over the period. This would lead to a reduction in the open unemployment rate from 1.9 per cent in 1996-97 to 1.47 per cent in the Plan's terminal year, that is, by about a million persons - from 7.5 million to 6.63 million.
- In other words, if the economy maintains an annual growth of 7 per cent, it would be just sufficient to absorb the new additions to the labour force. If the economy could grow at around 8 per cent per annum during the Plan period, the incidence of open unemployment could be brought down by two million persons, thus attaining near full employment by the end of the Plan period, according to the Plan.
- However, there appears to be some confusion about the figure of open unemployment. The unemployment figure given in the executive summary of the Ninth Plan, gives the figure of open unemployment at 7.5 million while the annual report of the Labour Ministry, for 1995-96, puts the figure for 1995 at 18.7 million. An internal government paper prepared in 1997 put the unemployment figure at the beginning of the Eighth Plan at 17 millions and at 18.7 million at the end of 1994-95. Perhaps the Planning Commission referred to

the current figure while the Labour Ministry figure referred to the accumulated unemployment backlog.

- Open unemployment is not a true indicator of the gravity of the unemployment problem in an economy such as India, characterised as it is by large-scale underemployment and poor employment quality in the unorganised sector, which accounts for over 90 per cent of the total employment. The organised sector contributes only about 9 per cent to the total employment.
- Underemployment in various segments of the labour force is quite high.
- For instance, though open unemployment was only 2 per cent in 1993-94, the incidence of under-employment and unemployment taken together was as much as 10 per cent that year. This, in spite of the fact that the incidence of underemployment was reduced substantially in the decade ending 1993-94.
- According to the Planning Commission, the States which face the prospect of increased unemployment in the post-Ninth Plan period (2002- 2007) are Bihar, Rajasthan, Uttar Pradesh, Kerala and Punjab.

Brain Drain

The Indian system of education follows a smooth hierarchy from basics to perfection. The school drop outs in India are very less as compared to other parts of the world. But still there remains a huge uneducated population that sometimes nullifies the effect of the good things that the intelligent minds of India do!

After completing their education in India, people often leave for foreign countries in search of better working environment and pay package on account of unemployment. This concept of taking education in a country but earning for another is known as brain drain. Asian countries have been a victim of such concept since the west opened up job opportunities for eastern countries. They get cheap and hardworking labour in this manner!!

Unemployment in India has been an overused excuse by the one's who are responsible for such brain drain and also by the ones who are desperately trying to contribute to the same. The opportunities inside the country suddenly seem small and worthless in front of the starry image of the west. More than anything else, better lifestyle and a developed country name to flaunt, has lead people into migrating their working areas from their native place to a western country. But the question remains is it really so starry as it seems? Are there seriously no "good" job opportunities in India? Well, had this question come a decade earlier the answer would have been a tragic yes, but today when many multi national companies are desperately trying to establish a branch in India, the verity differs! Going to foreign countries to earn can be beneficial for your native land only in case you are sending back money in foreign currency and adding to the countries funds and also going with an intention of returning.

Terrorism

Terrorism in India is primarily attributable to Islamic, Sikh, and Naxalite radical movements.

The regions with long term terrorist activities today are Jammu and Kashmir, Mumbai, Central India (Naxalism) and Seven Sister States (independence and autonomy movements). In the past, the Punjab insurgency led to militant activities in the Indian state of Punjab as well as the national capital Delhi.

As of 2006, at least 232 of the country's 608 districts were afflicted, at differing intensities, by various insurgent and terrorist movements.

a. Educational Problems : Equality of Educational Opportunity

The equalization of educational opportunities is essentially linked with the equality notions in the social system. The social system which intends to provide equal opportunities for the advancement of all has to make provisions for equal educational opportunities also. In modern industrial society education has become the main agency for socializing new born into law abiding citizens and productive members of the society. Formal education has become almost indispensable because to participate in economic production one needs to learn specialized skills which cannot be acquired through family or any other agency. Due to the indispensability of formal education in advanced industrial societies education is provided by the state as a matter of right for all its citizens. Formal institutions – schools, colleges and universities are organized for this purpose.

In most societies today legislations exist guaranteeing equality of the right of education. In fact to realize this ideal of equality of educational opportunities special efforts are made by the welfare states in industrial societies to provide compulsory education to the socially deprived. In developing countries like India state has assumed the responsibility to provide universal free education at the school level. Special policy measures have been developed to spread modern scientific secular education to rural areas and policy of protective discriminating has been adopted to encourage the traditionally deprived section like SC and ST to take to modern education. However in spite of the creation of a legal framework in most societies to ensure quality of educational opportunity such an ideal continues to be elusive in reality even in the industrially advanced societies.

Raymond Bourdon has investigated the problem of equality of educational opportunities. Bourdon has tried to analyze the relationship between social structure and educational attainment. Bourdon maintain that even if there were no sub cultural difference between classes the very fact that people start at different positions in the class system will produce inequality of educational opportunity. For example the costs involved and the benefits to be gained for a working class boy and an upper middle class boy in choosing the same educational course are very different simply because their starting positions in the class-system are different.

Bourdon also relates the costs and benefits of course selection to family and peer group solidarity. His work has important implications for practical solutions to the problem of inequality of education opportunity. Even if positive discrimination worked and schools were able to compensate for the primary effects of stratification considerable inequality of educational opportunity would remain.

Bourdon argues that there are two ways of removing the secondary effects of stratification. The first involves the educational system. If it provides a single compulsory curriculum for all students the element of choice in the selection of course and duration of stay in the system would be removed. The individual would no longer be influenced by his courses and remain in full time education for the same period of time. He argues that more the branching points there are in the educational system point at which the student can leave or choose between alternative courses the more likely working class students are to leave or choose lower level courses. The gradual raising of the school leaving age in all advanced industrial societies has reduced inequality of educational opportunity but the present trend indicate that his reduction will at best proceed at a much slower rate. Bourdon's second solution to the problem of inequality of educational opportunity is the abolition of social stratification. He sees moves in the direction of economic equality as the most effective way of reducing inequality or educational opportunity. As a result he argues that the key to equality of opportunity lies outside rather than inside the schools. Bourdon concludes: for inequality or educational opportunity to be eliminated either a society must be unstratified or its school system must be completely undifferentiated.

Problems Concerning Equality of Opportunities in Education

Education helps in establishing equality and ensuring social justice but the system of education itself can add to the existing inequalities or at least perpetuate the same. Inequalities of educational opportunities arise due to

- Poverty as the poor cannot afford to meet the expenses of education.
- Children studying in the rural schools have to compete with the children in urban areas where there are well-equipped schools.

- In the places where no primary, secondary or collegiate educational institutions exist children do not get the same opportunity as those who have all these in their neighbourhood.
- Wide inequalities also arise from differences in home environments. A child from a rural household or slum does not have the same opportunity as a child from an upper class home with educated parents.
- There is wide sex disparity in India. Here girl's education is not given the same encouragement as boys.
- Education of backward classes including SC and ST and economically backward sections is not at par with that of other communities or classes.

Attitude Change on Population Education of IX Standard Students

Population education is an educational innovation in response to population problems only about four decades ago, is now being experimented in over a hundred countries of the world. It has been introduced in the educational systems of different countries as an important component of the multi-pronged strategy employed to help nations in order to attain the goals of population stabilisation and sustainable development. The concept of population education emerged in the context of population and development-the two most pressing issues before humankind today. Both are closely interrelated and both encompass a number of complex factors.

Objectives

1. To study the separate and relative effectiveness of the three treatment groups in producing changes in attitude in the desired direction in sub-urban secondary school students.
2. To relate the initial attitudes and the changes in the attitudes produced by the treatments to sex and family size.

Method

Variables : The independent variable was the attitude change. The communication strategy employed in affecting attitude change took three treatment forms. Population education and family planning were the dependent variables. Recipient variables were also adequately controlled by systematic sampling technique and rotation design.

Population and Sampling

The effective sample for the experimental study consisted of 240 IX standard students drawn from sub-urban Zilla Parishad High School in Madhurawada, Visakhapatnam. Initially, 240 students were included. Due to the absence of some of them either for more than one session or for the post-test, finally 200 students were considered. The students were divided into three treatments groups, formed by systematic sampling, including every third name in the attendance registers in one group.

Procedure

Experimental method was adopted to change the attitude towards population education and family planning. All three strategies of verbal-visual, dramatized and combination of two strategies consisted of four kinds of activities each. The programme for attitude was planned to take four sessions, each of one hour duration, while actual treatment would take 45 to 50 minutes.

The rest of the time was to be used for report establishing, summing-up highlights, etc. The three treatments selected for the experiment were defined and designed. The tool used in the present study was developed, constructed and validated by Rao (1983). Visakha Students Attitude towards Family planning Scale (VISAF Scale) was constructed following the Linkert (1932) method.

Both Telugu and English versions were made with adequate control of language, though it was only the Telugu version that was administered. Pre-test was conducted and there was no time limit for answering the questionnaire. Detailed instructions were given for filling the questionnaire. After pre-test, experimental strategies were applied for the three treatment groups. Finally, post-test was conducted for the above three groups.

Statistical Analysis

Statistical software package (SPSS Windows version-11) was used to analyse the standard parameters like mean, t-test, standard deviation. The significance of acquiring more marks in post-test was observed. All the means of difference between pre-test and post-tests were positive, indicating gain in the direction of more positive attitudes in respect of all the treatments and the attitudes. The differences indicated that the quantum of change or gain were statistically significant in pre-test and post-test. All the treatments, therefore, proved to be quite productive and promising of change in attitude in the desired direction. All the mean differences between the final and the initial scores were positive. Hence, each of three treatments would produce substantial changes in the desired direction. In 200 samples of IX standard students of Zilla Parishad High School in Madhurawada area, a sub-urban of Visakhapatnam, boys (male) were 81 and girls (female) were 119. The small family size were numbered 73 where as large family were 127. Relationship between sex and family size taken as predictors on the one hand and the initial scores on the attitude scale taken as criteria on the other, was tested by the two-tailed 't' test for the significance of difference between means. Sub group mean followed by 't' values of differences between pairs of means. The differences by sex were not significant in any case.

Results

The effect of the three communication strategies (verbal-visual, dramatisation and combination) in changing attitude to population and family planning predicted that the three treatments would produce significant change in the desired direction. This was tested by the 't' test of significance of differences in means between initial and final scores on the attitude scales concerned. All the mean differences between the final and the initial scores were positive. Hence, in general, each of the three educational treatments produce substantial change in the desired direction. Hence, the research experiment was sustained in respect of the three treatments. All the means of the differences between pre-test and post-test scores were positive indicating gain in the direction of more positive attitude in respect of all the three treatments.

Wastage and Stagnation

Educationists in their zeal to say something different often fall back on the slogan of more socially productive manual work for school children. Some have even recommended reduction of school time to provide for more manual work and recreation in school. One of the arguments put forward for drop out, wastage and stagnation is the prevalent condition where the child helps the family in productive activities. If it is so, then instead of recognising that work for academic purpose, what good would it do to provide, soap, disinfectant, detergent powder, hair oil, brooms waste paper baskets', etc., are more socially productive manual work than helping the parents in food gathering, agriculture or cattle tending? Do the teachers have the competence to carry on 'experiment with different kinds of soil seeds and manure, vegetable propagation by breeding and grafting, making of jam, jelley, etc., bakery items, white washing of walls, door polishing, toy making, pottery and painting'? I am afraid that this will result in further polarisation of rural and urban, socially backward and the privileged. Lessening the school time will also harm the interests of the socially backward who cannot compete with children form middle class homes who have the benefit of home study. It is most unfortunate that educationists who are responsible for education being what it is are called upon to provide leadership for a new revolution. It is no wonder that they either play the number game dividing the school education in different permutations and combinations or in spite of paying lip sympathy to change become prisoners of old thinking and old habits.

So far midday meal is considered to be the prime motivating factor for children. The financial exercise made in the beginning of the Fifth Plan shows that the country's resources are not adequate to bear the entire burden of midday meals for all children. It is high time that alternatives, no matter in howsoever small measures, be sought to this helpless dependence on one incentive scheme. One suggestion is to convert a limited number of primary schools in each state on an experimental basis as parent-student education centres. Each school or cluster of schools should have craft teachers who could teach crafts to the mothers and sisters of the children enrolled. Teaching of craft, if imaginatively selected would not only be a motivating factor, but also can be self-paying. While the adult women can create interest in the children in work through their own examples, they can also read and write with them. Literacy for them, thus, would form an integral part of this education, which could benefit both adults and children. This way the community not only partly assumes responsibility for the education of their children, better integration of the home the education of their children, better integration of the home and the school could be achieved in the process. Women's literacy, and the enrolment of girls which is the lowest in the country could also be handled in a meaningful way through these centres. If this experiment in community biased human development succeeds, this can be further expanded and the character of primary education can be radically changed.

Traditional education has been a passive career of middle class values, through an arbitrarily chosen standard. Unless an academic strategy bridges the people' languages with the chosen standards the mosaic of values of a pluralistic society are unlikely to be reflected in education. The present education aims at the conversion of the past into the future. It does not bring both past and the future to the present. The present education system as well as the educationists do not appreciate the fact that experience is filtered through language and making this experience a cognitive structure is possible through evolving and implementing a rational language policy. Unless the new thinking veers away form the textbook centred teacher dominated class room instruction and accepts the learning child as the centre of curriculum, there is little hope of any qualitative change in the field of Primary Education.

Self Financing Pattern in Education

Knowledge is the driving force in the rapidly changing globalised economy and society. Quantity and quality of highly specialized human resources determine their competence in the global market. Emergence of knowledge as driving factor results in both challenges and opportunities. It is now well recognised that the growth of the global economy has increased opportunities for those countries with good levels of education and vice versa (Carnoy, 1999; Tilak, 2001; Stewart, 1996; Ilon, 1994). The benefits of globalisation accrue to the countries with highly skilled human capital and it is a curse for the countries without such specialised human capital. Developing and transition countries are further challenged in a highly competitive world economy because their higher education systems are not adequately developed for the creation and use of knowledge. Converting the challenges into opportunities depend on the rapidity at which they adapt to the changing environment. Though the higher education system and the pattern of financing in higher education vary a great deal across countries in terms of their size and strength and degree of diversification of higher education institutions, yet they all face a severe financial crisis in the public finances available for higher education.

India is no exception to this global phenomenon. As part of globalisation, the economic reform packages were introduced in India in the beginning of 1991. These reform packages imposed a heavy compression on the public budgets on education sector, more specifically so on higher education. Following the introduction of structural adjustment policies, that include macro economic stabilization and adjustment, a fiscal squeeze is experienced in all social sector investments in many developing countries, including in India. This has trickled down to public expenditure on education in general, and higher education in particular. With economic reforms, cuts in public budgets for higher education have been very steep, severely impairing the growth of higher education. Paradoxically, under the reforming economic conditions, integration of the Indian economy with world economy presupposes efficiency and competitiveness in the domestic front as well as in the international arena. As the process of globalization is technology-driven, and knowledge-driven, the very success of economic reform policies critically depends upon the competence of human capital. But, what is observed is the reverse. Even within the education sector, relative priority assigned to higher education has been on the decline. It is to be realized that higher education institutions play an important role in setting the academic standard for primary and secondary education. They are also responsible for not only providing the specialised human capital in order to corner the gains from globalisation, but also for training inside the country, provide policy advise, etc. With macro economic reforms resulting in severe cuts on the education budget on the one hand, accomplishing the long cherished goal of universal elementary education on the other hand, the government directs the shift of resources from higher to primary education. It can be noticed from the approach paper to the Tenth Five-year Plan and Tenth plan document that, "Since budget resources are limited, and such resources as are available, need to be allocated to expanding primary education, it is important to recognise that the universities must make greater efforts to supplement resources from the government" (Government of India, 2001, 2002-2007).

In a federal polity like India, education being concurrent subject since 1976, the commitment of the centre equally at all levels of education is important. Given the spill over benefits of higher education, it becomes mandatory for the centre to finance an increasing share of expenditure on higher education. But, this has been declining in the recent years. Even in secondary education, centre's share of expenditure is minimal ranging around 5 per cent. However, federal role in elementary education is on the rise since the middle of 1980s. Indeed, the momentum of interest in universalising elementary education began in the country in 1987 with a centrally sponsored scheme namely, Operation Blackboard to improve the educational infrastructure in primary schools all over the country. Around the same time another two important nation wide schemes have been initiated – on teacher education and non-formal education. As a result of all these efforts and initiatives by the federal government, the flow of plan transfers from central to statès in elementary education have improved since the late 1980s. It is to be realised that while primary education is fundamental to the nation, higher education determines its economic and technological progress in the globalised era, which are the necessary and sufficient conditions for growth and development respectively. Even for very low enrolment ratios in higher education in India, it is increasingly realised that public budgets cannot adequately fund higher education, particularly when sectors of mass education are starved of even bare needs. Hence, the resources from higher education are being diverted to the development of primary education. But it is stressed that while it is mandatory that the nation achieves universal elementary education and total literacy, it cannot at the same time afford to relegate to a neglected position to achieve global standards in higher education (UGC, 1993). With this perspective, the present paper attempts to examine financing of higher education in India during the previous two decades by looking at different sources of funds for higher education, highlighting the changes therein in terms of the hike in student fees, introduction of student loans operated by commercial banks and, rapidly increasing role of private sector and self-financing courses within public higher educational institutions.

Population Education

Population Connection's Education Program is the only national, population education program with a strong emphasis on teacher training for educators of grades pre-K through 12.

Since 1975, the program has developed age-appropriate curricula to complement students' science and social science instruction about human population trends and their impacts on natural resources, environmental quality and human well-being. We provide hands-on training to over 12,000 teachers and student teachers annually in North America. Tens of thousands of teachers are introducing important population concepts to their students using these outstanding resources and millions of students are benefitting from them.

With an emphasis on hands-on learning and balanced discussion of different viewpoints, our program has earned a reputation for educational excellence. All Population Connection curriculum materials are classroom-tested, rigorously evaluated and frequently updated to be leaders in their content and approach. They are interdisciplinary, well-suited for a cooperative learning environment and classroom-ready.

About Population Connection

Population Connection (formerly ZPG) is the national grassroots population organization that educates young people and advocates progressive action to stabilize world population at a level that can be sustained by Earth's resources. We believe that overpopulation threatens the quality of life for people everywhere. We seek to protect the environment and ensure a high quality of life for present and future generations. Population Connection's advocacy programs aim to influence public policies, attitudes, and behaviour on national and global population issues and related concerns.

What is Population Education?

It's all about people — how the human race has grown and shaped the world around us. World population has quadrupled in the past century, changing the way we use natural resources and function as societies. Population education is the ultimate multi-disciplinary field; it's ecology, human geography, anthropology, economics, biology, public health, sociology, environmental studies, history and civics all rolled into one, with a good bit of mathematics to help us understand where we've come from and where we might be headed.

How does Population Education fit in with my School Curricula?

Population studies are explicitly included in national and state content standards for science, social studies, geography and environmental education. The latest math standards emphasize drawing connections to real-world situations and integrating math with other subject areas.

Sex Education

A recent Reuters report brings up the question of sex-education in India's schools. Does educating school-going little kids about the carnal knowledge, help them prepare for safer sex practices, or does it make them go and try those newly-learned skills out before they are physically and psychologically ready? It's not an easy question to answer, and certainly an explosive political issue, considering the perpetual morality debate we seem to be having in our country. With 86% of this country's new HIV infections being contributed by unsafe sex practices, some more education on that front would certainly curb some of those HIV infections. On the other hand, there is a school of thought arguing that introducing the subject at the school level would somehow lead to Indian youngsters having sex at every posible corner.

Not that Indians need to know the basics of sex. Most fifth-graders probably already know what the government is trying to ban the teachers from teaching them. Television and Bollywood provide enough libidinous titillation to evoke curious questions about every possible aspect of carnal wisdom. So why the hullabaloo?

If the government really wants the schoolgoing kids to learn about sex but not to practise it, there is one real way to achieve this. Put all the sex-education in our mundane textbooks and then have the little children take long and hard essay-type exams on that topic, month after month, year after year. Make it a mandatory subject. Make those textbooks as boring as Geography or Science textbooks. Just suck all the fun out of it. Before long, India's schoolchildren will take such an aversion to sex that it will not only curtail HIV, it will also help limit the population as well.

Education for Gifted and Talented Students

In accordance with The Act of Special Education promulgated in 1984, gifted and talented students are divided into three categories- general abilities, scholastic aptitude, and special talents. Students of the first two categories are generally admitted into superior intelligence classes, while those with special talents are admitted into classes according to their individual talents (e.g., music, art, dance, athletics).

1. *Gifted and talented Student Classes:* In the early years, gifted and talented students were educated in

centralized special education classes. Since 1979, decentralized classes for gifted and Talented students were introduced. For example, in 1979 Taipei's Zhongxiao Junior High School introduced centralized classes to educate gifted and talented students of the general abilities category. Since the 1986 school year, decentralized classes replaced centralized classes. Gifted and Talented students were dispersed in four or five classes. In cases where students were grouped according to their scholastic abilities of different subjects (Mandarin, English, mathematics, and physics), they were taught depending on their abilities of the subject. The classes for these courses had to be arranged so that those gifted and talented students could attend the same classes at the same time. Currently, most general abilities and scholastic aptitude classes are resource classes.

Taiwan's first general abilities class was the centralized class for gifted and talented students established in 1971 by the primary school affiliated to Taichung Normal Junior College (the predecessor of National Taichung Normal College). The class reinforced students' Mandarin, math, and nature subjects with experimental courses. The centralized class selected gifted and talented students to form a class for special education according to students' abilities. A solid curriculum was designed to stimulate their creativity. Since 1979, in addition to the original centralized class, a resource class was introduced to provide gifted and talented students with guidance and assistance. It was called a decentralized class for gifted and talented students. As for students who excelled in scholastic aptitude, in 1979, Taipei's Zhongxiao and Datong Junior High Schools respectively introduced classes for gifted and talented students of the math and physics and language categories.

2. *Artistic Talent Classes:* Artistic talents fall into three categories- music, art, and dance. Experimental music classes were the first to be established. For example,

from as early as 1963, Taipei's private Guangren Primary School had an experimental music class. In addition, art classes were all centralized classes for gifted and talented students. Students were gathered together to form a special education class, with an emphasis on various kinds of artistic talents in order to cultivate outstanding artistic or performing individuals.

3. *Other Special Talent Classes:* Classes for students with special athletic abilities are most common.

In a word, one will find that special education has evolved from the earlier segregated special schools for the physically and mentally challenged, to centralized special education classes, decentralized resource classes, circuit guidance and assistance, and home education. In addition, past years' statistics have shown that more and more special education classes are transforming into resource classes for physically-, mentally-challenged students whose conditions are mild. Therefore, placement of special education students is moving toward the direction of blended education as advocated by the UN and international organizations.

Moreover, according to Article 13 of The Act of Special Education, "Educational placement of physically-, mentally-challenged students should meet the requirements of satisfying students' learning needs and minimized environment constraints. The office in charge of education administration of various cities and counties should each year reevaluate the adequacy of its educational placement." As a result, when deciding where to place a student, environment constraints are not the only consideration. The student's learning ability, social adaptability, scholastic accomplishments, and family needs, and parents' wishes also have to be taken into account. Moreover, to avoid causing harm to the student's body and mind as a result of wrong placement, the adequacy of the placement should be reevaluated each year. In case of wrong placement, the student should be reassigned immediately in order for the student to be placed in an environment best meeting his/her needs so he/she can fully develop his/her potential.

Special Education for the Challenged and Gifted

Special education is the individually planned and systematically monitored arrangement of teaching procedures, adapted equipment and materials, accessible settings, and other interventions designed to help either the truly disabled learners or those who are at-risk for school failures achieve a safe childhood rather than abuse in the past.

Students who are truly disabled such as those suffering from severe mental retardation are those whose needs are addressed within the special school. However, larger school districts are often able to provide more adequate and quality care for the truly disabled within their school system. This allows the district to save money on the cost of sending them out to a special school. Students who are at-risk for school failures due to learning differences, mental health issues , and giftedness are those whose needs are addressed within the regular school.

Providing access to basic education is a duty the Indian state that has taken upon itself. Therefore the government has taken various measures to provide access to education to all categories of students. Thus the differently able children are provided special education in India so that they can seriously engage in improving the quality of their life. With the advancement of technology, Special education in India for physically disabled or mentally challenged is also fast improving. But some recent research has thrown fresh insights on

Special education in India was present since the pre independence time, with very few schools or NGOs helping intellectually impaired children. Today India has come a long way and made a good progress in the field of disability rehabilitation. Presently India has four national institutes for effective implementation of this special education through various government schemes.

The popular national level institutes for disabled persons are the National institute for Hearing Handicapped, National Institute for the Mentally Handicapped, National Institute of the Visually Handicapped and National Institute for orthopedically handicapped. National Institute of Rehabilitation, Training and Research and The Institute for Physically Handicapped are other two national level institutes run by government.

Moreover, government has initiated District Rehabilitation Centre (DRC) scheme in ten states to make all-inclusive rehabilitation. Moreover, four Regional Rehabilitation Training Centres are there to train the staff and teachers who work with these institutes.

Today due to global competitiveness, education scenario in India is fast changing. Along with that, special education is also catching importance and various government agencies are working hard to make it available to masses. There are almost 37 diploma courses in the field of special education in India some of the institutes offer courses like B.Ed as well. All these courses are regulated and governed by the Rehabilitation Council of India (RCI)- a legislative body under the Ministry of Social Justice and Empowerment.

However over the years many scholars have questioned the importance of special education in India as they feel that it leads to segregation and isolation of the differently abled children. They argue that by segregating the children at young age the very purpose bringing all children to the mainstream of, the purpose of special education is defeated.

Therefore, to keep the special education at par with regular education, vocational courses are also initiated. Also, there has been a National Policy of Education, in which government has declared that education of children with gentle disabilities will be in regular schools. Due to such reforms and regulations, the quality and reach of special education in India has increased over the years giving new hopes and bright future for disabled.

Co-education

Mixed-sex education (also known as **coeducation**), is the integrated education of males and females in the same institution. The opposite situation is described as single-sex education. Most older institutions of higher education restricted their enrolment to a single sex at some point in their history, and since then have changed their policies to become coeducational.

Co-ed (or **coed**) is the shortened adjectival form of "coeducation", and the word co-ed is sometimes also used, in the United States, as a noun to refer to a female student at a coeducational college or university. This usage reflects the historical process by which it was often female pupils who were admitted to schools originally reserved for boys, and thus it was them who were identified with its becoming "coeducational".

The word is also often used to describe a situation in which both genders are integrated in any form (e.g. "The team is co-ed").

Main

Education of males and females in the same schools. A modern phenomenon, it was adopted earlier and more widely in the United States than in Europe, where tradition proved a greater obstacle.

Coeducation was first introduced in western Europe after the Reformation, when certain Protestant groups urged that girls as well as boys should be taught to read the Bible. The practice became especially marked in Scotland, the northern parts of England, and colonial New England, where young children of both sexes attended dame schools. In the latter half of the 18th century, girls were gradually admitted to town schools. The Society of Friends in England as well as in the United States were pioneers in coeducation as they were in universal education, and, in Quaker settlements in the British colonies, boys and girls generally attended school together. The new free public elementary, or common, schools, which after the American Revolution supplanted church institutions, were almost always coeducational, and by 1900 most public high schools were coeducational as well. Many private colleges from their inception admitted women (the first was Oberlin College in Oberlin, Ohio), and many state universities followed their example. By the end of the 19th century, 70 percent of American colleges were coeducational. In the second half of the 20th century, many institutions of higher learning that had been exclusively for persons of one sex became coeducational.

In western Europe the main exponents of primary and secondary coeducation were the Scandinavian countries. In Denmark coeducation extends back to the 18th century, and in Norway coeducation was adopted by law in 1896. In Germany, on the other hand, until the closing decades of the 19th century it was practically impossible for a girl to get a secondary education, and, when girls' secondary schools were introduced, their status was inferior to that of schools for boys. At present in many large municipalities, such as Bremen, Hamburg, and Berlin, coeducation at the primary level is the rule; at the secondary level there has been little change.

Antagonism to coeducation in England and on the European continent diminished more rapidly in higher education than in secondary. In England, Girton College at Cambridge was established for women in 1869, and the London School of Economics was opened to women in 1874. Germany permitted women to matriculate in 1901, and by 1910 women had been admitted to universities in The Netherlands, Belgium, Denmark, Sweden, Switzerland, Norway, Austria-Hungary, France, and Turkey.

Since World War II, coeducation has been adopted in many developing countries; China and Cuba are outstanding examples. There are many other countries, however, where social conditioning and religious sanctions have limited its success. In most Arab countries, for example, girls tend to drop out of coeducational schools at the age of puberty.

Supervision and Inspection

Supervision and inspection are considered to be the major planks of any strategy to improve the quality and standard of school education. The National Education Commission (1966), while analysing the reasons for the breakdown of super- vision programmes in most states, stressed the need for introducing the new system of supervision in our schools. The commission considered this as one of the main problems in the reform of school education.

The traditional concept of supervision and inspection was authoritarian and rigid and did not include the element of professional guidance to teachers. The modern concept of supervision and inspection is more scientific, professional and democratic in character and methods. The term supervision, accordingly, implies professional leadership by the head of the institution and senior teachers of the school in addition to similar guidance from outside supervisors. It is a dynamic function involving and stimulating the teachers while evaluating their performance with an ultimate view to improve the entire teaching-learning situation. Supervision, as such, involves demonstration teaching, observation lessons, organisation of seminars, meetings and workshops, guidance in the preparation of institutional plans etc. This is, however, the ideal situation. In fact, it is the inspecting officers who supervise class room instruction by virtue of their position in the educational administrative set-up. This also involves rating and indexing of teachers, finding out whether toe school has the prescribed number of qualified teachers, noting the state of the building and maintenance of accounts and records, looking into the observance of departmental rules and regulations, following the prescribed curricula and syllabi, proper utilisation of grants by private schools, and protection of the rights of teachers serving in them.

b. Justice for Women

In Indian households, often organized around extended families, violence can erupt in many forms. It occurs between siblings, sexual partners, in-laws, children and parents, young and old. While violence against women within a marriage has been a crime, the narrow scope of existing laws and lack of legal measures for victims led women's groups to campaign for a new and broader civil statute. In 2005, they successfully pushed through the Protection of Women from Domestic Violence Act.

The Lawyers Collective, one of the groups that led the campaign, will now use a grant by the UN Trust Fund to End Violence against Women to help the Indian legal system adjust the ways it handles domestic abuse cases.

The new law protects all members of a household, and it embraces the definition of violence adopted by the United Nations as being any form of abuse, whether emotional, physical, sexual or verbal. It also offers a wide range of new protection measures: injunctions, protection orders, and maintenance and custody orders. The common practice of throwing a married woman out of her home is now illegal, and while there is still no law making marital rape a crime, the 2005 act opens the door to make it so.

"We wanted to build on but also expand the existing legal framework," says Indira Jaising, a long-term activist and lawyer with the Lawyers Collective. "It is absolutely path-breaking, for example, that we were able to include sexual abuse under the definition of violence. A lot of reproductive rights will be strengthened."

First, however, groups like the Jaising's must contend with initial confusion about the new law, which calls upon members of the legal system to think and work differently. There are not many existing parallels to a statute that has both criminal and civil components: The violation of a protection order, for example, can be followed by arrest. The act also introduces a new category of court staff — the protection officer. Ideally this person should be a social worker with expertise in handling domestic violence, but Jaising points out that the tendency is to believe this is a job for the police.

The Lawyers Collective will use its Trust Fund grant to work with judges on developing a bench manual spelling out protocols for tasks such as issuing timely protection orders, developing safety plans and preparing counselling for abusers. A second part of the project will produce a training manual with comprehensive guidelines for protection officers and service providers. Training sessions in individual states led by peers will introduce both manuals to a spectrum of judicial staffs.

Jaising emphasizes that awareness about domestic violence has traditionally been very low in India, where the forms of abuse against women run the gamut from bride burning to female infanticide to the forced eviction of widows. "Domestic violence is so pervasive that women are not full partners in development or society," she contends. "You cannot talk about education or employment when you are trapped by abuse."

But the new law has already sparked a nationwide debate in the media. Jaising says the Trust Fund project will help keep this momentum going by continuing to build bridges with journalists, as well as exploring new means of public outreach such as text message campaigns and opinion polls.

The Lawyers Collective has spent more than a quarter century looking for ways to use the law as an instrument for social justice, working on homelessness, HIV, livelihood issues and discrimination against minority women. The UN Trust Fund grant will now help it deepen the impact of one of the most recent major triumphs for women's human rights.

Violence against Women

Violence against women is a technical term used to collectively refer to violent acts that are primarily or exclusively committed against women. Similar to a hate crime, this type of violence targets a specific group with the victim's gender as a primary motive. The United Nations General Assembly defines "violence against women" as *"any act of gender-based violence that results in, or is likely to result in, physical, sexual or mental harm or suffering to women, including threats of such acts, coercion or arbitrary deprivation of liberty, whether occurring in public or in private life."*. The 1993 *Declaration on the Elimination of Violence against Women* noted that this violence could be perpetrated by assailants of either gender, family members and even the "State" itself. Worldwide governments and organizations actively work to combat violence against women through a variety of programs. A UN resolution designated November 25th as *International Day for the Elimination of Violence against Women.*

History of Violence against Women

Some historians believe that the history of violence against women is tied to the history of women being viewed as property and a gender role assigned to be subservient to men and also other women.

Impact on Society

The World Health Organization reports that violence against women puts an undue burden on health care services with women who have suffered violence being more likely to need health services and at higher cost, compared to women who have not suffered violence. Several studies have shown a link between poor treatment of women and international violence. These studies show that one of the best predictors of inter-and intranational violence is the maltreatment of women in the society.

Human Trafficking-Legal Protection

The Republic of India is the second most populous country in the world, stretching from the Arabian Sea (W) to the Bay of Bengal (E), bordering Pakistan (W); China, Nepal, and Bhutan (N); Bangladesh (NE); and Myanmar (E). New Delhi is its capital and Bombay (Mumbai) its largest city. An estimated 400 million are children between 0 and 18 years of age. Although acceleration in economic growth has made India among the 10 fastest growing developing countries, the country's per capita income remains low and 26 per cent of the population live below the income poverty line.

India is a source, destination, and transit country for men, women, and children trafficked for the purposes of forced labour and commercial sexual exploitation. Internal forced labour may constitute India's largest trafficking problem; men, women, and children are held in debt bondage and face forced labour working in brick kilns, rice mills, agriculture, and embroidery factories. While no comprehensive study of forced and bonded labour has been completed, NGOs estimate this problem affects 20 to 65 million Indians. Women and girls are trafficked within the country for the purposes of commercial sexual exploitation and forced marriage. Children are subjected to forced labour as factory workers, domestic servants, beggars, and agriculture workers, and have been used as armed combatants by some terrorist and insurgent groups. India is also a destination for women and girls from Nepal and Bangladesh trafficked for the purpose of commercial sexual exploitation. Nepali children are also trafficked to India for forced labour in circus shows. Indian women are trafficked to the Middle East for commercial sexual exploitation. There are also victims of labour trafficking among the thousands of Indians who migrate willingly every year to the Middle East, Europe, and the United States for work as domestic servants and low-skilled labourers. In some cases, such workers are the victims of fraudulent recruitment practices that lead them directly into situations of forced labour, including debt bondage; in other cases, high debts incurred to pay recruitment fees leave them vulnerable to exploitation by unscrupulous employers in the destination countries, where some are subjected to conditions of involuntary servitude, including non-payment of wages, restrictions on movement, unlawful withholding of passports, and physical or sexual abuse. Men and women from Bangladesh and Nepal are trafficked through India for forced labour and commercial sexual exploitation in the Middle East. Indian nationals travel to Nepal and within the country for child sex tourism.

Protecting Women from Domestic Violence

Perpetrators of domestic violence against women beware! The Protection of Women from Domestic Violence Act 2005 has come into force.

Primarily meant to provide *protection to the wife or female live-in partner* from violence at the hands of the husband or male live-in partner or his relatives, the Act extends its protection to women who are sisters, widows or mothers. Domestic violence under the Act includes actual abuse or the threat of abuse whether physical, sexual, verbal, emotional or economic. Harassment by way of unlawful dowry demands to the woman or her relatives would also be covered under this definition.

Ministry of *Women and Child Development had issued a notification to bring it into force from 26th October, 2006*. The Act was passed by the Parliament in August last year and assented to by the president on 13th September, 2005. But implementation was pending as detailed consultations will required with the State and other agencies for framing the rules.The Ministry has simultaneously issued another notification laying down the rules framed for the implementation of the Act. These rules provide for, among other things, appointment of protection officers, service providers and Counsellors. Action to be taken in the event of the respondent breaching the protection order passed by the Magistrate in favour of the aggrieved woman is also prescribed in these rules. Both the notifications are now available on the Ministry's website www.wcd.nic.in.

The Act will go a long way to provide relief to the women from domestic violence and get their due. The Ministry has requested all State Governments and Union Territories to ensure that the necessary administrative arrangements are immediately put in place for the commencement of the Act.

The salient features of the Protection from Domestic Violence Act, 2005 are as follows:

> *The Act seeks to cover those women who are or have been in a relationship with the abuser where both parties have lived together in a shared household and are related by consanguinity, marriage or a relationship in the nature of marriage, or adoption; in addition relationship with family members living together as a joint family are also included. Even those women who are sisters, widows, mothers, single women, or living with the abuser are entitled to get legal protection under the proposed Act.*

'**Domestic violence**' includes actual abuse or the threat of abuse that is physical, sexual, verbal, emotional and economic. Harassment by way of unlawful dowry demands to the woman or her relatives would also be covered under this definition.

Indian Constitution Provisions relationg to Women Personal Laws

Whenever talk revolves around gender equality, women's right or their empowerment people are found to be indifferent toward 70 million Muslim women in India who have been facing the most humiliating aspect of their lives like polygamy and divorce. They are compelled to bear this pang of social humiliation for centuries under the water tight compartment of Shariat (Islamic law). A number of Muslim-majority countries like Turkey, Morocco and Indonasia have already reformed this medieval law and allowed much freedom to their women citizens befitting the rapidly changing social environment all over the world. However, the diehard Mullhas in the name of Muslim identity still maintain that Shariat is a permanent ingredient of Islam which is not subject to any scrutiny. Therefore, Muslim women owing to the deeper and different layer of discrimination under this law are more vulnerable than their counterparts in other religions. In the absence of any law to protect their rights under the provision of gender equality in the constitution the larger majority of them are destined to the fate of 'Gudiya' and 'Imrana'.

Erosion of Muslim Women's right in India as pointed out in 'The study of Muslim women in India –"Inching towards Equality" suggested that "Muslim Personal Law as practiced in India contravenes the Convention on the Elimination of All forms of Discrimination Against Women (CEDAW) in several respect". Article 5(a) of the CEDAW asks all states to take appropriate measures for "elimination of prejudices and customary and other practices which are based on the idea of the inferiority or superiority of either of the sexes or on stereotype rules for men and women".

India ratified the CEDAW in 1993 but declared its reservation on this particular article on the plea of its conformity with its policy of non-interference in the personal affairs of any community without its initiative and consent.

Although larger majority of Muslim women are silent due to suppressed state of mind and educational backwardness, a section of educated women in the community is found to be expressing views against the stand of the Islamists. In conformity with the provision of gender equality in the Indian Constitution, articles of CEDAW and commonly understood basic spirit of equality and justice for women in Islam they maintain that Muslim Personal Laws as practiced in India are against these provisions and have come forward in exploring the possibilities to bring about progressive changes in the customary practice of Shariat. Sayeda Saiyidain Hameed, convener of the Muslim Women's forum in her article "Adultery in Islam" dated September 13, 2002 maintained that "Islam does not sanction the punishment of stoning to death for adultery". She has quoted Surah 17, Al Isra verse 32 and Surah 24 Al Nur, verse 2 to prove her point.

Disgusted with the indifference of the democratic institutions towards their cause some of the Muslim women activists took initiative to fight for their cause and formed a separate All India Muslim Women Personal Law Board (AIMWPLB) parallel to All India Muslim Personal Law Board (AIMPLB) in February 2005 with Shaista Ambar as President, Parveen Abidi General Secretary, thirteen-member executive committee, 42 members and 22-member advisory committee. With main focus on resolving the marital problems like divorce, maintenance and desertion of wives by husbands, the avowed objectives of the board include employment generation for women, marriage of destitute girls, equal rights to the daughters in ancestral properties etc. Parveen Abidi maintained that "Muslim women are doubly disadvantaged as the Maulanas never come to the rescue of harassed, divorced or victimized women while the administration refuses to interfere terming it a religious matter" (India Together dated 21 September 2006).

AIMPLB refused to recognize the separate personal law board for Muslim women and its senior member Maulana Sajjad Nomani termed its formation as a 'joke'. However, AIMWPLB is not ready to back out of its commitment. In fact it refused to accept the fatwa of Darul Uloom Deoband annulling the marriage of Imrana who was raped by her father-in-law and supported the victim in her legal battle in which the accused was convicted for ten years imprisonment by the district court. Demanding separate mosque for women AIMWPLB has even released a separate Nikahnama (Marriage deed) on March 16, 2008 which rejects divorce through SMS, e-mail or phone and also recognized the right of the Muslim women to seek divorce (Khula) are the guidelines for marriage under the Shariat for bride and groom. The key issues of new Nikahnama are as under:

Triple talaq said in one go will not be acceptable

Talaq to be spaced out over a period of 3 months

Talaq not to be allowed via phone or SMS

New Nikahnama insists on free will for the girl in case of nikah

Talaq cannot be given under the influence of alcohol

Talaq given to pregnant woman should be considered illegal

Although, in absence of some effective and assertive leadership the voice of AIMWPLB is yet to jerk the conscience of the community or to draw due attention of political class or media, the issue has at least attracted the people believing in the concept of gender equality. Since AIMWPLB is facing the challenge mainly from AIMPLB, All India Ulema Councils and the Maulanas, the leadership in the women board needs the support of the masses so that they could put pressure on the political class in the country to initiate dialogue with them. As the board is fighting on the basis of the gender equality provision of Indian constitution it should also initiate a dialogue with the government for implementation of article 44 of the constitution regarding uniform Civil Code in the country. A Supreme Court order in October 2007 has made the registration of marriages mandatory for all and this could be another rallying point for the Muslim women.

Much publicised introduction of Women's Reservation Bill in Rajya Sabha is an attempt for empowerment of women but it is doubtful that Mullhas would allow their women to derive its benefit by reforming the Shariat. The historical surrender of state power to the pressure of Islamists in Shahbano case in mid nineteen eighties by amending the constitution and neutalising the Supreme Court judgment was a signal of its helplessness towards the cause of Muslim women. In fact the state power owing to the mutual profit game between Mullhas and the vote-seeking political class is indifferent towards a sizeable section of its citizens simply on the plea that it is committed to the principle of non-interference in the personal laws of any community. Now the time has come for the Muslim women to come forward and put pressure on the government for intervention in the anti-women laws of Shariat. Once they take the lead the non-Muslim organisations in the country would also support their cause for social evolution in conformity with the changing global scenario.

UCC, Constitution and the Supreme Court of India

The Supreme Court has time and again suggested that the Parliament should frame a Uniform Civil Code for the country, as that will help the cause of national integration. The Supreme Court is the upholder of the Constitution and interprets it in the light of the spirit of the same. While Article 25 guaranteed freedom of conscience and free profession, practice and propagation of religions, Article 44 has divested the religions from social relations and the personal law. Thus Article 44 is not in conflict with Article 25 and 26 of the Constitution. These are reflected in the various Supreme Court exhortations over the years on this sensitive and contentious issue. The Court has gone to the extent of saying that Article 44 has remained a dead letter, thereby expressing their anticipation as to the possibility of the existence of a Uniform Civil Code. Laws relating to marriage, divorce, inheritance, maintenance etc. are of a secular nature and therefore a uniform system of law governing them is a possibility and is consonance with spirit of the Constitution.

The Challenge and the Debate

It is ironic that a constitutional provision intended to bring people closer in a secular order has become an object of divisive, often acrimonious debate. The Challenge today is to separate the core issues from the dross and the reactionary. Personal laws relate to marriage, divorce, maintenance, succession, and adoption. They also have tax and other implications. While the domain of these of these laws should not be exaggerated, self-evidently a secular and democratic society requires the common law to "invade" all aspects of human relationships. However, the matter is not as simple as it sounds. As democratic women's organizations have been pointing out, the concept of a uniform, or rather equality, between communities and equality within communities, that is, between men and women The unfortunate truth is that personal laws, as they exist in India, tend stubbornly to discriminate against girls and women. This is not to deny the gains made by various attempts that are reforming these laws and the progressive contributions made over the long term by the higher judiciary in moderating or lessening the iniquitous impact of the personal laws. It cannot also be denied that, for a complexity of reasons, the personal laws of some religious than the counterpart laws of other communities. Muslim women are about the worst off, but the essential problem does not concern Muslim women alone. Women—Hindu, Muslim, Christian, Sikh and so on – are invariably the losers under the personal law regime. The embryo of a common civil code is seen in such progressive enactments as the Special Marriage Act, 1954 but such instances are few and far between. Gender discrimination is the critical issue. Pious advocacy of a uniform civil code as an instrument for ushering in "national integration" and communal campaigns that use Article 44 as a stick to intimidate minorities with fail to address this issue. The democratic women's movement is absolutely right when it proposes that call for a uniform civil code, which must eventually be put in place by any society that calls itself secular and democratic, must be "preceded" by the demand for equal rights and equal laws that ensure gender justice. The task is well cut out.

History and Codes and Codification in India

According to Oxford dictionary, 'code' means *'a systematic collection of statutes, body of law, so arranged as to avoid inconsistency and overlapping'*. Legislature seems to be the most important source of law in modern times. By legislation, sometimes, a new law is made, sometimes, a custom or an usage is embodied in a statute, and it is put in a coherent and systematic form. The law put in this form is called code. The law making and putting it in this form is called codification. Thus codification means promulgation, compilation, collection and systematization of the body of law in a coherent form by an authority in a state competent to do so.

There have been codes since very ancient times. In India, the Code of Manu is a very ancient code. There were many other law givers who gave their codes as Yajnavalkya, Brihaspati, Narada, Parashara etc. These various codes applied in different parts of the country. Though these codes cannot be said to be codes in the modern sense of the term, they are important because they made a beginning out of which the modern codes evolved in course of time.

During medieval period personal laws and customs governed people. When the Britishers came here, they too, as a matter of policy, recognized personal laws and local customs, and justice was administered in accordance with that. But after they had consolidated their position here, they paid their attention to codification. Under the provisions of the Charter Act of 1833 the first Indian Law Commission was appointed with Lord Macaulay as its chairman. They drafted a number of codes such as the Indian Penal Code, the Civil Procedure Code and the Indian Limitation Act. A Second Law Commission was set up under Charter Act of 1853. The Indian Penal Code was passed. Later on, the Criminal Procedure Code and some other Acts were drafted and passed. Law Commissions were set up again in 1861 and 1879, which drafted and revised many Acts. Thus the criminal law, civil law, in most part, And procedural laws had been codified. Now the personal laws remained operative in respect of limited fields only. With the introduction of legislatures in Provinces and the Centre the codification was expedited. After nation became independent, various Law Commissions made recommendation in regard to personal laws which are still pending.

Codification of Personal Laws: The Panacea

India is a developing country facing numerous problems. Planning has been resorted to for a comprehensive development. The planned development of legal jurisprudence is possible only through codification. A nation cannot make the desired development if the people are left to regulate their relations in different and divergent ways. By codification there comes uniformity and the desired development is speedily achieved.

For the national unity and integrity, which unfortunately are very grave problems of India, the uniformity of the law is very necessary, which can be achieved only through codification. Perhaps it was keeping this objective in view that Article 44 of the Indian Constitution that is, 'Directive Principles of State Policy'. It runs as:-

"The State shall endeavour to secure for the citizens a uniform civil code through out the territory of India".

Thus in India, though much has been done towards codification, there still remains more to be done as far as personal laws are concerned.

Codification brings about certainty. Laws no longer remain vague and uncertain as it is generally in precedent and custom. It makes law simple and accessible to everybody. It can be said that law is logically arranged in a coherent form. There are little chances of any conflict or inconsistency arising among the different provisions of the law. Thus the law is harmonized and systematized in the code. This would in a sense prevent frivolous petitions filed before Courts regarding personal laws and their implementation and thus preserving precious time.

The codification makes the law stable. The law which comes into existence through other sources has not that much of stability. Stability is very essential for law so that the people may have confidence in it and legal transaction may be made easily and smoothly. Also, it is an instrument of forging unity among the people. Codified laws have uniform and wider application. The persons governed by the same laws, in course of time, develop an affinity amongst them and they come closer to each other. Thus, it helps in creating unity and integration in a country like India, which is a land of diversities. This is one of the major arguments for promoting the idea of uniform civil code in India

It is pertinent to note that most of the demerits of the codification have been magnified and exaggerated. Codification of personal laws has undoubtedly some demerits but they are very insignificant in comparison to the merits it has. Codification causes planned developed of law. It enables the law to fulfil the purpose for which it is meant. Many of the demerits have been attributed to it due to mistaken view that codification means the complete abolition of case law and customary law. Contrary to it, these case law always work as a supplement to the code by interpreting it, reconciling it and filing up the lacuna, if any because in code, howsoever meticulously prepared they might be, some defects generally find their place. If case law functions side by side with the code, most of the demerits would not come into being at all.

India needs a Uniform Civil Code. The Constitution says, bit only in a manner of speaking –in the soft part labelled "Directive Principles of state Policy", which include such tall promises as the "right to work [and] education", "free and compulsory education for all children", and so forth. Article 44 "directs", non-bindingly of course, that the state shall make an effort to bring about uniform civil code. Even Italy has one, as do the rest of the developed world. Nowhere is a scenario in India, of various personal laws jostling together. It needs to come on the heel of a political consensus, which has been a long term demand. We all know that this has to be marked by consensual politics. But when and how.... these questions still remain unanswered?

Labour Laws

Bidi making is a highly labour intensive activity dominated by home workers. They are not expected to possess much knowledge about the specific provisions of various labour laws. Awareness about important provisions among the employers and the employees can bring in a lot of improvement in the implementation of the minimum wage legislation. Accordingly, during the course of the study an effort was made to collect information on prevailing wage rates, date of revision, working hours, trade unions activities, associations, sex-based wage differentials, prescribed limits for rejection of bidis, enforcement machinery, etc. The extent of awareness displayed by the employers and the employees on the relevant provisions of the Minimum Wages Act, 1948; the Bidi and Cigar Workers (Conditions of Employment) Act, 1966, and the Equal Remuneration Act, 1976 is being discussed in the following paragraphs.

Employers

The employers were expected to have full knowledge about the provisions of various labour laws applicable to the Bidi Making Industry. During the course of survey, it was found that all the employers covered by the study were not only aware of the prescribed rates of minimum wages for different categories of employees but were also conversant with the important provisions of the Minimum Wages Act, 1948; the Beedi and Cigar Workers (Conditions of Employment) Act, 1966, and the Equal Remuneration Act, 1976.

The employers disclosed that the bidi making activity was dominated by female labour who were mostly engaged as Bidi Rollers and were paid on piece rate basis as wages prescribed by the Government. This was confirmed by field officers who did not come across any situation wherein female workers were engaged in any other operation. The employers were also familiar with enforcement machinery, inspection procedure, permissible limits of rejection of sub-standard bidis (Chhat) and the exemptions granted to smaller bidi manufacturers under excise laws. All the employers had taken licences in the names of Contractors engaged by them.

Contractors

The system of getting the bidis rolled through Contractors was prevalent in all the Strata in one form or the other. It was more predominant in Stratum-I as the clusters of Bidi Rollers were widely spread over the villages in this area and the Contractors frequented these areas in large numbers to engage them. Further, the agriculture was also not dependable in this Stratum.

In certain other Strata bidi industry was relying more on the purchase of un-branded green bidis from middle men even from across the State borders rather than engaging their own Contractors for enhancing their production. All the Contractors studied were familiar with the provisions of the relevant labour laws and related matter of their interest. The Contractors were registered with the establishments for whom they got the bidis rolled and collected the rolled bidis.

Bidi Workers

The work culture of bidi workers within the premises was similar to an organized industry. The information collected during the field study revealed that, only 25.4 percent of them were aware of the prescribed rates of minimum wages while 58.2 percent were aware of the existence of the enforcement machinery. The low proportion of awareness about prescribed wages as well as about the existence of the enforcement machinery was attributed to lack of unionisation amongst the bidi workers, prevalence of practices like assigning the jobs of checking, sorting, labelling, wrapping, etc. on contract to a team of workers and the petty establishments widely scattered in remote areas, which escaped the notice of the enforcement officers. It was also observed during the Study that the Enforcement Officers just inspected the records maintained by the Employers and perhaps did not devote time to understand the problems of bidi workers and enquire about the wages actually paid to them. It was also observed that although the workers had proximity to both the management and the employers, yet such contacts had not at all influenced the employers in terms of better service conditions.

Bidi Rollers

The extent of compliance with the implementation of the prescribed minimum wages depends on the awareness about the labour laws and related matters, level of education, unionisation among the workers and the enforcement effort. The study revealed that the Bidi Rollers, mostly home workers, were lagging behind in this respect. They mostly belonged to the fair sex, who were more concerned about supplementing their family incomes without neglecting their domestic duties, rather than fighting for the prescribed wages. They were earning around Rs.36/-per day for continuous sitting of seven to eight hours. They were living in clusters, monopolised by one or two bidi manufacturers offering identical terms of employment. The study revealed that since all the Bidi Rollers were home workers they did not enjoy the advantage of a regular and close contact with their colleagues as well as proximity with the employer or his representatives. They collected the raw materials, rolled bidis with the help of their family members and deposited the finished product at the centres setup by the employers or their representatives. Most of these home workers were free to draw large quantities of raw materials from different sources and to supply higher output of bidis to them. Bidi Rollers generally lacked awareness about the laws governing their conditions of service, the wage rates prescribed by the Government and existence of the enforcement machinery.

During the course of the study, it was also observed that a very large number of female home workers, belonging to a particular community, accepted to work at much lower than the prescribed rates of minimum wages as they could not undertake outdoor activities due to religious and social restrictions. Sometimes it became difficult even to identify the employers for whom they had been rolling the bidis because they were ordinarily reluctant to talk to the enforcement officers and divulge the facts about their employment and earnings. They were, therefore, highly vulnerable to exploitation by the Contractors, middlemen and agents dominating the bidi industry in different parts of the country.

The information collected reveals that home workers alone constituted 73.5 percent of the total number of employees in bidi making establishments. The proportion of helping dependants of the home workers in rolling bidis worked out to about 106.5 percent. These home workers were the most vulnerable section of the bidi employees, while their dependants who made an impressive contribution towards the overall production of the industry as 'invisible workers', remained unprotected by labour laws. The very nature of their work, conditions of employment and family compulsions were also responsible for their plight. Though the extent of unionisation among the Bidi Rollers was 34.7 percent yet they displayed complete ignorance about the prescribed wage rates and the labour laws governing their work.

It can be concluded that the Bidi Rollers, although constituted a large proportion of bidi employees, yet they failed to get their due share as most of them were keen on having an additional source of income within their homes alongside their domestic or other responsibilities. Generally they were not aware of the wages prescribed for them and wherever they were aware, they did not demand for the same. Thus, there was wider scope for exploitation of the home workers at the hands of the petty establishments producing un-branded bidis and their contractors, agents and the middlemen.

Family Courts

The State Government, after consultation with the High Court and by notification shall establish a Family Court. However such courts shall be established only for a city or town whose population exceeds 1 million. The State Government with the concurrence of High Court may appoint one or more judge or judges of a Family Court and the Act lays down the provisions relating to terms of office, salary, allowance etc. of such judge/judges.

The State Government in consultation with the High Court may also provide for associations/welfare agencies to enable the Family Court to exercise its jurisdiction more effectively. It has to be noted that this provision is not mandatory. The use of word "may" indicates that it is the discretion of the State Government whether to provide for such associations or agencies or not.

The Act also authorizes the State Government to make provisions regarding the number and categories of counsellors, officers and other employees required to assist a Family Court and the terms and conditions of their service and employment.

Family Courts in India have been set up in several major cities and towns. Broadly, all matrimonial disputes like divorce, maintenance, alimony, custody of children, etc. are tried by the Family Courts. The concept of Family Courts in India imply an integrated broad based service to families in trouble. It stipulates that the Family Court structure should be such as to stabilize the marriage, to preserve the family, and where a marriage has been broken down irretrievably, to dissolve it with maximum fairness and minimum bitterness, distress and humiliation. The Family Court system also visualizes assistance of specialized agencies and persons.

Trends in Law Enforcement

The problem of integrity is not confined to the police force. However, it is society's responsibility to assert itself through motivating police officers and evolving a practical code of conduct for the entire service.

THE customary annual review of police performance at the national and State levels is usually dismissed by cynics as an exercise in futility. They strongly believe that the police and other agencies charged with maintaining peace and promoting a respect for the law are so much driven by arbitrary political direction that they can hardly benefit from analysis or introspection. According to the school of thought they represent, forces of deviance and evil are strongly entrenched in our milieu, and they emasculate the whole criminal justice system-not merely the police-so much that the principal players can hardly learn from past mistakes. The suggestion here is that, since the polity is managed by people to whom self-aggrandisement at any cost was the sole criterion, values such as professionalism and personal integrity are irrelevant. Events in our country since the watershed year of 1975, when one saw a national Emergency imposed on the flimsiest of grounds, lend credibility to such an assessment, however warped it might seem. This palpable loss of faith in the law enforcement machinery is a serious situation. It is an entirely different matter that such lack of faith in a crucial state instrument ignores the many significant achievements (such as counter-terrorism, dignitary protection and conduct of peaceful elections in four States during the recent Assembly elections) to its credit during the year. The stark fact, however, is that popular despondency, unchecked, can bring a constitutional government down on its knees. It is against this backdrop that we need to analyse the happenings of the year that has gone by.

It is not my intention to chronicle all the events of 2003. I would be content with identifying some major trends that should cause concern to most of us. In doing so, I would refer to a few incidents alone that would help to clarify myself and bring home to the reader the substance and significance of a particular trend.

In the early years of the Republic, we were not very confident that the Centre would be able to quell all fissiparous tendencies that were in full play at that time in some parts of the country. The northeastern States, Nagaland and Mizoram in particular, gave us anxiety for nearly two decades. Both the Army and the police were used to great effect to bolster the efforts initiated on the political front. The combination of diplomacy and firmness did not bring immediate dividends. However, over a course of time, the strategy did succeed to convince the polity and the public in the two States that their destinies were inextricably linked to New Delhi and not to a place outside the country. As a result, we can confidently say today that Nagaland and Mizoram have been nearly totally integrated with the rest of the country. Manipur remains a disturbed region but not to the extent that will arouse a fear that separatist forces there will eventually prevail. In sum, the situation in the northeastern region is one that infuses confidence in us in the ability of the political machinery to use selectively the security agencies for sending a strong message to those trying to disrupt national unity. This lengthy preamble is required only to put recent happenings in Assam in the right context. Here is a situation in which the Railways had to abandon a routine process of recruitment to one of its low level positions, all because of the fear of the local population that most of the vacancies were being gobbled up by people from neighbouring Bihar at the cost of the locals. The Railways' decision came after brutal attacks in a few parts of Assam on whoever was suspected to be a Bihari. Murders were committed at will and the Assam Police appeared totally unprepared for the orgy of violence. At least one case of rape was reported. What do you make out of this intolerance that cuts at the root of nationhood? It is entirely possible that a few Bihari youth had used irregular methods to get priority in recruitment at the cost of some Assamese. Did this justify the violence against the so-called outsiders? Nothing can be more galling if we remember that this is happening 53 years after we became a Republic.

There are two aspects of the Assam incidents that are worrying. First, they send out the signal that the country's integration is fragile. As a result, in the future also, sensitive economic issues could trigger major inter-State violence capable of destabilising law and order. More important, such happenings pose the danger of igniting parochial feelings among the police. The consequence? In such an environment, professionalism could yield place to expediency and chauvinism in an agency that has to remain scrupulously objective if we are to hold together as a nation.

The mere creation of paramilitary and central police forces will not help to reverse this trend as, under the Constitution, it is the State police that is the pivot around which law enforcement revolves. I find it difficult to exaggerate the import of the Assam happenings. They point to the need for training programmes that would build a national outlook among policemen who are rooted to regions and States. We have excellent programmes in central institutions such as the National Police Academy, Hyderabad, aimed at the Indian Police Service (IPS) and central police organisations. Their spirit will have to be captured in full and transmitted to State police training establishments that traditionally offer instruction in law and its enforcement in the restricted State setting without bringing a national perspective. I am of the view that a mere study of the Indian Penal Code (IPC) and the Indian Evidence Act (IEA) does not impart to policemen a national outlook. One has to go beyond this to tell State police officers that policing transcends the boundaries of a State and it has necessarily national links. The sooner State police training syllabi are reoriented to accommodate this imperative the better, because, we do not know when Assam will repeat itself elsewhere in the country.

The stamp paper scam is still very much in the news. Its dimensions are mind-boggling. It is possible that there will be a few more startling revelations about men in public life before it actually goes to court in the form of a chargesheet. There are two features of this sordid episode that should make us sit up and ask a few questions. A fraud of this magnitude was not detected until it was a decade old. This is what Finance Minister Jaswant Singh is rightly worked up about. His ire is against intelligence agencies, especially those within his own Ministry.

He is quite justified in his indignation. The charge of intelligence failure is all too familiar to us. Even the mighty Central Intelligence Agency (CIA) and Federal Bureau of Investigation (FBI) have been accused of failure to predict 9/11.

The point is, are we in India doing anything more than what the Americans have done to sharpen intelligence performance? I am quite alive to the tireless efforts made by New Delhi and some of the States in this direction. When this is so, why were we found wanting in the stamp paper scam, a nationwide fraud that has the severest implications for our economy? While our intelligence outfits have done reasonably well in keeping track of the machinations of our principal adversary operating from across the border, how is it that we have been ignorant of individuals like Telgi who can cause tremendous damage to our economy? I personally know how quick we were to react to Pakistan's action in pumping fake five hundred rupee notes into our country with a view to wrecking our economy.

The swift coordinated efforts in this matter neutralised the mischief greatly. Why did we then fail in the case of Telgi? There seems to be preponderant evidence that some politicians and many policemen had knowledge of the goings on. They either actively gave protection to him and his associates or turned a blind eye in return for a consideration. My concern is, how are we going to prevent future Telgis from corrupting the polity and the civil service. I know I am being idealistic because the whole of human history is replete with scandals of such proportions at periodic intervals. I am not for a moment going to suggest the creation of new agencies or strengthening the existing ones. What I am asking for is a simple inexpensive mechanism to monitor individuals and organisations that are suddenly flush with money. Our energies need to concentrate on this deceptively simple yet frustratingly complicated mission. Here, there has to be a synergy between intelligence agencies and organisations in the private sector that deal in money, not merely banks but asset management and insurance companies as well. It is the latter who interact with people who have come by a lot of money in quick time and who need to launder it.

What I am suggesting has possibly been tried out unobtrusively but without much structure. We need to give precisely that to ongoing or fresh efforts to track down and neutralise depredators like Telgi. My belief is that the stamp paper scam was the most important happening of the past year that has immense potential to cause national harm at a time when our economy has been looking up tremendously.

The second feature of the scam that causes even greater anguish is the ease with which Telgi was able to buy up policemen and other members of the bureaucracy. Civil service and police corruption is not a new phenomenon. When the higher echelons of the police are accused of it, we need to take more than a mere notice of it. Two senior IPS officers in Maharashtra, one in the rank of an Additional DGP (the former Mumbai Police Commissioner) and the other an IGP (an alumnus of the Indian Institute of Technology and Indian Institute of Management) are now languishing in jail for their alleged Telgi connection. While they cannot be condemned before they are tried judicially, the fact that there is enough evidence for their detention under the draconian Maharashtra Control of Organised Crime Act (MCOCA) speaks volumes for the misconduct. It is not very material whether they received personal consideration from Telgi or their acts of omission and commission now under the scanner were at the behest of some political bigwigs.

That they placed themselves in a situation where they had to be arrested and lodged in jail is enough to bring shame to the Indian Police Service as a whole. The New Delhi Television ran a story the other day listing the many Haryana IPS officers who had been charged with corruption in the recent past. Possibly, in many other States the picture is more appalling. What do we, as a community, do to stem the rot? Are we going to depend only on the Ministry of Home Affairs, which is the Cadre Authority for the IPS, to initiate a major exercise that will aim at correcting the alarming situation? It is not my case that it is only the IPS that has problems of integrity. Many other services that give leadership to the various wings of the bureaucracy have the same disease. But when the police is afflicted with it, complacence (arising out of penal action against just a few officers like in Maharashtra) or "masterly inactivity" (from an assessment that the evil is traditional and nothing much can be done about it) cannot be condoned. It is society that has to assert itself through motivating upright IPS officers and evolving a practical conduct for the whole service for strict adherence. The existing All India Services Conduct Rules (AISCR) have proved inadequate to the task.

Finally, a crucial question with regard to the autonomy that the police should enjoy came to the fore again during the year. Bihar DGP (Director-General of Police) D.P. Ojha was unceremoniously removed by the Rabri Devi government without the courtesy of telling the public the rationale for what appeared to be a capricious and petulant action. Before this, we were no doubt privy to the battle that the hapless officer was waging against a ruling party MP who had first been accused of illegal conduct and, thereafter, arrested and remanded to judicial custody.

Ojha's charge was that the State government was treating the MP with a kid glove and was giving him facilities in jail that he was not entitled to. Ojha went public with the accusation and RJD (Rashtriya Janata Dal) president Laloo Prasad Yadav was quick to denounce the former. What was most shocking was Laloo Prasad Yadav's statement that Ojha was appointed as DGP in spite of an adverse report from the Central Bureau of Investigation.

There are two principal issues here. The first is, why did the State government appoint Ojha to this sensitive position if the CBI report had been unfavourable to him? Now, to the second issue. Assuming that Ojha was found suitable otherwise, why was he removed arbitrarily? Did he prove to be inconvenient to the ruling party bosses when he went for one of its MPs? These questions should agitate many of us who stand for enhancing police autonomy without diluting police accountability to the law. If such a fundamental issue is not resolved-the National Police Commission (1977) had indeed given a concrete scheme in the matter-there is little point in talking about police performance or IPS integrity.

Human Rights Defenders Face Intimidation from Police after People's Tribunal

FORUM-ASIA is deeply concerned over incidences of harassment faced by members of a Kolkata-based human rights organisation-the Banglar Manabadhikar Suraksha Mancha (MASUM), The organisation coordinated a People's Tribunal on Torture in Moulali, Kolkata, where 1,200 victims were present and 82 people deposed in front of the Tribunal. This tribunal is part of the National Project on Preventing Torture in India (NPPTI), and was a collaboration with FORUM-ASIA's member organisation in India, People's Watch. According to MASUM, the harassment began a few days before the Tribunal, on June 7. Despite a visit by a police officer to MASUM's office earlier, and his refusal to accept the legality of the Tribunal, MASUM went ahead with the Tribunal.

On June 10, after the event successfully concluded, a police officer trespassed into the venue and took photographs of the premises without permission. When questioned, the officer revealed he was under order from the Detective Department.

MASUM contacted the Commissioner of Police Gautam Mohan Chakrabarty, who informed the former that a criminal case had been lodged against the organisation's President and NPPTI state director, Mr. Kirity Roy. Gautam refused to give further information or details. Later, People's Watch and MASUM found out that the case was filed against Mr. Kirity Roy and others by the Detective Department of Police at Taltolla under sections 170 (Personating a public officer)/ 229 (Personation of a juror or assessor) and 120B (Criminal Conspiracy) of the Indian Penal Code.

Meanwhile, on June 12, about 12 plain clothes policemen searched MASUM premises, while 10 armed officers waited outside. Although the officers had a search warrant, MASUM did not know what was the investigation for. The organization felt that the number of police force and timing of the raid induce that the action aimed in repression and intimidation rather than law enforcement. Currently, plain clothes police personnel are visiting houses of victims of torture, who deposed before the tribunal to get their statements. Police officers also visited the office and house of the decorator, who supplied chairs, tables, and cooking utensils, and threatened them so that they will issue a statement against the organization.

Meanwhile, on 29-30 May, during the People's Tribunal on Torture in Tamil Nadu, People's Watch also faced intimidation and harassment from police forces, and false cases were registered against four members of the organization, including its Executive Director, Henri Tiphagne.

On 26 June, in conjunction with International Day in Support of Victims of Torture, about 40 human rights and women's organizations held a large people's convention in front of Calcutta University to protest the police raid at MASUM's office. Participants included several judges, advocates, doctors, professors, news magazine editors, victims and their families, who rallied together with Justice Malay Sengupta and the jury/ panel members of the Peoples Tribunal.

However, that meeting also saw plain clothed policemen present to take photographs. We also understand that Kirity Roy's mobile phone is tapped.

FORUM-ASIA is appalled by the intimidation and threats which hamper the conduct of the Public Tribunals, including the judicial harassment faced by the human rights defenders involved.

India was elected at the UN Human Rights Council in 2007, for a three year term, and agreed, for this purpose, to uphold the highest standards of promotion and protection of human rights in the country. The acts committed by the police forces and judicial instances are anything but in line with this commitment.

Once more, FORUM-ASIA urges the Government of India to comply with the provisions of the Declaration on Human Rights Defenders adopted by the UN General Assembly on December 9, 1998, in particular Article 1, which states that "everyone has the right, individually or collectively, to promote the protection and fulfilment of human rights and fundamental freedoms at the national and international levels", as well as Article 12.2, which provides that "the State shall take all necessary measures to ensure the protection by the competent authorities of everyone, individually or in association with others, against any violence, threats, retaliation, de facto or de jure adverse discrimination, pressure or any other arbitrary action as a consequence of his or her legitimate exercise of the rights referred to in the present Declaration".

Extrajudicial Killings, Disappearances, Torture and Other Forms of Gross Human Rights Violations Still Engulf in India

India has not ratified the Convention against Torture and Other Cruel, Inhuman or Degrading Treatment or Punishment (CAT) with torture remaining rampant as a method of criminal investigation in the country. Even in more developed areas of India, from the point of view of the educational level of the people, like Kerala, torture is still common. The widespread use of torture occurs despite commendable judicial decisions, such as the famous Basu vs. the State of West Bengal, which laid down detailed rules on arrest, detention and the like, which, if applied, would lead toward the elimination of torture. The prevalence of torture is also not due to the lack of forensic facilities or forensic training available to the Indian police; for in recent years, there has been considerable sophistication achieved with regard to equipment and training. Torture though remains endemic due to other factors, such as bribery and corruption and the lack of a speedy and efficient disciplinary control mechanism. The tolerance of torture by higher-ranking officers and some prominent politicians of the central government as well as various states has not ceased. The failure of the Indian government to ratify CAT is itself a manifestation of the irresoluteness on the part of the state to bring this evil practice to an end. In addition, India's record on delays in adjudication, including matters of criminal justice, are among the worst in the world. Court cases may go on for five or 10 years or even longer—delays in the judicial system that virtually distort the whole process of justice. The prevalence of these delays prevents the possibility of judicial enforcement of the basic rights of the people. While the higher courts still produce significant judgments, the justice that the average litigant receives is still of a primitive nature. Delays allow corruption and negligence. Accusations of corruption among some of the judiciary of all ranks are now an open accusation that has not been reputed in any credible way. Another major problem facing the country is the caste system. Despite many commitments expressed by India's best-known leaders since independence to end this great social divide, it is still one of the greatest obstacles to progress in Indian society. Dalits, or "Untouchables," for instance, are among the worst victims of torture and other abuses of human rights in the country. Dalits also suffer from delays in justice and the absence of access to justice. Thus, their misery is specifically linked to serious defects in the criminal justice system. The absence of justice also contributes to deeply entrenched poverty and starvation. The AHRC's studies on starvation deaths have revealed that there have been deaths caused by starvation even due to the negligence of magistrates who have particular responsibilities relating to these matters. In short, the neglect of justice in India is of such a proportion that it challenges India's claim of being a vibrant democracy. India's democracy, in fact, is fundamentally flawed and is unable to maintain the rights of its ordinary folk. The powerful, for the most part, are still above the law.

Enforcement Machinery

The judiciary is a major means for the protection of rights. It has the power to receive complaints of the violation of rights, to hear evidence, and to provide redress for violations, including punishment for violators. The judiciary can only perform this function if the legal system is strong and well-organized. The members of the judiciary should be competent, experienced and have a commitment to human rights, dignity and justice. They should be independent of the legislature and the executive by vesting the power of their appointment in a judicial service commission and by constitutional safeguards of their tenure. Judicial institutions should fairly reflect the character of the different sections of the people by religion, region, gender and social class. This means that there must be a restructuring of the judiciary and the investigative machinery.

More women, more under-privileged categories and more of the Pariahs of society must by deliberate State action be lifted out of the mire and instilled in judicial positions with necessary training. Only such a measure will command the confidence of the weaker sector whose human rights are ordinarily ignored in the traditional societies of Asia. The legal profession should be independent. Legal aid should be provided for those who are unable to afford the services of lawyers or have access to courts, for the protection of their rights. Rules which unduly restrict access to courts should be reformed to provide a broad access.

Social and welfare organizations should be authorised to bring legal action on behalf of individuals and groups who are unable to utilize the courts. All states should establish Human Rights Commissions and specialized institutions for the protection of rights, particularly of vulnerable members of society. They can provide easy, friendly and inexpensive access to justice for victims of human rights violations. These bodies can supplement the role of the judiciary. They enjoy special advantages: they can help establish standards for the implementation of human rights norms; they can disseminate information about human rights; they can investigate allegations of violation of rights; they can promote conciliation and mediation; and they can seek to enforce human rights through administrative or judicial means. They can act on their own initiative as well on complaints from members of the public. Civil society institutions can help to enforce rights through the organization of People's Tribunals, which can touch the conscience of the government and the public. The establishment of People's Tribunals emphasizes that the responsibility for the protection of rights is wide, and not a preserve of the state. They are not confined to legal rules in their adjudication and can consequently help to uncover the moral and spiritual foundations of human rights.

Police and Judiciary Human Rights as Womens Rights

In most Asian societies women suffer from discrimination and oppression. The cause of their oppression lies in both history and contemporary social and economic systems. The roots of patriarchy are systemic and its structures dominate all institutions, attitudes, social norms and customary laws, religions and values in Asian societies, crossing the boundaries of class, culture, caste and ethnicity. Oppression takes many forms, but is most evident in sexual slavery, domestic violence, trafficking in women and rape. They suffer discrimination in both public and private spheres. The increasing militarization of many societies in Asia has led to the increase of violence against women in situations of armed conflict, including mass rape, forced labour, racism, kidnapping and displacement from their homes. As female victims of armed conflict are often denied justice, rehabilitation, compensation and reparation of the war crimes committed against them, it is important to emphasis that systematic rape is a war crime and a crime against humanity. To end discrimination against women in the field of employment and the right to work, women should be given the right to employment opportunities, the free choice of profession, job security, equal remuneration, the right to compensation in respect of domestic work, the right to protection of health and safe working conditions, especially in safeguarding of the function of reproduction and special protection in times of pregnancy from work that may be harmful.

Women should be given the full right to control their sexual and reproductive health, free from discrimination or coercion, and be given access to information about sexual and reproductive health care and safe reproductive technology. There are few legal provisions to protect women against violations of their rights within the domestic and patriarchal realm. Their rights in public law are seldom observed. Affirmative measures should be taken to ensure full and equal participation of women in the political and public life of the society. A considerable increase in the presence of women in the various institutions of state power and in the fields of business, agriculture and land ownership must be provided for by way of affirmative action. The political, social and economic empowerment of women is essential for the defence of their legal rights.

Unit-IX

Social Values and the Teacher

The Concept of Values

Values are concepts or beliefs that determine how we live in our life. At work, they are major influences on how individuals approach to work. Values drive our decisions and cause us to summon up energy to preserve what we believe in or what we want to defend. As such, they can be principal determinants of behaviour and will influence our views about people, situations or events. When team members share the same values, the team will have the energy to deliver outstanding performance. Where individual values clash, conflict will occur and teams are unlikely to reach their full potential. Work related demands appear in literature on the subject as *work values*.

These can be readily characterized as relatively time-resistant and comprehensive interpretation patterns regarding work per se. Work values represent our personal relation to what we want to achieve through our work and career (S¡ verko 1999). They are acquired early in the process of socialization and are relatively stable in the personal system of values of each person.

There has been growing interest, in recent years, in the analysis of human values in general (Levy 1990; and Shwartz and Bilsky 1990) and of work values specifically (Elizur *et al.* 1991). Work values can be defined as generalized beliefs about the desirability of certain attributes of work (e.g. pay, autonomy, working conditions), and work-related outcomes (e.g. accomplishment, fulfilment, prestige). Like general values, work values act as the criteria that an individual uses in selecting appropriate work-related behaviours and goals. The match between teachers' work values and supplies offered by the schools is important for teacher's outcomes like job involvement, work motivation, and turnover intentions. Values related to work have received considerable scholarly attention for many decades (Hofstede 1980). Work values are linked to motivation and job satisfaction, and others have demonstrated a strong link between having a high achievement value and being aggressiveness in and showing initiative in one's work. Work values have also been related to organizational commitment (Elizur and Koslowsky 2001), vocational choice (Super 1970), ethical decision making (Shafer et al. 2001) and cross-cultural management (Mellahi 2001). Tarnai (1995) indicated that various authors have presented theoretical drafts of work value structures. Rosenberg distinguishes a further construct termed social oriented, people oriented and value complex and categorizes work values using three components. The social oriented value complex represents the need for contact with others and activities benefiting society. Classifications of work values structurally similar to Rosenberg's have been produced by Elizur (1984) and others. Alderfer introduces the three needs-existence, growth and relatedness, whereas Elizur distinguishes material or instrumental, cognitive and affective work values. Pawlowsky differentiates between acquisitive, non-acquisitive and social oriented dimensions. The concepts developed by Rosenberg, Alderfer, Elizur and Pawlowsky differ more in semantics and less in structure.

Work values are goals that one seeks to attain to satisfy a need; they may be satisfied by more than one kind of activity or occupation. Theory of work values includes three categories, instrumental, affective and cognitive (Elizur 1999, p. 77; Elizur and Kowslowsky 2000, p. 594). In order to analyse work values systematically, two basic facts of the domain were distinguished: modality of outcome, and system performance contingency (Elizur 1984). Modality of outcome includes various values.

Instrumental (material) values have some material return or outcome, such as pay and benefits. These values are more salient than other values and are associated with Maslow's physiological/safety/security needs. Various work outcomes are of material or instrumental nature. This class of outcome can be defined as material, or instrumental, in a sense that they are concrete and of practical use. Affective values deal with interpersonal relationships, which are less salient than the instrumental needs, and relate to Maslow's interpersonal need categories of belongingness, love, and esteem. Most studies include items that ask about relations, and others. These items relate to social relations, and they are affective outcomes rather than material. Cognitive values include items that deal with contribution to society, achievement, personal growth, responsibility, independence, interest, and use some of the same descriptive words and concepts as Maslow's levels. These items represent psychological rather than social or material outcomes. In today's world, the efficiency of a country's system represents the most important standard of assessment and comparison for societies.

The present study extends the existing empirical research about work values in the educational sectors by examining the influence of age and subject taught on work values of high school teachers. The aim of this study is to enable teachers to see themselves in perspectives and to identify and to explain features which seem to them to be significant for their country's educational policies.

Democracy and Socialism

Social democracy is a political ideology of the left or centre-left that emerged in the late 19th century from the socialist movement and continues to exert influence worldwide.

The concept of social democracy has changed throughout the decades since its inception. Historically, social democratic parties advocated socialism in the strict sense, achieved by class struggle. In the early 20th century, however, a number of socialist and labour parties rejected revolution and other traditional teachings of Marxism and went on to take more moderate positions, which came to characterize modern social democracy. These positions often include support for a democratic welfare state which incorporates elements of both socialism and capitalism, sometimes termed the mixed economy. This differs from traditional socialism, which aims to end capitalism altogether. Social democrats aim to reform capitalism democratically through state regulation and the creation of programs that work to counteract or remove the social injustice and inefficiencies they see as inherent in capitalism.

In many countries, social democrats continue to exist alongside democratic socialists, who stand to the left of them on the political spectrum. The two movements sometimes operate within the same political party, such as the Brazilian Workers' Party and the French Socialist Party. More unusually, social democrats occasionally share parties with politicians of the centre-right, as in Forza Italia in Italy.

The Socialist International (SI) is the main international organization of social democratic and socialist parties. It affirms the following principles: first, *freedom*—not only individual liberties, but also freedom from discrimination and freedom from dependence on either the owners of the means of production or the holders of abusive political power; second, *equality and social justice*—not only before the law but also economic and socio-cultural equality as well, and equal opportunities for all including those with physical, mental, or social disabilities; and, third, *solidarity*—unity and a sense of compassion for the victims of injustice and inequality. These ideals are described in further detail in the SI's Declaration of Principles.

In recent years, several social democratic parties (in particular, the British Labour Party) have embraced more centrist, Third Way policy positions. This development has generated considerable controversy. The Third Way aims to synthesize socialism and capitalism, rather than create a crude mixture or compromise between socialism and capitalism.

Ralph Alvarez, 83, works out at the Joyce Raye Patterson Senior Citizens Centre on Thursday. Mr. Alvarez has been getting checks through Social Security — the federal government's largest program — since he was 62.

The federal government is in the business of redistributing the wealth. Or of providing services its citizens value, depending on who's running your presidential campaign. "Redistributing the wealth" became an October rallying cry to link President Obama with socialism. People who work for a living would give more money to more people who do not work for a living.

Indeed, the largest federal program does go to people who don't work. And the program is sure to grow. But it deals less with giving from rich to poor and deals much more with giving from young to old. America, for more than 70 years, has chosen to take care of its elderly with Social Security benefits. While this system is billed as workers accruing benefits over their lifetime, in reality the current workers are paying the benefits for the elderly. Social Security is the country's greatest expenditure. Retiree pay alone is greater than the entire federal government's payroll — $369 billion, compared to $253 billion in 2007 — according to the U.S. Census Bureau's Consolidated Federal Funds Report. Total Social Security benefits — including retirement pay, survivor pay, disability and supplemental pay—exceeded $623 billion in 2007.

Tom Hutton can sympathize with workers' pain of seeing Social Security dollars sliced from paychecks. "They probably complain then, but it's been very good to me," Mr. Hutton said. "Thank God for it." Mr. Hutton, 80, of St. Joseph, operated an optical company here for about 50 years. He said he began collecting Social Security at age 64. Last week, he was grateful to receive a $250 check from his uncle — that is, Uncle Sam.

Dr. Patrick McMurry, economics professor at Missouri Western State University, said one of Social Security's goals is to create "social equity." "There is a redistributionist element to Social Security," Dr. McMurry said. But do people think about it that way? "No. People simply don't understand that the money they put in is not set aside in some little account for them."

Medicaid and Medicare are the more urgent programs, he said, and both they and Social Security are in need of policy solutions. But when Dr. McMurry thinks about whether the country is becoming more "socialized," he said it is, but not with regard to social programs. "I don't like that word, but when government takes control of banks and can fire CEOs, it is," he said. "We don't have a term for this new paradigm." The roots of Social Security could be traced to the 10 Commandments: Honour thy mother and father.

American Revolutionary leader Thomas Paine argued for an inheritance tax to give benefits to every person older than 50 and a one-time payment when a person turned 21, according to the Social Security Administration. The notion was to not just provide security for all, but to guarantee a ground floor for the broader economy. Indeed, the bottom would have to fall out of the economy before federal retirement payments began in America. During the Great Depression, "radical calls to action" threatened capitalism and wealth, according to the Social Security Administration. In 1935, President Franklin D. Roosevelt took a middle-line approach with the federal government's creation of Social Security. It relied — and still does rely — on worker contributions rather than explicit taxes on the rich.

Looking forward, that political salve may be the system's downfall. The children of the Depression, like Mr. Hutton, now give way to the children of post-World War II. The first "boomers" began collecting Social Security in 2008 (born in 1946, and reaching reduced-benefits eligibility at age 62). Many estimates from both sides of the aisle point to 2040 as the year the system goes broke in its current form. Unless things change, it appears that you'll receive benefits if you were born before about 1978.

Secularism

During the freedom struggle and during the deliberations of the sessions of the Indian National Congress, prior to independence, there was little, if any, debate on secularism and on what character the State of India was to take. It was no doubt accepted that India, inhabited by many religions, will not discriminate against any religion and will allow freedom of religions to the followers of different religions. Independent India was anointed in a bloodbath consequent to communal riots that rocked the sub-continent for nearly two years. The

Muslim majority areas of the British India were constituted into Pakistan, a theocratic Islamic State – a concept that was duly incorporated later in the Constitution of Pakistan. It should be remembered that in the history of the world Pakistan is the first and the only Islamic (indeed a theocratic) State born or established as such. Other Islamic States were States already existing that came to acquire Islamic character. This development has certain political and social consequences that should form the subject of a separate study.

Because of the generally non-communal character of the political party that spearheaded the freedom struggle and the wise leadership that guided Indian polity at the initial stages, India fortunately did not become a religious or a theocratic State. The debates in the Constituent assembly that framed the Constitution of India show that there was unanimity on the point that there would be no discrimination based on religion, though there was no common understanding what secularism meant. Surprisingly or otherwise, there was no discussion on this subject at least in the public till the sixties. Apparently there was no judgement either of a High Court or of the Supreme Court dealing with the subject – or else there would have been some debate among our alert academicians.

Studies in Indian Secularism

In 1963 there appeared what has been regarded as a pioneer study on secularism in India. This was **'India as a Secular State'** by Prof. Donald E. Smith of Princeton University, New Jersey. Around the same time there was another study on the subject made by Ved Prakash Luthera of University of Delhi, India, which was awaiting publication. It was published in 1964 as **'The Concept of the Secular State in India'**. In the Preface to his book Luthera mentions that when Donald Smith's India **'As A Secular State'** appeared, his study had gone to the press but Smith had read the manuscript of Luthera's study. As will be mentioned later, the two authors take contrary views on the subject.

Thereafter, for reasons which are not clear, regular discussion and debates took place on this subject, namely,

Secularism and India. It would be in order to take note of some of the earlier studies which were published. In November 1965 The Indian Law Institute, New Delhi, had organised a seminar on '**Secularism: Its Implications For Law and Life In India**' and the papers presented at the seminar along with the inaugural address by the then Chief Justice of India were published in a volume under the same title.

Challenges to Secularism

Prof. A.B. Shah, the Founder-President of the Indian Secular Society, Poona, wrote some articles in a newspaper which brought forth some responses. A Muslim friend put some questions to Shah and he responded to them in his characteristically frank and outspoken manner. Then there was his correspondence with Shankaracharya of Puri. All this material has been published in 1968 in a book under the title '**Challenges to Secularism**'. This book deserves much wider reading than it seems to have enjoyed. Sample the following headings: The Challenge from Hindu Obscurantism; The Challenge from Muslim Obscurantism; Dialogue with a Hindu Obscurantist (i.e. Shankaracharya of Puri).

A collection of essays in the form of a symposium has been edited by Prof. V.K. Sinha and has been published under the title of Secularism In India on behalf of International Association For Cultural Freedom. The readers will be interested to note that this volume contains criticism of Prof. Smith's book by two other academicians viz. Prof. Marg Galanter of University of Chicago and Prof. John T. Flint at the State University of New York at Binghamton, New York, and Prof. Smith's rejoinder to the same.

During the forty years or so secularism has been a supremely debated, discussed and contested subject. In India everyone says he is a secularist. Hindutvavadis insist that they are the true secularists and the Congress is pseudo-secularist; some Muslim scholars – notable among them Dr. Rafiq Zacharia and Asghar Ali Engineer – propound a theory that Islam based upon the Holy Quran is secularist. Moreover so many topics and sub-topics related – directly or indirectly – with secularism have been the subject of secular discourse in India that it is not possible to survey it within the space permitted for this essay. I intend to cover the debate in so far as it deals with three questions, which I formulate as follows:

1. What is the true meaning of secularism?
2. Is the Republic of India, as per the Constitution of India, a secular State?
3. Is secularism desirable or possible in India?

Nonviolence

Nonviolence is a philosophy and strategy for social change that rejects the use of physical violence. As such, nonviolence is an alternative to passive acceptance of oppression and armed struggle against it. Practitioners of nonviolence may use diverse methods in their campaigns for social change, including critical forms of education and persuasion, civil disobedience and nonviolent direct action, and targeted communication via mass media.

In modern times, nonviolence has been a powerful tool for social protest. Mahatma Gandhi led a decades-long nonviolent struggle against British rule in India, which eventually helped India win its independence in 1947. About 10 years later, Martin Luther King adopted Gandhi's nonviolent methods in his struggle to win civil rights for African Americans. Then in the 1960s Cesar Chavez organized a campaign of nonviolence to protest the treatment of farm workers in California. These three leaders proved that people can bring about social change without using violence. As Chavez once explained, "Nonviolence is not inaction. It is not for the timid or the weak. It is hard work, it is the patience to win." Another recent nonviolent movement was the "Velvet Revolution", a nonviolent revolution in Czechoslovakia that saw the overthrow of the Communist government in 1989. It is seen as one of the most important of the Revolutions of 1989.

The term "nonviolence" is often linked with or even used as a synonym for pacifism; however, the two concepts are fundamentally different. Pacifism denotes the rejection of the use of violence as a personal decision on moral or spiritual grounds, but does not inherently imply any inclination toward change on a sociopolitical level. Nonviolence on the other hand, presupposes the intent of (but does not limit it to) social or political change as a reason for the rejection of violence. Also, a person may advocate nonviolence in a specific context while advocating violence in other contexts.

Permit me to begin with the recent survey that is being conducted by the **International Forum for India's Heritage**, which has issued a questionnaire to a number of Indian schools so as to elicit responses from students in regard to their experience of our current educational system. I had recently an occasion to study a few illustrative samples of answers that have been received from students from different parts of the country. Three general remarks are common: (i) the present system of education is not at all inspiring; (ii) it does not contribute to the all round development of personality; (iii) there is keenness to study Indian heritage. I am sure that when this survey will be completed and results are brought out, educationists in our country and NCERT in particular, will have valuable material for reflection and action.

Cry of the National Soul

There is, unmistakably, a cry among our students to bring about a radical change in our system of education, so as to make it more meaningful, more purposive, more value-oriented, more skill-oriented, more interesting and less burdensome. There is a cry of the soul of India, it appears, which wants to communicate itself with the coming generations so that its wisdom and its value-systemcan be nourished, strengthened and developed further in the light of the needs of the critical conditions through which humanity as a whole is passing today. This is not a new cry; this cry was reflected throughout the freedom struggle, when the greatest educationists of India proposed and inspired experiments in education so as to combat the Macaulayan system of education, which had come to be imposed under assumptions which were entirely antagonistic to the national system of values and national system of education.

What is, however, new at present is the cry of the students, and we need to discern in it a deep call to educationists to undertake a fresh journey of research ¾ research in objectives of education, research in contents of education and research in methods of education. (...)

Integration

Social integration, in sociology and other social sciences, is the movement of minority groups such as ethnic minorities, refugees and underprivileged sections of a society into the mainstream of the society. Members of the minority groups thus gain full access to the opportunities, rights and services available to the members of the mainstream.

In sociology, social integration usually goes hand in hand with social solidarity.

National and International Value Education in Schools

There is, unmistakably, a cry among our students to bring about a radical change in our system of education, so as to make it more meaningful, more purposive, more value-oriented, more skill-oriented, more interesting and less burdensome. There is a cry of the soul of India, it appears, which wants to communicate itself with the coming generations so that its wisdom and its value-system can be nourished, strengthened and developed further in the light of the needs of the critical conditions through which humanity as a whole is passing today. This is not a new cry; this cry was reflected throughout the freedom struggle, when the greatest educationists of India proposed and inspired experiments in education so as to combat the Macaulayan system of education, which had come to be imposed under assumptions which were entirely antagonistic to the national system of values and national system of education.

What is, however, new at present is the cry of the students, and we need to discern in it a deep call to educationists to undertake a fresh journey of research ¾ research in objectives of education, research in contents of education and research in methods of education.

Teachers Personal Values and Code of Conduct for Teachers

Preamble

Goal of Education in Our Country: The basic purpose of education is to create skill and knowledge and awareness of our glorious national heritage and the achievement of human civilization, possessing a basic scientific outlook and commitment to the ideals of patriotism, democracy, secularism, socialism and peace, and the principles enunciated in the Preamble to our Constitution. The education sector has to produce leaders of society in all areas of activities with a commitment to the above ideals. Education should strive for academic excellence, and progress of the arts and sciences, education, research and extension should be conducted in conformity with our national needs and priorities and ensure that our best talents make befitting contributions on societal needs.

The Code of Professional Ethics

Teachers and their Responsibilities: Whoever adopts teaching as a profession, is under an obligation to conduct himself in accordance with the ideals of the profession. A teacher is constantly under the scrutiny of his students and society at large. Therefore, every teacher should see that there is no incompatibility between his precepts and practice. The national ideals of education which have already been set forth and which he/she should seek to inculcate among students must be his/her own ideals. The profession further requires that the teachers should be calm, patient and communicative in temperament and amiable in disposition.

Teachers should:

(i) adhere to a responsible pattern of conduct and demeanour expected of them by the Community;

(ii) manage their private affairs in a manner consistent with the dignity of the profession;

(iii) strive for continuous professional growth through study and research;

(iv) express free and frank opinion when participating in professional meetings, seminars and conferences;

(v) maintain active membership of professional organisations and strive to update their knowledge through them;

(vi) perform their duties in the form of teaching, tutorials practical and seminar work conscientiously and with dedication;

(vii) cooperate and assist in carrying out functions relating to the educational responsibilities of the schools, the Board of School Education such as: assisting in appraising application for admission advising and counselling students as well as assisting in the conduct of Board and School examinations, including supervision, invigilation and evaluation; and

(viii) participate in extension, co-curricular and extra-curricular activities including community service.

Teachers and Students

Teachers should:

(i) respect the right and dignity of the student in expressing his/her opinion;

(ii) deal justly and impartially with students regardless of their religion, caste, political, economic, social and physical characteristics;

(iii) recognise the differences in aptitude and capabilities among students and strive to meet their individual needs;

(iv) encourage students to improve their attainments, develop their personalities and at the same time contribute to community welfare;

(v) inculcate among students a scientific outlook and respect for physical labour and ideals of democracy, patriotism, and peace;

(vi) be affectionate to the students and not behave in a vindictive manner towards any of them for any reason;

(vii) pay attention to only the attainment of the students in the assessment of merit;

(viii) make themselves available to the students even beyond their class hours and help and guide students without any remuneration or reward;

(ix) aid students to develop an understanding of our national heritage and national goals; and

(x) refrain from inciting students against other students, colleagues or administration.

Teachers and Colleagues

Teachers should:

(i) treat other members of the profession in the same manner as they themselves wish to be treated;

(ii) speak respectfully to other teachers and render assistance for overall professional betterment;

(iii) refrain from lodging unsubstantiated allegations against colleagues to their higher authorities; and

(iv) refrain from allowing considerations of caste, creed, religion, race or sex to influence their professional working.

Teachers and Authorities

Teachers should:

(i) discharge their professional responsibilities according to the existing rules and adhere to procedures and methods consistent with their profession in initiating steps through their own institutional bodies and/or professional organisations for change of any such rules detrimental to the professional interest;

(ii) refrain from undertaking any other employment and commitment including private tuitions and coaching classes which are likely to interfere with their professional responsibilities

(iii) cooperate in the formulation of the policies of their institution by accepting various offices and discharge the responsibilities which such offices may demand.

(iv) cooperate through their organisations in the formulation of policies of the other institutions and accept offices; as necessary;

(v) cooperate with the authorities for the betterment of the institutions keeping in view the overall interest and in conformity with the dignity of the profession;

(vi) give and expect due notice before a change of position is made; and

(vii) refrain from availing themselves of leave except on unavoidable grounds and as far as practicable with prior intimation, keeping in view their particular responsibility towards the completion of the academic schedule.

Teachers and Non/Teaching Staff

(i) teachers should treat the non teaching staff as colleagues and equal partners in a co-operative undertaking, within every educational institution; and

(ii) Teachers should help in the functioning of the Joint Staff Councils covering both teachers and the non teaching staff.

Teachers and Guardians

Teachers should try to see through teachers' bodies and organisations that institutions maintain contact with the guardians of their students, send reports of their performance to the guardians whenever necessary and meet the guardians in meetings convened for the purpose for mutual exchange of ideas and for the benefit of the institution.

Teachers and Society

Teachers should:

(i) recognise that education is a public service and strive to keep the public informed of the educational programmes which are being provided;

(ii) work to improve education in the community and strengthen the community's moral and intellectual life;

(iii) be aware of social problems and take part in such activities as would be conducive to the progress of society and hence the country as a whole;

(iv) perform the duties of citizenship, participate in Community activities and shoulder responsibilities of public offices;

(v) refrain from taking part in or subscribing to or assisting in any way, activities which tend to promote feeling of hatred or enmity among different communities, religious or linguistic groups but actively work for national integration.

Note.-Regarding Tailoring/Knitting/Embroidery and Bringing/use of help books. The Govt. has imposed a complete ban on the following activities in the offices/ institutions vide letter No. Shiksha-IIGA(10) 1/94 dated 8-11-94.

1. Bringing of Tailoring/Knitting/Embroidery material and allied work.
2. Use of help books/keys to text books in all its institutions.
3. Use of Radio/Transistor in the offices and institutions is completely prohibited.
4. Teaching Staff will not perform any tuition work either before or after the school hours.

Non-teaching Staff

The code of conduct specified for teachers shall apply to other employees as well

Personal Development of the Teachers

Who are the excellent teachers, and what do they look like? Well, this talk is only going to address part of that question. Specifically, this empirical report is based on self reported data, from teachers who have been identified as "Excellent Teachers". While all such teachers might not be excellent in terms of prizes for teaching and learning, they were selected by relatively knowledgeable, independent and experienced arbiters. Hence, it is hoped that this group may be informative of teachers who are very good practitioners of teaching and learning, within the secondary school structure, to inform a discussion of the nature and development of excellence in teaching.

Unit-X

Health Education

The Concept of Health

Health education is defined as the principle by which individuals and groups of people learn to behave in a manner conducive to the promotion, maintenance, or restoration of health.

Motivation

Education for health begins with people. It hopes to motivate them with whatever interests they may have in improving their living conditions. Its aim is to develop in them a sense of responsibility for health conditions for themselves as individuals, as members of families, and as communities. In communicable disease control, health education commonly includes an appraisal of what is known by a population about a disease, an assessment of habits and attitudes of the people as they relate to spread and frequency of the disease, and the presentation of specific means to remedy observed deficiencies.

Health education is also an effective tool that helps improve health in developing nations. It not only teaches prevention and basic health knowledge but also conditions ideas that re-shape everyday habits of people with unhealthy lifestyles in developing countries. This type of conditioning not only affects the immediate recipients of such education but also future generations will benefit from an improved and properly cultivated ideas about health that will eventually be ingrained with widely spread health education. Moreover, besides physical health prevention, health education can also provide more aid and help people deal healthier with situations of extreme stress, anxiety, depression or other emotional disturbances to lessen the impact of these sorts of mental and emotional constituents, which can consequently lead to detrimental physical effects.

Teaching

Health education is included in the curriculum of most schools. In the United States some forty states require the teaching of health education. A comprehensive health education curriculum consists of planned learning experiences which will help students achieve desirable attitudes and practices related to critical health issues. Some of these are: emotional health and a positive self image; appreciation, respect for, and care of the human body and its vital organs; physical fitness; health issues of alcohol, tobacco, drug use and abuse; health misconceptions and quackery; effects of exercise on the body systems and on general well being; nutrition and weight control; sexual relationships, the scientific, social and economic aspects of community and ecological health; communicable and degenerative diseases including sexually transmitted diseases; disaster preparedness; safety and driver education; life skills; choosing professional medical and health services; and choices of health careers.

The Concept of Health Education

One of the most important achievements for peace among peoples, and is given the opportunity to serve the area in need of health care and social after they had been denied them during the long years ago.

Those in need of such care is every person suffering from a disease attendant for the rest of his life can not be cured, as well as Hello hereditary diseases transmitted from generation to generation, and affect the community in a clear and the spread of disease, which cost the state sums of money as well as working to destroy the society, family and individual who is the backbone of this family in all respects.

Also multiple disabilities exist in the community that needs with special care to care unspeakable.

Here, a group of concerned citizens of this benevolent society for the advancement of culture and good health of the Jordanian and Arab citizens alike in all areas.

Nutrition and Health

America is committing increased dollars and resources to remedy the negative effects of poor dietary choices and unhealthy lifestyles, foodborne illnesses, and the potential for terrorist-related and other threats to the food supply. At the same time, millions of Americans struggle to obtain sufficient food, while U.S. food suppliers scramble to keep up with changing food trends. Through program leadership and funding opportunities, CSREES' Food, Nutrition & Health programs strengthen the nation's capacity to address issues related to diet, health, food safety, food security, and food science and technology.

While the American food supply is among the safest in the world, millions of Americans still fall victim to foodborne illness. Each year, foodborne diseases cause an estimated 325,000 serious illnesses resulting in hospitalization, 76 million cases of gastrointestinal illnesses, and 5,000 deaths. The nation faces new food safety challenges because of new and emerging foodborne pathogens and because familiar ones are growing resistant to treatment.

The goal of food safety programs in CSREES is to reduce the incidence of foodborne illness to the greatest extent feasible. CSREES' food safety programs increase the understanding of disease-causing microorganisms, their products, naturally occurring toxicants and chemical contaminants in meats, poultry, seafood, and fresh fruits and vegetables. Food safety concerns cover a broad spectrum, from on-farm production, postharvest processing, distribution, and food preparation, selection and consumption. Programs increase the understanding of the ecology of foodborne pathogens and their products so better intervention strategies can be developed. CSREES' food safety programs also encourage public and private sectors to work collaboratively to identify and implement preventive measures that reduce the risk of foodborne illness while making the best use of public and private resources. And finally, the food safety program focuses on addressing the safety of a national food supply that is threatened by both incidental and deliberate contamination.

The value-added sector of the food industry—processing, packaging, marketing, and distribution—accounts for about three-fourths of the consumer's food dollar. CSREES supports research and education in talue-added food processing and quality improvement through formula grants, competitive grants, and special research grants. These include: thermal processing, irradiation, hydrostatic processing, ohmic processing, reverse osmosis and ultrafiltration, bioproces 02/20/2008drying, and refrigeration. Maintenance and improvement of quality of the nutrients, flavour, texture, and phytochemicals/nutraceuticals are integral parts of these processes. Processing methods to improve the physical, chemical, and microbiological safety of food are an important component of the research supported.

Sanitation

School Sanitation and Hygiene Education, widely known as SSHE, is a comprehensive programme to ensure child friendly water supply, toilet and hand washing facilities in the schools and promote Behavioural change by hygiene education. SSHE not only ensures child's right to have healthy and clean environment but also leads to an effective learning and enrolment of girls in particular, and reduce diseases and worm infestation. SSHE was introduced in the RCRSP programme in 1999 both in TSC as well as in allocation based component. At present, SSHE is implemented under Total Sanitation Campaign (TSC) and given special thrust by following the proven route of teacher-children-family-community where child is a change-agent playing an effective role on sustained basis to spread the message of improved sanitary and healthy practices. TSC has made provision for toilet facility and hygiene education in all types of Government Rural Schools i.e. Primary, Upper Primary, Secondary and Higher Secondary schools with emphasis on toilets for girls. Central Government, State

Government and Parent Teachers/GP share the cost in the ratio of 60:30:10. Govt. is committed to cover all uncovered rural schools with water and sanitation facility and also imparting hygiene education by 2005-2006.

Communicable Diseases

India is undergoing an epidemiologic, demo-graphic and health transition. The expectancy of life has increased, with consequent rise in degenerative diseases of aging and life-styles. Nevertheless, communicable diseases are still dominant and constitute major public health issues. The research strategy adopted by the Council is a balance between the upstream (fundamental and basic) and downstream (product development/ evaluation and operational) research. Through the network of its disease-specific Institutes/Regional Medical Research Centres and extramural research programme, the Council is supporting and encouraging biomedical research in communicable diseases. New viral and bacterial infections have been identified. Monitoring of anti-microbial resistance to commonly used drugs is being extended to include more organisms. Disease surveillance at the molecular level has been expanded and strengthened. Studies to assess disease burden not only in terms of morbidity and mortality but also economic are high on the Council's agenda. Feasibility of effective strategies under field conditions for control of infectious diseases is being demonstrated. Research support to eradicate target diseases has been intensified. Development and evaluation of diagnostic tools, drugs and vaccines is being undertaken. Programme relevant research to strengthen the national health programmes and human resource development are an integral part of the efforts of the Council towards control of communicable diseases.

Safety And First Aid

Injuries are the number one cause of death for children and adolescents ages 1 to 21. There are important steps for parents, pediatricians, and communities to take to keep injuries from happening. When an injury does occur, quick action to give appropriate first aid can reduce the consequences of the injury.

Car Safety Seats and Transportation Safety

Motor vehicle crashes are the number one cause of death for children and adolescents ages 1 to 21. The AAP has information on topics ranging from car safety seats to school buses to teen driving.

Water Safety

Drowning is the second leading cause of unintentional injury death for children and adolescents. The AAP has information on how to keep children in all age groups safe in the water at home, in swimming pools, on boats, and in open bodies of water.

TIPP: The Injury Prevention Program

TIPP is an educational program for parents of children newborn through 12 years of age to help prevent common injuries from a variety of causes. TIPP is designed to provide a systematic method for pediatricians to counsel parents and children about adopting behaviours to prevent injuries.

Health Services and Health Supervision in School

The scheme is headed by Dy. Director/Chief Medical Officer to carry out the day to day functioning of School Health Scheme, which includes planning, implementing, administration and monitoring. School Health Clinics are situated within the school premises. Each School Health Clinic cater to about 8 to10 thousand children, from the cluster of 8 to10 schools located around radius of 3-4 k.m.

Functioning of School Heath Clinic

School Health Clinic provides comprehensive integrated health care services to school children to achieve the objectives of the school health program. The services provided to the students include:

- Routine complete physical health checkup of each student
- Curative services through OPD services.

- Immunization against tetanus at the age of 10 and 16 years.
- Referral of students who require attention of a specialist, to referral centres and subsequent follow up of these cases.
- Health Education and Counselling.
- Advising the school authorities for maintenance of healthy and safe environment.

The school medical team report to their respective clinics in the morning and set up the clinic as per their plan schedule and call the children of respective class for routing medical examination. Commutative Health Record is filled for each child. Cumulative Health Record contains details of health profile of the student, treatment, advices and follow up. This record will be given to student at the time of leaving the school. During the routine examination of students, health education is also been given at individual level and in a group. Children needing specialist services are referred to specialist with subsequent follow up. First Aid and Emergency Services are provided as and when required along with OPD services. Incidental health education is also been provided.

When needed, class teachers and parents are informed about the condition of the child and are advised for regular treatment and follow up. Parents and teaches are also given health guidance and counselling along with the school children during parent teacher meetings.

Health education is an ongoing activity carried out during O.P.D. medical examination, immunization, in the prayer meeting, in classes or in assembly hall. Topics are chosen on the basis of need and current problem in the community. Various A.V. Aids are used to impart Health Education.

Every year all the children of 10 and 16 years of age are given booster dose of tetanus-toxoid.

Sanitation survey school is being done by school medical team and suggestions are given to concerned school authorities for its improvement. A close liaison is maintained by the school medical team with the school authorities.

The school medical teams submit their progress report of every month, annual report and special report if any to the School Health Scheme Head Office.

Pediatric Health Supervision Guidelines

You will be making less frequent visits to your Pediatrician now. Age specific topics that should be discussed at well child visits include toilet training (eighteen months to three years), school readiness in preschool age children, and school performance in school age children. Remember that by the middle childhood years, it is important to talk about avoiding drugs and alcohol and to begin sexuality education. In general, you can expect the following topics to be covered at each visit:

- Examination of your child's growth and development.
- Review of feeding and sleep schedules.
- Screening height, weight, head circumference (up to age three) and/or blood pressure (usually routine after age three years).
- Counselling for effective discipline, injury prevention, dental health (first visit to the dentist by age three unless high risk), and diet.
- Immunizations: MMR, DTaP and IPV boosters at the four to six year checkup.
- Screening test: vision (formal test by three years), hearing (formal test by four years), blood level to check for anemia (at two years), screening questionnaire for lead poisoning risk (routinely at nine months and two years), tuberculosis test if high risk.

Elements of Comprehensive Health Examinations Relating to School Health

1. An assessment on entry into school should include a review of the medical history with attention to physical, emotional, orfamily problems that might influence school achievement. Previousparticipation in preschool experiences should be included in the history. The assessment should include a careful evaluation oflanguage, motor, social, and adaptive development

and immunization status. Private physicians or physicians and mid-level health professionals used by the school system should collaborate with designated school officials to design protocols. These protocols should be used to initiate appropriate referrals available in the school or the community and provide placement in the educational system as deemed appropriate by the findings of the medical history, physical examination, and developmental assessment.

2. Subsequent visits should include a history that focuses on new medical problems, medications, changes in the child's developmental and psychosocial status, and an update on school progress and problems. The frequency of subsequent health assessments will vary depending on the child's functional status but should be in compliance with the AAP-recommended periodicity schedule for child health supervision visits.
3. A complete age-appropriate unclothed physical examination should be performed by a physician or mid-level professional. It should include, but not be limited to, the assessment of height, weight, physical and sexual maturation, and blood pressure. A screening evaluation should be performed to evaluate visual acuity, auditory acuity, emotional maturity, language, dental condition, and motor skills. Any abnormal findings should be monitored by the physician.
4. In the United States, children of various ages participate in sports or physical education sponsored by the school. It is important for the health care professional to be familiar with the physical assessment and requirements to appropriately approve participation in such activities. This assessment should be combined with the health examination and interval history when possible, although it may be performed separately. In any case, the uniqueness of a detailed comprehensive physical examination that include sendurance and muscular assessment must be recognized. Specific descriptions of such an assessment are available.

5. The health examination should identify specific health needs and problems that might require cooperation among community resources, and school officials may want to organize the community health professionals and community resources to integrate services available and provide easy access to these services. These services may support administration of medications, physical therapy, problems with access to buildings, anticipated absences, Behavioural and emotional needs, special location in class (e.g, for visual or auditory problems), or other conditions requiring the assistance of the classroom teacher or school nurse. Easy access to the services will become more important as increasing numbers of chronically ill or disabled students or students with special needs attend classes in their neighbourhood schools. The frequency with which these issues are reviewed will depend on the student's specific needs. Direct communication among school personnel, parents, and the physician should occur to determine the requirements of children with special health care needs.
6. Anticipatory guidance for students and parents for physical fitness, nutrition, cardiovascular risk reduction, injury and violence prevention, sexual development and sex education, stress management, alcohol and other drug abuse, and tobacco use should be provided. Anticipatory guidance should be provided for parents about their role in promoting school achievement and learning as priorities in their child's life. Guidance also may be provided to assist parents in helping their child develop responsibility, independence, and self-reliance in the educational process.

Blood and Eye Donations

There are three major kinds of donations. An *allogeneic* (also called *homologous*) donation is when a donor gives blood for storage at a blood bank for transfusion to an unknown recipient. A *directed* donation is when a person, often a family member, donates blood for transfusion to a specific individual.

The third kind is when the donor gives blood that is used for further manufacturing into medicines, usually plasma for fractionation. A person can also have a unit of blood stored that will eventually be transfused back, usually after surgery. This is called an *autologous* donation.

An event where donors come to give allogeneic blood is sometimes called a *blood drive* or a *blood donor session*. These can occur at a blood bank but they are often set up at a location in the community such as a shopping centre, workplace, school, or a local house of worship.

Blood Donation Organization

On 23rd May 2003 when a patient in one of the city hospitals died because he did not receive blood on time, Sankalp was born.

The commitment was simple. Whenever there is any requirement of blood which the blood banks in the city fail to satisfy, we requested them to forward it over to us. Sankalp **24 X 7 X 365** emergency blood helpline has been working since then taking up all emergency blood requests that come up.

The fragmented nature of the blood transfusion services led to un-necessary competition and seclusions. Blood banks did not work as one unit. We conceptualized and eventually realized a single helpline number that gave information about blood availability in various blood banks in Bangalore. **Need Blood-Call 1062** Every time the donor went to donate, he/she was doubtful about his/her safety. Is this the right place to donate? Am I safe? Will they sell my blood? These questions were raised frequently and there were no sure answers.. Each party blew it's own trumpet. We explored, we studied and we came up with solution. We came up with information that answers the donor's questions and ensures the safest of all donations. The blood banks across the country face a problem in delivering good quality of service to the people. They are many time unable to deliver the gift of life. To ensure safe and sustainable supply of blood it was realized that enrolment of **Voluntary Non-remunerative blood donors** was a must. People wanted to donate blood. But there was little organized help to conduct camps. We are working on Rakta Kranti, the road to 100% Voluntary Non-Remunerative Blood donation. We are slowly changing attitudes. We are slowly pushing in reforms. We are providing help, but at the same time we are empowering people to help themselves. Read on to explore **Sankalp Blood Donation Organization.**

Eye Donation

In India, thee are approximately 120 lakh blind in both eyes and 80 lakh blind in one eye, which is about one fourth of the total blind population of the world. This means 14.9 out of every 1000 people in India are blind compared to just 3 per 1000 in the developed countries. Blindness in most cases is avoidable that is, either preventable or curable. Of the 120 lakh blind, approximately 103 lakh are curable by relatively simple operations, unfortunately yet they remain uncured. About 96 lakh persons suffer from cataract which can be cured by a simple operation. About 7 lakh Indians suffer from corneal blindness, mostly children in their early childhood, can be cured by corneal transplantation.

What is Corneal Blindness?

Corneal blindness means that the cornea, which is the transparent and thin outer layer of eye, becomes cloudy due to nutritional deficiency, injury or diseases such as trachoma, corneal ulcer, degeneration, dystrophies, etc. leading to loss of vision. This blindness can be cured in most cases by corneal transplant. Corneal transplant or grafting is performed on a patient when a voluntary donor pledges and donates his or her eyes after death.

What is the Status of Donated Eyes in India?

There is a severe lack of donor eyes in India and only 4.500 operations are being performed every year, while 30,000 new cases are added each year to the long list of 7 lakh patients already waiting to be cured. Although there are enough qualified surgeons and plenty of potential patients, corneal transplantation cannot be carried out due to lack of donor corneas. Eye donation means people pledging to donate their eyes after death to be used for corneal grafting for restoring sight to corneal blind people. In India there are more than 80 lakh deaths every year but sadly the corneal donations do not exceed a few thousand.

What is an Eye Bank?

An eye bank collects, medically evaluates and distributes eyes donated by caring individuals for use in corneal transplantation, research, and education. Eye banks are non-profit organizations.

Eye Donation-How does it Work?

Usually eyes have to be removed within six to eight hours to death; therefore the nearest eye bank or eye collection centre must be informed of the death immediately

The donor or the diseased need not to be taken to the eye bank, the eye bank team will come to take the eyes wherever the donor is, at no cost to the donors family. Removal of eyes usually is a quick and simple procedure. On reaching the eye bank, the donated eyes are evaluated, processed and then used for a corneal transplant surgery. The donated eyes are used on patients who are on the waiting list in accordance with the priority based on the guidelines.

Will Eye Donation Affect the Appearance of the Donor?

No. Great care is taken to preserve the donor's appearance. Funeral arrangements, including a viewing if desired, may proceed as scheduled.

Personal Hygiene

Personal hygiene is the first step to good grooming and good health. Elementary cleanliness is common knowledge. Neglect causes problems that you may not even be aware of. Many people with bad breath are blissfully unaware of it. Some problems may not be your fault at all, but improving standards of hygiene will control these conditions. Dandruff is a case in point. More often than you know, good looks are the result of careful and continuous grooming. Every external part of the body demands a basic amount of attention on a regular basis.

Here are some grooming routines and some complaints associated with neglect.

Personal hygiene pertains to hygiene practices performed by an individual to care for one's bodily health and well being through cleanliness. Motivations for personal hygiene practice include reduction of personal illness, healing from personal illness, optimal health and sense of well being, social acceptance and prevention of spread of illness to others.

Personal hygiene practices include: seeing a doctor, seeing a dentist, regular washing (bathing or showering) of the body, regular hand washing, brushing and flossing of the teeth, basic manicure and pedicure, feminine hygiene and healthy eating. Personal grooming extends personal hygiene as it pertains to the maintenance of a good personal and public appearance which need not necessarily be hygienic.

Personal hygiene is achieved by using personal hygiene products including: soap, hair shampoo, hair conditioner, toothbrushes, tooth paste, cotton swabs, deodorant, chapstick, cream, lotion, facial tissue, hair clippers, nail clippers, mouthwash, nail files, skin cleansers, razors, shaving cream, skin cream and toilet paper. Other personal hygiene and grooming products can be used to improve health and well being.

Bibliography

Aggarwal, J.C.: *Landmarks in the History of Modern Indian Education*, Vikas Publishing House (Pvt.) Ltd., Delhi,1984.

Ahmad, Imtiaz : *Caste and Social Stratification Among Muslims in India*, New Delhi, Manohar, 1978.

Banerjee, Hiranmay : *The House of the Tagores*, Calcutta, Rabiondra Bharati University, 1968.

Birley Derei: *Planning and Education*; Routledge and Kegan Paul, London and Boston, 1972.

Chaklader, Snehamoy : *Sociolinguistics: A Guide to Language Problems in India*, New Delhi, Mittal, 1990.

Donaldson, Gordon A. : *Cultivating Leadership in Schools*, New York, College Press, 2001.

Erickson, Erik H.P. : *Gandhi's Truth: On the Origins of Militant Nonviolence*, New York, Norton, 1970.

Gibson, R. : *Critical Theory and Education*, London, Hodder & Stoughton, 1986.

Grace, G. : *School Leadership: Beyond Educational Management*, London, Falmer, 1995.

Hasan, S.nurul: *Challenges in Education,Culture and social Welfare*, Allied Publishers (Pvt.) Ltd. Delhi, 1978.

Jeffs, T. and Smith, M. : *Using Informal Education*, Milton Keynes, Open University Press, 1990.

Kamat, A.R.: *The educational Situation and other Essays on Education*, Peoples' Publishing House, New Delhi, 1973.

Kochar, S.K.: *Pivotal Issues in Indian Education*, Sterling Publisher (Private) Ltd., Allahabad, 1981.

Lovett, T. : *Adult Education, Community Development and the Working Class*, London, Ward Lock, 1975.

Mohan, Radhey : *Education and National Development*, Indiana Publications, New Delhi, 1976.

Mohanty, J.: *Indian Education in the Emerging Society*, Sterling Publisher Private Limited, Banglore, 1982.

Naik, J.P.: *The Education Commission and After*, Allied Publishers (Pvt.) Ltd., New Delhi, 1982.

Nazareth, M. RIA: *Education: Goals, Aims and Objectives*, Vikas Publishing House, New Delhi, 1984.

Nuna, S.C. : *Education and Development*, NIEPA, New Delhi, 1987.

Paliwal, M.R.: *Social Change and Education: Present and Future*, Uppal Publishing House, New Delhi, 1984.

Premi, M.K.: *Educational Planning in India*, Sterling Publishers (P) Ltd., New Delhi. 1972.

Saxena, Sateshwari: *Educational Planning in India*, Sterling Publishers (pvt.) Ltd., Bombay, 1978.

Setranjiwalla : *Current trends in Indian Education*; S. Chand & Co. (pvt.) Ltd., New Delhi. 1973.

Shrimati, K.L.: *A search for values in Indian Education*, Vikas Publications, Delhi. 1971.

Shukla, P.D.: *Towards New pattern of Education in India*, Sterling Publishers (Pvt.) Ltd., New Delhi. 1976.

Simkins, T. : *Non-formal Education and Development*, Manchester, Manchester University, 1977.

Steele, T. and Taylor, R. : *Learning Independence, A political outline of Indian Adult Education*, Leicester, National Institute of Adult Continuing Education, 1995.

Sundram, P.S. and Shah, A.B.: *Education or Catastrophe*, Vikas Publishing House (Pvt.) Ltd., Delhi, 1976.

Thrupp, J. & Willmott. : *Educational Management in Managerialist Times: Beyond the Textual Apologists*, Maidenhead, UK, 2003.

Venkatasubramanian, K.: *Issues in Education*; Macmillan India Ltd., Delhi, 1982.

Index

□□□